Why Do Good People Suffer Bad Things?

Discovering the Root Causes of Human Suffering—
and What You Can and Cannot Do about It!

TR Williams

FriesenPress

Suite 300 - 990 Fort St
Victoria, BC, V8V 3K2
Canada

www.friesenpress.com

ISBN
978-1-5255-3155-2 (Hardcover)
978-1-5255-3157-6 (eBook)

Library of Congress Cataloging Data: 2018910172

1. Religion, Christian Life, Inspirational
2. Self-Help, Recovery & Personal Growth
3. Psychology, Grief & Loss

Distributed to the trade by The Ingram Book Company

Quantity discounts are available to your company,
organization, educational institution, or specific group for
the purposes of textbooks, counseling, therapy or reading
materials, promotion and subscription incentives, study
tools, gifts, or fundraiser campaigns. You may contact us at:
www.empowerlifebooks.com

This book is dedicated to all of those who have suffered the unpredictable, the unimaginable, the inconceivable, the unexplainable, and have asked the question *Why!*

Table of Contents

Acknowledgments

THIS BOOK GREW OUT OF A PERSONAL QUEST AND DRIVE TO understand and to explain in practical terms why so many adversarial hardships happen to so many good people, and to try to make sense out of all the unwanted, unpredictable, often unexpected, and sometimes unexplainable pain, distress, misfortune, and suffering we all encounter in life. There isn't always a complete narrative behind every story, so we're often left without fully knowing *Why!* We can't always find the obvious reasons, nor come up with simplistic answers to suffering. Many of those for whom I write are for the most part resolute in their faith, love, and devotion to God; they are driven to do His will, fulfill their purpose, and do the right thing while living in this world.

The perennial, moral life question of why good people suffer bad things has been debated and discussed by people from all walks of life, in every culture, and throughout civilization of humanity for almost as long as sin and suffering have been in the world. It has been the subject of a myriad of books written by a multitude of individuals down through the ages. There is no possible way that a multi-tiered question such as this, with all its facets, possibilities, complexities, and ramifications, could ever be adequately explained in one book, or even in a series of books. I am under no such illusion.

With this book, however, I have endeavored to make a practical attempt to explain the root causes, origin, and process of human suffering, to offer sound biblical counsel on how to learn and grow from it, to provide dynamic wisdom principles for successfully navigating through it, and to help readers discover how to minimize the effects and scope of suffering as much as possible, while maximizing their purpose and maintaining a winning spirit that enables them to move forward in life. I am fully aware that none of us on this earth can totally escape suffering and adversity in this mortal life. However, we can all learn to overcome life's suffering and hardships by taking positive actions to make life better for ourselves and those who follow in our footsteps.

There are a few people I wish to acknowledge for their voluntary but valuable contributions to this book. No author's book is ever the fruit of his own effort and hard work alone. I could not have earnestly succeeded in producing this work without the support, enthusiasm, advice, commitment, and sacrifice of these individuals.

First, my wife and best friend, Sabrina, who, for many years, has challenged and inspired me to transform my messages into book form. The timeless and universal principles gleaned over the years through much careful study, which I have imparted to thousands—as a challenge for them to trust God—I have watched their faith grow exponentially as they applied to their daily lives the practical truths of God's life-changing Word. Sabrina has been instrumental in enhancing certain materials and, most of all, as a sharp sounding board as I developed my thoughts and writings into chapters. I am truly grateful for her love, support, discernment, and faith in the unique capabilities and gifts with which God has endowed me. She has seen more potential and destiny in me than I have ever seen in myself. Her confidence in my assignment has made all the difference in the world. Thank you from the bottom of my heart for your tireless commitment to reading, rereading, critiquing, correcting, and refining my manuscript until it was finally ready for book format.

Second, I extend a special word of thanks to John, a freelance writer and author, who worked endlessly to help develop the initial stylistic concept of the book, researched materials, and also helped to assemble the foundation of the book's beginning. John is very gifted, creative, and talented in his own right. He graciously and insightfully assisted me in matching particular stories to certain themes and principles in my writings. John has been a real friend and resource for making this project possible—exceeding my best efforts. In addition, he created the design for the front cover of the book. I have enjoyed working with him over the years on several different projects; I greatly appreciate his friendship, genuine hard work, and spirit of humility. You are an awesome man of God. Great blessings to you, John, for your time and commitment to this undertaking.

Finally, a very warm thanks to my copyeditor for her detail-oriented skills, used to ensure that my manuscript was clear, cohesive, and consistent before the final project was sent to the publisher. Words can never express the depth of my appreciation for the wonderful support you have extended on this project. When I think of the goodness of God in my life, I think of people like you. He has graced you with a mighty gift of precision to help advance another person's vision. You are one of the most beautiful people God has placed upon the earth. Thank you for all you have done. I will never forget your strength, love, and sacrifice. You are truly a blessing.

Introduction

CHRISTA MCAULIFFE BEAT THE ODDS IN EDGING OUT MORE than 11,000 other applicants when she was awarded the position of the first non-astronaut to fly into outer space. A gifted educator, wife, and mother of two (a six-year-old daughter and a nine-year-old son), she was selected to participate in then-President Ronald Reagan's "NASA Teacher in Space Project."

The announcement of her selection left the country buzzing with excitement. McAuliffe took a one-year leave of absence from teaching to prepare for her journey into space, during which time she would conduct science experiments and teach two lessons from the space shuttle *Challenger*. Upon being chosen to participate in the program, her popularity grew quickly. She developed an immediate rapport with the media, which helped the Teacher in Space Project establish a very large following and receive constant attention. McAuliffe appeared frequently on popular television programs such as *Good Morning America, CBS Morning News,* The T*oday Show,* and *The Tonight Show Starring Johnny Carson.*

On January 28, 1986, she, along with six other crew members, boarded the space shuttle Challenger for the historic flight. During her year of training, McAuliffe, 37, had captured the attention of the entire nation. As the Challenger rocketed into Florida's clear blue sky, hundreds of bystanders gathering at the Cape Canaveral launch site stood transfixed, their gaze riveted on the rapidly diminishing orbiter sitting majestically atop its columns of smoke and flame. Joining them around the nation were millions of others glued to their television screens to watch the late-morning event. Everyone knew they were witnessing history in the making.

Roughly 73 seconds into the launch and 10 miles into the air, NASA abruptly lost radio contact with the shuttle. As millions of viewers watched worldwide, Challenger disintegrated in mid-flight, and all seven crew members were killed. In sudden horror, shocked onlookers stared in silence at the huge, blossoming cloud of white smoke that marked the doomed shuttle's final position, not fully comprehending the disaster unfolding before their eyes. In a single tragic instant, seven intrepid travelers, including beloved teacher-turned-astronaut Christa McAuliffe, were gone forever.

How could it happen? How could such a proud, shining moment in our nation's history suddenly turn into a mind-numbing, heart-wrenching national tragedy? Just as important, why did it happen? Why did such a horrible mishap occur and snuff out, like a candle in the wind, the lives of seven such incredible and exceptional people as Christa McAuliffe and the other members of Challenger's crew? In the weeks and months following the loss of Challenger, an intensive investigation of protocols, procedures, and technical components identified the cause of the disaster. An O-ring on one of the solid fuel booster rockets had failed, thus allowing the burning fuel to blow out sideways, which ignited the liquid fuel tank attached to the orbiter. That explained the "*how.*" But the "*why*" remained a mystery, which left a sorrowing nation and the grieving families of those who died with no real answers, only the age-old question: *Why do good people suffer bad things?*

Sudden tragedies or suffering of this magnitude routinely challenge our faith in God and His goodness. They confront us with the need to understand why suffering, pain, misfortune, disaster, and death are inescapable parts of life, and require us to reassess our understanding (or misunderstanding) of why God allows bad things to happen to good people.

Whenever we are thrust into suffering or pain, especially through no apparent fault of our own, it is only natural that we ask the question: W*hy?* The only thing we can be certain of is that bad things *do* happen to good people. And while we sometimes eventually learn the basic causes behind our hardship, there are many other times when we never receive all the answers to our question of why bad things happen to us. It is a universal question because pain, misfortune, suffering, and hardship are universal experiences of humankind.

1

LIFE IS FRAGILE

"'How frail is humanity! How short is life, how full of trouble! We blossom like a flower and then wither. Like a passing shadow, we quickly disappear.'"

— Job 14:1–2 (NLT)

"Unfortunately, mortal life is very fragile, and very short."

— Rachel Caine

LIFE CAN BE BRUTAL, FEROCIOUS, AND AT TIMES DOWNRIGHT unfair. One of humanity's perennial questions existing beyond the reach of memory has been an inescapable reality: Why does God allow so much suffering, evil, pain, misery, misfortune, and injustice in the world? Other similar queries have been posed: Why do so many good people suffer bad things? Why is this world in such a big mess? Why does it seem like God hides His face from so much egregious suffering? In order to gain insight into the ***root causes*** of these questions, we must first understand the following areas: the origin of evil and suffering, why God has allowed this disorder to exist and even to flourish, and how to live our lives effectively, productively, and victoriously in the midst of and in spite of evil and suffering as we navigate through these adverse conditions. Even when we can neither explain nor make sense of the evil, suffering, and pain of life, or when our joy is eclipsed by sorrow, we can still place our absolute trust and faith in the Almighty God. Our understanding in the grand scheme of life and why we experience suffering and attacks by evil forces can only come as we view them through the lens of human frailty while also realizing the consequences of our conscious choices. We must also consider our individual purpose and calling on the earth, alongside God's ultimate plans, purposes, and pursuits. Acknowledging the brevity and fragility of life will not stop bad things from happening to you, nor will it block evil and hardship from arriving at your doorstep. Embracing life's fragility, however, will produce a different mindset—different thinking, actions, and choices—and awaken the desire to live a more meaningful life, and one that really counts. Because, ready or not, trouble *is* coming—if it has not already arrived. That's not a negative statement—it's just the real deal!

The Fragility of Life

Gary was a corporate businessman and found his path to success in the financial industry. His honesty and integrity made him a sought-after advisor in financial investments and securities. Gary found it eminently easy to build his personal relationships in much the same way as Microsoft creates software—by focusing on extraordinary details. Gary valued his closest clients and friendships; he spent much of his free time building and nurturing them.

At one point, Gary went through an extremely tough season when his life changed drastically over a very short period of time. First of all, a dear friend from his community church had passed away unexpectedly—possibly suicide. It was such a devastating, shocking, and tragic event because Gary had just spent the previous weekend camping with him. Both loved nature and the outdoors; they shared a common bond from their childhood experiences. During a weekend camping trip, Gary's friend had shared with him how much he was looking forward to building his private company and spending the rest of his life with his family (a wife and two daughters) whom he passionately adored. This dear friend often expressed the excitement he felt for his daughter's future, but all of this was left behind when he suddenly and unexpectedly died. Bereaved, one of his closest friends was now gone, and his death was beyond Gary's deepest comprehension. Gary had a tight-knit relationship with his friend's entire family; he even taught the 11-year-old daughter in Sunday school. Gary questioned God about his friend's death because he was never able to fully understand it, and never received a sufficient answer as to why his friend passed prematurely, and so abruptly.

A few weeks later, Gary suffered a second big blow when another close friend tragically passed away from a bike accident. Struck from behind by a drunk driver while riding his bike to work, he was propelled some 30 feet into the air and landed on his head, which killed him instantly. This was Gary's business mentor. He left behind three children, and a wife—who was an incredibly amazing and strong person. Gary had always admired her for her great optimism and courage, although she had been unable to move forward in life since her husband's tragic death. Gary often said that this family was the epitome of some of the most beautiful people he had ever met in his life. He did not understand why something so horrific had happened to such good people. Grief-stricken, Gary grappled with the trauma induced by the loss of his friends, whose deaths seemed so meaningless to him.

Gary soon experienced a third mournful loss. Approximately three months later, after the death of his second friend, another very close associate (a fellow cancer warrior with whom Gary played golf weekly) had passed away from a long, difficult battle with melanoma. It had spread from his deep-skinned tissue to his lymphoid tissue, and death soon followed. He also left behind a wife and four young children. Gary remembered that a couple of months earlier, his hypnotherapist had told him during a session, "Look, you have the same odds of survival as your friend or anyone else." She said, "Gary, you could have a car wreck tomorrow and be gone, or you could very well not die from this melanoma! You might live to an old age or you might not. NOBODY knows what will happen to you, except God. I don't have that answer!"

After the passing of his third colleague, Gary began to reflect on his memories. This friend had been especially hopeful and positive, despite the grim prognosis of terminal cancer that had spread to his lymphatic system. Through the entire illness, his friend had believed God for divine healing in his physical body. Gary had no idea that one of his closest friends, a fellow melanoma patient, would be gone only nine months after receiving his diagnosis, and even undergoing a series of chemo treatments. Considering that he himself was battling a similar condition, Gary eventually recovered from his cancer and was profoundly thankful to be alive. It was at that moment he became fully aware of just how fragile life is, and how brief it can be. He also realized that he needed to make the best of his life, however long or short it might be.

Unexpectedly, life can change in the blink of an eye. It has happened so many times in the past. One day you have a steady job, the next day you are out pounding the pavement seeking work. One day you're holding your healthy, newborn infant, the next day he is fighting for his very life. One day you're living a fairly normal life with routines centered around getting your day-to-day tasks accomplished, the next day some unknown crisis strikes. Life can change so quickly. Life is extremely volatile and delicate at times. Life is very fragile!

Many people today act as if they believe they are somehow indestructible, that they are physically immortal, and that life will somehow continue without any decay, pains, disparities, or other bumps in the road. This flatly contradicts the reality of life experience. Much of our learning as individuals comes through trial and error, which sometimes involves pain. We also learn from, others who show us all the things we should and shouldn't do. As we grow to maturity, we are regularly exposed to the sorrow, pain, and regret experienced by others, in addition to our own painful experiences. Understood properly, these experiences help us learn to navigate through life successfully. The journey to adulthood normally involves a paradigm shift from childish ways of thinking, talking, and acting to more mature attitudes and behavior. Some people, however, never seem to make that shift. Ignoring their own vulnerability, they continue to make unwise or foolish decisions that put them into precarious situations that endanger themselves and others. Throughout life, their trajectory never changes. They continue to behave as though they will live forever on this earth, regardless of what they do, while often blundering and ill-considered decisions propel them into severe consequences that will impact them for the rest of their lives, and for all eternity.

Tragically, humans today are leaving the earth in record numbers before discovering their purpose or fulfilling their destiny. There are approximately 160,000 people who die every day. I often wonder how many of those who that died left their earthly assignments uncompleted. How many died without the salvation of Jesus Christ applied to their eternal spirit? Some of them died prematurely because they spent their time living life for themselves. Society is complicit in this modern philosophy and worldview which consist of playing up pop culture mindsets and sayings such as "*Keep it one-hundred,*" or "*Do you,*" or "*Do what thou wilt,*" and "*Ride or die.*" What this rationale leaves out of the equation is that life will surely come to an end. God will one day call everyone's life into judgment. More specifically, while you are living your life for yourself on the earth, the unknown in the spirit world picks up on sense-lessness and reckless behavior. As long as you are "*Riding and dying*" or "*Doing what you wilt,*" you are not preparing for the "*moment*" of eternity. If you are so busy in this life "*Doing you*" and "*Keeping it one-hundred,*" then you are not thinking about the life that is to come. Suffering, pain, evil, tragedy, mis-fortune, injustice, and an avalanche of other heartaches in this world should all serve as warning signals to unbelievers and believers in Christ alike. Your eternal destiny looms on the horizon. Your primary motivation in life should be to do your very best to prepare for your life to come.

As I've said, it's as though we have forgotten how fragile life really is. Even worse, many have either forgotten that there is an afterlife or are trying their best to put it out of their minds and not think about it. But the afterlife is what matters. This life is merely a prelude and preparation for the next life. Every created human spirit will live forever somewhere. Heaven and hell are eternal realities, and they are the only two places where the human spirit is destined to spend eternity. Every one of us will spend eternity in one place or the other; no one will miss both places. Don't be fooled! In case you're thinking, "Well, maybe there is a chance someone might end up somewhere else," think again; hell is the only guaranteed destination by default. You can bank on it!

Tragedies, injustices, suffering, misfortune, and pain abound in our world. We all experience them in some form or fashion and at one time or another. Life on earth is shorter and more fleeting than we often realize. While everybody wants to enjoy life and be happy, the sad reality is that many good-hearted Christians are in as bad or worse shape than unbelievers in this regard; they are consciously choosing to strive for the fleeting and temporary seductions of success, fame, fortune, and the delusional bliss of material happiness. Oftentimes, many well-meaning Christians have very poor performance records of their commitment to Christ regarding their living and giving. How about you? Have you forgotten that life could end at any moment and that tomorrow is not promised to you? Yes, the believer has a great hope *in Christ*. However, the frailty of life should prompt you to strive to focus on the essentials of living a Spirit–filled life and becoming the person Christ designed you to be. Don't allow anyone to sell you a bill of goods of superficial happiness only to find yourself holding an empty bag of promises in the end. You need to live every day as a precious gift given by Almighty God; focus your time, energy, gifts, and resources on your purpose, doing God's will, proclaiming and advancing the kingdom of God. Everything in this life is transient and will eventually fade away.

Let's drill down to your *everyday life*. In your day-to-day comings and goings, you often take for granted that you will indeed be here to carry out your daily business of the day. Sometimes the unexpected funeral of a loved one or friend brings you face-to-face with the reality of just how easily you can leave this world. The shock of that sudden death impels you to shift your attention from the matters of this temporal life into proper focus on the weightier matters of preparing yourself for the life to come. How long does that last? It doesn't last long enough—not nearly long enough! I cannot overemphasize how extremely important it is that you spend time building your spiritual life, embracing your assignment, and following God's Word while on the earth because this mortal life of yours and mine will surely come to an end. Child of God, build your hopes on things that are eternal. The apostle Paul said it best when he told us to set our main focus on things above, rather than on earthly things or material things of this world:

> So if you're serious about living this new resurrection life with Christ, act like it. Pursue the things over which Christ presides. Don't shuffle along, eyes to the ground, absorbed with the things right in front of you. Look up, and be alert to what is going on around Christ—that's where the action is. See things from [H]is perspective. Your old life is dead. Your new life, which is your real life—even though invisible to spectators—is with Christ in God. He is your life. . . . Meanwhile, be content with obscurity, like Christ. (Col. 3:1–4 MSG)

As believers, our desires, thoughts, motivation, and thinking, as well as our emotional, intellectual, and spiritual energy, should be directed toward eternal things, even while we live out our temporal lives on this planet. In fact, this life has a very limited dimension; again, our number one priority in life should be preparing for the next life. Only those things that are eternally purposed will have lasting effects and great rewards. The Word of God never promotes adopting a dysfunctional attitude about life that disregards the responsibilities and duties which are a part of the hustle and bustle of everyday life. However, as a believer in Christ, your ultimate concern in this life is of those realities and values that have their roots in the kingdom of God. Ultimately, it is your decision whether or not to focus on the more important things of life or on the mundane and simple objects of this five-physical-sense world.

Still, the day-to-day humdrum of earning a living, dealing with the contingencies of family life, staying on top of the bills, obsessively following friends on Facebook, and watching your favorite television shows, all derail you many times from keeping your mind focused on things above. So many distractions arise to draw your attention away from your assignment, your purpose, and your destiny. The Bible teaches that God ordains your steps and that nothing befalls us that He is not aware of (Ps. 37:23). With this in mind, you need to understand that tragedies, misfortune, injustices, pain, and suffering all serve to wake you up and to jump-start your mind back into thinking about how you can best fulfill your purpose and serve the kingdom of God while still on this earth. You are only here for a short time. It will certainly pass!

Surely, you need to feed and clothe your family as well as take care of all the other necessities of life, but your time spent also needs to reflect your understanding that this world's prosperity and pleasures will neither fulfill nor satisfy the hunger of the human heart. Your heart hungers for a relationship with your Creator. That hunger can serve as a spiritual barometer to help you immensely in making better choices in every facet of your life. Life in this world is temporary, but eternity is forever. Don't ever forget this fact. Messages like this one often get diluted over time by worldliness, busyness, and by embracing false belief systems. For this reason, I will repeat it, because if you live your life as if you truly know this, then it will change your internal compass: *Life in this world is temporary, but eternity is forever.*

Life is fleeting. Life is very short. Life is challenging. Life is delicate. Life is uncertain. Life is fragile. However, with God, life can be great! Life is precious! Life is extraordinary! Life is beautiful! Life is a gift; what are you doing with yours? God gives you only one life to live. The award-winning author Dan Simmons said, *"God is found in this life . . . to wait for another is folly."* Are you burying your life or selfishly hoarding it? If your life is not producing good fruit and you are not fulfilling what God sent you to earth to do, then you are burying your gift alive! Someday God will bring your life into examination. He will say, "I gave you a life. What did you do with it?" The bottom line is this: Life is very fragile, so you should be discernibly careful to avoid wasteful living, focus on maximizing your purpose, and remember to never sweat the small stuff.

Avoid Wasteful Living

A recent survey conducted by "Productivity-501" found that the biggest time wasters are watching TV, not having a game plan for life, procrastinating, thinking about unimportant things, being busy without accomplishing anything, not learning from mistakes, and being consumed with worry and fear. Productivity-501 later admitted that, although surfing the internet/social media sites was not part of the survey, it undoubtedly would have made the list as well.

Your free time is precious and valuable; how you spend it reveals much about what your core beliefs and values truly are. Productivity-501 got it right. Watching too much television, not having a game plan for life, being ignorant of your assignment on the earth, being a chronic procrastinator—especially regarding important, conscious decisions, being preoccupied with unimportant things that will not make your life any better, staying constantly busy but not accomplishing anything, repeating the same mistakes because you failed to learn from your past errors, and perpetually worrying about things you can't change are all unhelpful issues which jeopardize your life spiritually, emotionally, financially, and intellectually.

Spending a majority of your precious free moments and resources on excessive, unimportant, nonsensical endeavors is what I call wasteful experimentation, in other words—buffoonery!

The troubling part of all of this is that you may feel that you have a super-abundance of time, so you tell yourself that it will take a little while for you to incorporate a more efficient way to live. The reality is that you *don't* have a plethora of time to waste. Your time has already been measured, and every moment that passes brings you closer to your last moment on this earth.

American society today is addicted to instant gratification. This is a *fast-paced* age. The average person in the western hemisphere hates to wait for anything or even plan for the future. Our New Age mindset is to get as much as we can as quickly as we can, to consume and hoard as much as we can, and to dispose of whatever is necessary as quickly as we can. "*Don't waste your time planning for the most important things in this life and the afterlife (which may not even exist); just live for today*!" That's what the world tells us. As a whole, we are a generation of people who desire instant credibility without accountability, yet, at the same time, we squander opportunity—great time wasters.

If you disagree, then consider this definition of "*time waster*," recently included in the Urban Dictionary:

> A person who either consciously or unconsciously tries to engage you in a fruitless investment of your energy, time, money or attention. These people can be "takers" or simply abject individuals. The truth [of the matter] is that engaging in these types of interactions is an act of free will on our part so each of us can only blame ourselves for getting sucked in once again.

Wow, think about that! Wasting time is an act of your free will. No one compels you or me to waste time; if you do waste time, it is because you choose to do so on your own. There are undeniable pernicious effects of wasting the precious time afforded to you on this earth. As a society, we have been fooled into labeling them under categories such as entertainment, free time, or social events. Millions of sophisticated and well-informed Christians today are spending an inordinate number of hours chatting gregariously on Facebook and being fascinated with other social media sites, spending countless hours and resources on entertainment, playing video games, watching television, surfing the Internet, and spending an exorbitant amount of energy on scheduling pleasure and leisure. They are doing unscrupulous activities that do not help them better themselves spiritually, emotionally, physically, or intellectually. They spend more time living for the moment and waiting for the next "*good time*" to roll around than they do seeking the things of the kingdom of God. Many modernized Christians, desiring the easy life, spend far too much valuable time and too many resources on the pursuit of material things, leisure, and entertainment. I am neither denouncing free time nor advocating that we should spend our lives in a vacuum and not enjoy life. However, the Bible is clear in expressing that where our hearts are, there we will find our treasures also (Matt. 6:21).

Too often, modern-day believers don't value the spiritual things of God as did many of our parents and grandparents. Some rarely attend church, and when they do attend, they are unable to sit and listen for more than 20 minutes at a time without getting bored, restless, and trapped by the barrage of texting on their phone. However, most have no problem watching a three-hour movie with rapt attention. Our modern, anemic church culture (which too often mirrors the secular culture) has produced a generation (or more) of Christians who want material stuff, bling–bling, fun, fads, and gimmicks more than they want God. For them, Jesus Christ has become a once-in-a-while sidekick whom they keep on hand to ensure that they skip hellfire! Many modern believers' minds have never truly been renewed with the Word of God; many have never truly fallen in love with Jesus and His Word. It is a crying shame to witness how the bulk of God's chosen people spend their free time. On the whole, very little of it is devoted to God or their spiritual lives. There must be a higher and better purpose for Christians, who have received salvation and who possess a free will (decision-making power), to spend their time and resources more admirably. Much selfishness and self–centeredness have become the dominant and preferential mindsets of our day. If it doesn't make us happy, comfortable, and excited, then we don't participate or don't want to belong and be committed—even if it's good for us.

What consumes you? What captivates your thoughts? What do you constantly contemplate? What drives your decisions? Where is your heart's desire? What are your passions in life? What and who gets the full value of your time and resources?

Too many of us spend too much time on what should have been or what could have been. More specifically, how often do you sit down with your morning Starbucks coffee or tea and continue to reflect on past mistakes, failures, missed opportunities, or misappropriated priorities instead of planning how to best maximize your talents or gifts for God's kingdom and His purpose for you? How much time do you waste comparing yourself to others or fantasizing about the life of stardom you desire to have? What good can come from this? Don't waste, squander, and ransack the precious time given to you by your Creator. Use your time effectively and efficiently, because once it's gone, you can't get it back. The apostle Paul admonishes the believers at the church of Ephesus to use their time wisely and to make every situation count because the time they have on the earth is short-lived; evil and suffering are continually increasing. Paul the apostle gives us the proper perspective:

> *Be careful then how you live, not as unwise people but as wise, making the most of the time, because the days are evil. (Eph. 5:15–16 NRSV)*

Undeniably, as believers, we should be people who live in the light of Christ and His Word in this world. We should pay careful attention to behave like wise people—not like those who are ignorant or naive, nor like those who are foolishly wasting their time, energy, and purpose ravenously consuming their resources in life like famished wastrels. Every one of us should be applying our God-given wisdom to the practical matters of life by seizing and using every opportunity to invest in what is good and making the most of our time. We must always remember that the world's system in which we live is under the control and dominion of the devil who tempts and entices us to waste our most precious commodity—time; ripping away from us our time, which we will eventually come to deeply regret, because time cannot be recovered.

Fear is often the culprit behind why we are not seeking and using wisdom to extract the complete worth of our time. Fear has a crippling effect. Have you ever lived through a truly frightening experience, one in which you were in genuine fear for your life? Typically, your muscles constrict and leave you immobile for a period of time. We call this *paralyzing fear*. Too many of us are still crippled by years of fear. Even decades after giving our lives to Christ, we have not progressed beyond it to any significant degree. Many Christ-professing believers are crucially behind schedule. Fear has been described as

False Evidence Appearing Real, and many times that is the case. Most of our fears are paralyzing anxieties of what might happen in the future. We allow our minds to erect imaginary, colossal walls that we are afraid to climb. Many believers know the Lord and the awesome truth of His Word, but somewhere in the recesses of their minds is a deeply entrenched fear or doubt that renders them immobile, wasteful, and ineffective for God's kingdom. Neil Gaiman said, "You're alive. That means you have infinite potential. You can do anything, dream anything. If you change the world, the world will change." Sitting back and not doing anything is not God's plan for your life. God wants His people standing, not sitting. He wants you to be strong, not weak; overcoming your adversity. He wants you *chomping at the bit* to do His will. It is the will of the Father that you move toward your purpose, destiny, and the completion of your earthly assignment. Once you realize how truly great God is, that epiphany will shed a new light on the fear that the devil has tried to use like paralyzing venom to stunt your spiritual growth in order to burn God's vision and mission from your life. God has great things invested in your future!

More often than not, many individuals precariously believe they will live out their full lives, banking on their good health—until it fails. Life can be short— very short! We all want and plan to live a long life, but that doesn't always work out the way we plan. We all want to believe that we will know when we will breathe our last breath, but when we do, we won't have a second chance to redo or expand each precious moment of time we were given.

Assuredly, I do not want to obscure this simple but profound important message, so let me be perfectly clear: *It is time to stop wasting your time!* Stop reflecting on things of the past. Your past has passed at last. Stop holding on to grudges against others. Stop contemplating on things that you can do nothing about, because it only consumes fleeting moments and erodes your peace of mind. Stop feeling guilty for things you have not done and cannot change. Start operating in your calling and purpose. It's very likely you have made serious mistakes in your life, but now God wants you to succeed His way. Give God praise and glory because through Christ, your heavenly Father sees you as blameless and spotless! It is time to stop allowing guilt to hold you prisoner. Develop the habit of regularly meditating and thinking on the goodness and greatness of God. Your life will always follow your consistent thoughts. It is

Satan's *job* to inflict you with guilt; why help him along by doing his job for him and inflicting it on yourself? Submit yourself to God! Resist and rebuke the devil! Whoever the Son has set free is free indeed!

The following excerpt is from "a Duke University study on '*peace of mind*'" which identified significant "factors found to contribute greatly to the emotional and mental stability" associated with moving forward in life:

1. *The absence of suspicion and resentment. Nursing a grudge was a major factor in unhappiness.*

2. *Not living in the past. An unwholesome preoccupation with old mistakes and failures leads to depression.*

3. *Not wasting time and energy fighting conditions you cannot change. Cooperate with life, instead of trying to run away from it.*

4. *Force yourself to stay involved with the living world. Resist the temptation to withdraw and become reclusive during periods of emotional distress.*

5. *Refuse to indulge in self-pity when life hands you a raw deal. Accept the fact that nobody gets through life without some sorrow and misfortune.*

6. *Cultivate the old-fashioned virtues: love, humor, compassion, and loyalty.*

7. *Find something bigger than yourself to believe in. Self-centered, egotistical people score lowest in any test for measuring happiness.*

Paul the apostle gave credence to these conclusions when he wrote on how to activate and maintain peaceable fruit in our lives as follows:

> Fix your thoughts on what is true, and honorable, and right, and pure, and lovely, and admirable. Think about things that are excellent and worthy of praise. Keep putting into practice all you learned and received from me—everything you heard from me and saw me doing. Then the God of peace will be with you. *(Phil. 4:8–9 NLT)*

Invest in Maximizing Your Purpose

These days it is not unusual to hear stressed-out individuals bemoan the fact that there are simply not enough hours in the day to accomplish all that needs to be done in this life—trying to do more with less. Millions of people spend millions of dollars and countless hours learning time-management techniques in order to live a more effective and productive daily life. However, the term *time-management*, like most secular terms, may appear harmless, but it has a subtle and potentially hazardous undercurrent that Christians may unknowingly slip into and follow when they try to manage their time and resources.

God has given you a purpose and an assignment to live out in the earth, and a time frame in which to do it. However, instead of learning time-management, I propose that you learn *purpose-management*. When you focus each day on fulfilling the purpose God has for your life, you will spend your time more productively and beneficially. I believe God is pleased with a purpose–filled life. Time-management fads will give you a sense of accomplishment if all you're looking for is a checklist of tasks to do in a given day, but that is just not enough for God's people. Your reward is not just the satisfaction of completing routines, objectives, and tasks. You should live to serve and carry out the King's business and purpose on the earth. Your time spent needs to be fueled by your God-given individual purpose, assignment, and calling. Otherwise, you will be nothing more than a task-checking master who has let your destiny slip by the wayside. Which person do you think God wants you to be? Why do you think the devil has you so distracted in life? Why are you behind schedule in your earthly assignment? Why are your plans not moving forward?

Purpose-management is good management according to Matthew:

> "'But seek first his kingdom and his righteousness, and all these things will be given to you as well.'" (Matt. 6:33 NIV)

Matthew said that everything you need to eat, drink, and wear will be given to you by your heavenly Father when you seek Him first. God's kingdom should be your primary concern on this earth before you concern yourself with anything else. Managing your time does have merit; however, when you manage your purpose by submitting yourself to God's rule in your life and by doing what He requires, you bring glory to the Lord, and He will reward you in this life as well as in the life to come. Child of God, you cannot spend your time listening to the wrong people. This also includes good-hearted, well-intentioned, but uninformed people and many so-called Christians!

Author Lavaille Lavette takes a different approach to maximizing your time in her book *86,400: Manage Your Purpose to Make Every Second of Each Day Count* (86,400 is the number of seconds in a 24-hour timespan). Lavaille said, "The question you should ask yourself each morning isn't: 'How many tasks can I squeeze into my allocated time?' Rather, it is, 'how closely can I use each second of the day to live my purpose?'" It is time for a paradigm shift in how you plan your day, week, month, and year. By its very definition, the word *purpose* echoes that it is not accidental. Unless you learn to maximize your time, resources, and opportunities, you will likely fail to fulfill your God-given purpose in the earth. It will not happen automatically.

Now is the time to take aggressive action to eradicate the things that move you away from your calling and purpose. You can exchange your erroneous and self-defeating focus on the past and on trivial matters for making positive choices that maximize your energy and resources. Your goal as a believer is to become Christ-like; Christ was all about His Father's business (purpose). Christ is the one who we must emulate. We need to be about fulfilling our purpose. Everybody has one!

Being ignorant of this truth will not change things for you. Make a resounding declaration over your life that you will not be the type of person who repeatedly experiences wrong or excessively bad things simply because you failed to manage your time and your purpose. Keep etched in your mind the frailty of life. Declare that you will stop embracing poor lifestyle choices and wasting valuable time on the unchangeable past.

Some of you are reading this book because you are in great need of an epiphany about your suffering, pain, and misfortune. Well, here is one:

> *"Your life will never make total sense, have real significance or meaning until you come to grips with your true assignment and purpose and begin to walk it out on this planet."*

Never Sweat the Small Stuff

When I was a young man growing up, my mother often told me, "*Son, you have to learn to roll with the punches in life.*" She said that whenever I would experience adverse circumstances or seemingly insurmountable, hostile, or unfavorable obstacles and wanted to quit or give up. Many times I resented it because I really didn't want to hear it. However, as I developed into a mature man, my mother's wisdom and grit about life and its hardships helped to shape my personal philosophy about God, life, and how to endure suffering. I was better able to understand how to keep moving with life's ebbs and flows, overcome obstacles, and not look back or sweat over the small stuff in life.

My mother certainly had more than her fair-shake of obstacles and punches of adversity with her back against the wall. Nevertheless, she always managed to hold her head up and keep her life moving forward while looking for a brighter day. Sometimes, I wondered how in the world she always seemed to grin and bear it, as she made it through each crisis one step at a time. She always survived them with God's help, a personal determination, and a refusal to give up. She exudes a real inward bedrock of strength, tenacity, and courage toward life that is a rare quality, absent from many people today—especially many modern Christians. Many of the individuals that I meet and interact with today can't harness much pressure or adversity. The least bit of trouble, which in many cases doesn't amount to a hill of beans, renders them hysterical. Often, they are immediately ready to give up and throw in the towel. Life is too fragile—and too short—to waste time worrying about things that don't matter or being frantic and frustrated over things you can't change. On the one hand, my mother was invariably trying to get me to view life through a bigger lens without allowing the thin veneer of trivial things to impede my progress and optimism. On the other hand, she was preparing me to pierce and penetrate through the inescapable disappointments, enormous hardships, and jaded complexities of life.

Today, we live in a technologically advanced culture that is growing increasingly oversensitive, mendacious, and politically correct. *Micro-aggressions* are the latest insult claimed by the easily-offended; they quickly label any viewpoint that differs from their own as "*hate speech*" or old-school tactics.

Many are often reckless in attaching labels to their identities by often claiming some-kind of hereditary disorder or debilitating syndrome that justifies shirking their crucial responsibilities or accountabilities; they also have a sense of entitlement or seek subsidy-perks. In the trivialized, petty, snappy, egocentric, perpetually-offended, frenzied thinking, and whiny complaints of many in society today, molehills become mountains and motes become logs. Having drifted away from God—even deliberately rejected—absolute or objective truth with no moral courage or energy. Many people waste their lives on frivolous pursuits that they falsely believe are fundamental priorities. What a terrible waste!

Don't let yourself fall into that insidious mental trap. Nothing is more tragic than a life of potential greatness wasted in the vain pursuit of trivial matters. If you are in Christ, then He has called you to higher things, and even greater things. You are called to reign (excel or ascend) in this life by Christ Jesus. Don't make up scenarios, or make the little irritations and the disappointments in your life bigger than they ought to be. We've all heard the catchphrases: "*Don't blow it out of proportion,*" "*Don't make a mountain out of a molehill,*" and "*Don't make a federal case out of it.*" Or, in more modern jive, "*Don't sweat the small stuff.*" The small stuff is just a part of life. Multilayered problems and obstacles are endemic to life. Some are large, some are small, and some are trivial; learn to know the difference. Irritations and inconveniences are inevitable; learn how to process them in a healthy manner that doesn't allow them—or your response to them—to spiral out of control. Don't allow the little stuff, unimportant things or insignificant issues, to pervade and overtake your life. The petty things can often riddle your world with so much stress, annoyance, and bitter frustration that they will extract every bit of your happiness and peace. Decide early on to never sweat over the small stuff; otherwise, the insignificant stuff will control your life, and it will not be pretty. Yes, and Amen!

It is important to understand that not sweating the small stuff does not necessarily mean *ignoring* the small stuff. It means learning to keep everything in proper perspective; to keep everything in its proper place. Sometimes, the small things are important because they affect larger issues. Benjamin Franklin, writing in *Poor Richard's Almanac* in 1758, said, "A little neglect may breed mischief. . . for want of a nail, the shoe was lost; for want of a shoe the horse was lost; and for want of a horse the rider was lost." This aphorism, which has many variations, illustrates the reality that sometimes seemingly insignificant incidents can lead to much greater consequences than their apparent size would indicate. So, don't automatically ignore the *small* irritations, frustrations, inconveniences, problems, or troubles that come along. At the same time, however, don't give them more attention than they deserve. Some *small* problems need to be addressed quickly before they escalate, while others can be safely set aside without having any long-term impact. The difficulty is in knowing which to address first. Ask the Lord to give you discernment and perception so you can recognize the problems in your life that really matter, wisdom and grace to deal with them effectively, and the peace and presence of mind to let the others—the truly *small stuff*—inadvertently work themselves out. You can't wrestle with every small issue of life and expect to keep your sanity. Sweating over the *small stuff* simply is not mentally healthy.

Unquestionably, the way you react to the bad things that happen in your life—large or small—will often affect your life going forward more than the negative event that provoked your reaction. Overreacting to a small issue will often hurt you far worse than the issue itself. That is why it is so important to learn how to recognize the truly *small stuff*, and then not sweat over it. Not sweating over the small stuff means not always reacting or overreacting to every bad thing that happens—the disappointments, pain, suffering, and adversity that come your way—in a manner that threatens or alters your whole attitude and perspective on life. Always being chronically irritated, agitated, annoyed, and angry, as well as thinking negatively with the tendency to exaggerate and overdramatize your problems by blowing them all out of proportion, are the wrong habits to cultivate if you want to build a successful, satisfying, and fulfilling life. Your success in resolving life's issues, whether great or small, will not be determined by what happens to you, but by how you react to what happens to you. And how you respond to life's issues today will affect the course, quality, and fruitfulness of your life tomorrow—especially your attitude. In the whole scheme of things, life isn't as bad as we sometimes make it out to be. It's not worth letting little nuisances dampen your day or spoil your future. Refuse to allow yourself to keep falling into the same dire-straits of always zeroing in on what's not working, what you have failed to fix, or on what you are unable to change. Learn to live every day in the present. Keep it moving. Never sweat the small stuff!

Reflections on the Fragility and Brevity of Life

If you do not understand life's frailty, then you will find it existentially difficult to grasp why you have suffered some things, as well as find it difficult to move forward in life. You must first come to grips with avoiding wasteful living, maximizing your purpose, and not allowing the small things in life to trip you up. Below are five proven mindsets that can enormously change the scope of your perspective. They will help you set a better posture regarding human frailty and how to handle your affairs during difficult deprivations. Putting into practice this simple five-step process will assist you in balancing your mindset during all seasons of life.

1. **Examine your lifestyle choices:** Always remember that life is about the choices you make! All choices have consequences—good or bad! You always have a choice, even when bad things happen to you. You choose to move from the bad experiences of life to the better ones. Let the unfortunate events in your life, eclipsed by your poor choices, give you wisdom to make better choices in and for the future. Learn to see your mistakes and failures as stepping-stones. Use them as learning opportunities from which to grow and further develop, instead of getting overwhelmed or lost in the chaos. Your life experiences can either make you bitter or better.

   It may be immensely helpful to take an inventory of the common choices you make in your daily life. Set aside some time, however long you need, to navigate through the choices you have made on a recurring basis, and reflect back on those choices. You may even want to brainstorm and compile a list by writing them down. How did you make those choices? And why? Try to identify the results or consequences that came from those choices. This inventory should make it easier for you to distinguish between the positive, healthy choices you made and those that were negative or harmful. There may be times when you will need to shift from where you presently are to where you need to be. Inflexibility often creates an enormous amount of tension and confusion. Taking a census and reflecting on the choices you have made in order to make better ones will begin to produce gigantic strides. However, this process will not happen overnight. Next, identify positive choices you could have made instead of the negative choices you did make. Ask yourself: What can I do to change my lifestyle choices and my neurotic behavior from negative to positive? Jot down a few ideas that will help you. It's never too late to change your direction.

2. **Look at the "Big Picture" of life:** Don't allow the small stuff in life to constantly rattle your cage. Yes! You are going to have issues and problems that surface in your world. I'll be the first to admit that life can be somewhat unfair and a bummer at times. Suffering is a part of life, and at the same time it is very fragile. Don't concentrate all your energy on your rigorous hardships, or you will become increasingly annoyed, angered, and agitated. This will leave you discouraged and deplete your capacity for ingenuity and innovative thinking. There are many good things in life. Focus on what is going right. Stop talking about the bad things that happened to you 10 years ago or even 20 years ago as though they just happened today; all that does is constantly drag your past into your future. Jesus said that we should never worry about tomorrow because we cannot change it, and because the day has enough trouble of its own (Matt. 6:34). The same holds true for yesterday. You cannot change what happened in your past by regretting it any more than you can change your future by worrying about it. You can, however, affect the way your future unfolds by the attitude and perspective you take today, and each day as it arrives. The past is the past. Quit fussing about it! It is as good as dead, so *bury it*!

Realize the dynamic power of persistency. When your focus is not on the *"Big Picture"* of life, it slows down your motivation and perseverance. Don't allow yourself to get trapped into the habitual, chaotic complexities and hardships of life. This will only bring additional bitter frustration, inner conflict, stress, and anger. If you continue to have an attitude of defeat and failure, then you will only produce more results of the same. It's time for you to move on. Stay away from asking never-ending questions and probing into the meaning of life's troubles. All of life's answers don't come at one stage in the game. Your destiny awaits you! Concentrate on living for today and building your future with positive thinking and enthusiasm. Focus on the ultimate rewards that are up the road. Start thinking in line with the following questions: What is my purpose here on earth? What is my calling in life? What are the gifts and talents that God has placed inside me? What are the most important things in life? Once you begin to embrace this type of thinking, your life will not fixate on things of your past.

3. **Reevaluate your core belief system:** Many well-meaning Christians are falling for the new cultural, politically correct agendas that are pegged with false belief systems and false ideologies. Many believe that there are no moral absolutes, just different strokes for different folks. Most of these philosophies, values, and beliefs are neither rooted in nor consistent with the Word of God; therefore, they are an enemy to your faith. Believe it! Many contemporary believers are misled by a plethora of false teachings that are not essentially based or rooted in Scripture. Still, many others don't really know God's Word and don't know what they believe.

    Things in this life are transient and fleeting. Bad things will happen. It's a fact! Your core belief system must remain constant even while other things change and flex. Make sure your actions and reactions are congruent with your core beliefs, and that your core beliefs are also congruent with the Word of God. Your core belief system and values will drive your decisions and lifestyle behavior. One of the biggest dangers you face as a Christian is the tendency, usually unconscious, to drift away from dependence on the Word of God as your constant and daily guide for living; instead, you begin to favor superficial and worldly influences. Don't let that happen! Take stock in your own life's busyness right now to see how highly you value God's Word and spiritual matters on your list of priorities. Make sure you are getting into the Word of God on a regular basis, without the façade of the deep spiritual mumbo-jumbo stuff. Objectively reevaluate and reorientate your priorities. Humbly ask the Lord to give you understanding about His Word and insight into life's challenges; ask Him to increase your faith, and to help you align your core beliefs and your lifestyle with the teachings of His principles.

4. **Master the hand you have been dealt in life:** It's not so much the inadequate hand you have been dealt in life, but what you are doing with that hand. The point of life is not for you to always be dealt a perfect hand,

but for you to build and work with what you have. Increase it for the good, and make it better. The world, with all of its insidious hardships, will never fluidly hand-over to you the life you desire to have, but it will always reveal the real you! A cardinal rule in golf is to *"play it where it lies."* Whether in the rough, the sand trap, or on the green, you proceed with the game from where your last stroke placed you. You can't go back; all you can do is play forward. In playing the hand you have been dealt in life, stop wishing you had someone else's life—it's foolishness. The grass always looks greener on the other side. Don't be fooled by the appearances and images of other people. No matter who they are or what they have, no one makes it through life unscathed. Live the life God gave you to the best of your ability. Enjoy life from where you are presently, and move forward. Don't expect the world to give you jovial happiness; make your own happiness along the way. Grasping this insight will pay tremendously rich dividends in your life.

Start planning now how you can best change or use the bad things that have happened to you for your good. Put yourself in a position to take advantage of all your life's experiences—the good, the bad, and the ugly! Everybody's life has purpose. Concentrate on building your strengths and deflating your weaknesses. The secret to this is to develop the capacity for true contentment, which is not found in circumstances that are always fluctuating, but in Christ—who never changes and who is always faithful. This is the lesson the apostle Paul (and I) had to learn; Paul knew how to be content regardless of his circumstances (1 Tim. 6:6). It is a lesson you can learn as well. Stop worrying and being anxious about things that are not within your power to control or change. Consider making the well-known "**Serenity Prayer**" your prayer:

> *Lord, grant me the serenity to accept the things I cannot change, the courage to change the things I can, and the wisdom to know the difference.*

5. **Focus on setting the right priorities and moving forward in life:** One of the greatest pieces of the puzzle to moving forward in life is the ability to press the reset-button. You need to be prepared to reset at all times, especially when there has been severe suffering, residual chaos, or

devastating hardships in life. Don't continually allow yourself to always get frustrated, worked-up, and stressed-out over life's setbacks. Nobody *"bats 1000 percent"* in life, no matter how great they are—nobody except God. Don't be fooled. Always keep the proper perspective, do your very best, and keep moving forward. Set the importance of your priorities in life, and make plans to activate them. Direct your focus on how you will spend your time, energy, and resources on rejuvenating yourself and moving forward. Don't allow the bad things that happen to you take you off course. If you do not set your priorities, dreams, and visions, then someone or something else will set them for you and inevitably take you in a direction you don't want to go. I know it was a horrible thing that happened to you. Okay! What's next? Where do you go from here? How do you pick up the pieces and move on? Don't wish for *"old times"* or the *"good old days"* living in past memories. Let the past stay where it is—in the past. There are wonderful new memories awaiting you on the horizon. Learn from your experiences and memories, but move on.

The future lies ahead of you, and that's what is important. If you have seen the movie *Cannonball Run,* then you will remember how one of the drivers, getting ready for the big car race, rips the rearview mirror off of his car. When asked why, he replied, "I don't care about what's behind me; I only care about what's ahead of me." Paul the apostle had the same mindset in view when he said that he was forgetting what lay behind him and was pressing forward to what lay ahead: the prize of the upward call of God in Christ (Phil. 3:13–14). There is a glorious future in God that awaits you, and it will be far better than anything you have ever imagined or experienced. The famous poet Robert Frost said, "In three words I can sum up everything I've learned about life—it goes on."

2
THE FALL OF HUMANITY

"For everyone has sinned; we all fall short of God's glorious standard."

— Romans 3:23 (NLT)

"One thing is certain: man is not what he was meant to be."

— G. K. Chesterton

Chaos and Death in the Earth Realm

THE CONTINUING EXISTENCE OF EVIL AND SUFFERING IN THE world has always been and remains one of the greatest barriers to people's belief in a loving and caring God. On one side, are Christians who long to strengthen their faith in God and in the Bible, but struggle with the troubling conundrum of the undeniable reality of pain and suffering, especially in their own lives or in the lives of those they love. The stubborn persistence of this hurtful state of affairs raises many serious doubts in their minds regarding the goodness of God. If God loves us, why does He seem to be so absent from us? Why is He often silent in our pain? If God loves us, why doesn't He immediately do something about it? What's really the whole point of it all?

On the other side, are the skeptics, the atheists, and others who find it impossible to believe in a supposedly all-powerful, all-knowing, and all-loving God who also seemingly allows so much misery, grief, pain, heartache, disease, violence, and injustice to exist in the world. This apparent contradiction is the greatest obstacle to their belief in God and acceptance of the Bible as His infallible Word, consisting of *"truth that is non-negotiable."*

At heart, the stumbling block is the same for both groups. How can incorruptible good and intractable evil coexist? In the face of seemingly unremitting evil, pain, and suffering in the human experience, how can anyone claim that there is a loving and caring God who governs the world? Let's face it: all we have to do is open our eyes to see a litany of malignant evils in the world. No matter how we look at it, life's awful experiences such as injustices of every kind, the horrendous bloodshed of war, terror, genocide, ethnic cleansing, and death, terrible atrocities with catastrophic devastation and destruction of natural disasters, pestilential plagues of global poverty, widespread hunger and epidemic starvation even when sufficient food is available for everyone, diabolical sicknesses that roam the planet, pain, abuses of every kind, scourges of human ailments and grievous sufferings that are unyielding to medical interventions, congenital birth defects, devastating and unrelenting communicable diseases, deprivations and desertions, crippling and disfiguring injuries of all kinds resulting from repulsive accidents which leave an array of debilitating disabilities, including all other kinds of horrific evil, and seemingly insurmountable nuisances and nemeses that plague the planet and the human body to an unimaginable degree. All of it seems to belie the presence of a benevolent God who personally cares about the human beings He created. Again, many ask: If God is really there and if He cares for and loves us, then why doesn't He do something right now about all the suffering in the world? Why does He allow it to continue when He could swiftly take it all away with a single word? What is the point and purpose of continuing to bring innocent children into this twisted world under such egregious conditions?

The Fall of the Human Race

Conspicuously, before we can hope to arrive at any measure of rational understanding of why God continues to allow so much suffering, pain, misfortune, and tragedy to afflict the world, we must first understand clearly that these things were absent in the original state of man's environment that God had created for him. Suffering of any kind was never part of God's original design for the world nor for the human beings He created in the uniqueness of His own image. In the beginning of creation, the earth was free of weeds, predators, calamities, diseases, chaos, deprivations, violence, misfortune, natural disasters, and most of all—death. Everything that God made was good and in perfect harmony with everything else. Adam and Eve, the first man and woman, walked in harmony with each other, with the created environment of the Garden of Eden and its creatures, and with their Creator. This idyllic state of affairs would have continued forever if they had not fallen prey to the deception of Satan, the enemy of God and humanity. When they did, the result was disastrous: a fallen world and a fallen human race which was corrupted and almost unrecognizable from the way they were before. As David Breese writes in his book *Living for Eternity*:

> Had Adam and Eve retained their original state, they never would have died. But Eve and then Adam yielded to the serpent's temptation, and death came into the world. Before that moment, they were in a beautiful, pristine state. They existed on a level far above the present condition of the human race. It is difficult to imagine what man was like then by viewing him as he is now. It would require something like trying to reconstruct the original version of an aircraft from its wreckage. If we knew nothing of flying, we would hardly suspect that it had once soared above the earth. The material would be the same; the capability of flight, however, would be lost.

Simultaneously, when Adam fell, the whole human race and the world fell into darkness and chaos that has ever since subjected the entire planet and its inhabitants to an agonizing litany of diabolical destruction, calamity, and death. The original sin of Adam stained and infected us all. In the words of *The New England Primer*, "In Adam's fall—we sinned all." And as a more contemporary sage put it, "Adam was the driver of the bus of humanity. When he drove the bus over the cliff, we went down with him." So, we see that the ills of the world—pain and poverty, sickness and disease, chaos and calamity, destruction and death—are not God's doing; He did not put them here. Whenever we think of suffering, pain, evil, loss, and misfortune, we must trace it all back to Adam and Eve's conscious decision to purposely disobey God. Understandably, this doesn't seem fair to the unregenerate mind (many well-intentioned Christians frequently struggle with the same thought), but it is a reality. Of course, the devil has his foot in it also. These things are the natural byproducts of human sin. The consequences of humanity's fall were so catastrophic that they not only destroyed our perfect relationship with God, but they also affected every aspect of our physical, mental, and spiritual world. The whole world has been stained by Adam's fall and humanity's sin.

In the beginning, God gave Adam and Eve His wisdom and authority, to enable them to exercise dominion over the created order, yet they rejected these in favor of a counterfeit authority and an alien wisdom which were actually satanic. The moment they introduced that dark wisdom into their lives, a radical corruption occurred in their nature. We could liken it to a computer virus, a worm, or a piece of malware, that, when insidiously introduced into one computer, rapidly spreads to every other computer connected to it until the entire network is corrupted, resulting in a catastrophic systems failure. In a similar manner, the sin that corrupted the hearts and nature of Adam and Eve has been unfailingly replicated into the human genome in every generation from that day on. We are all born corrupted by sin and spiritually disconnected from the Author of life. Because of the fall, we have lost our way and no longer know who we are or who we were originally created to be.

When Adam and Eve disobeyed God's moral law, sin entered the world, and they lost the blessing of God's total protection. Every other human being born into this world has faced the same loss. Adam and Eve's moral disobedience violated God's moral will and brought with it the consequences of evil and suffering in the earth. The recklessness of their actions gave permission for evil and suffering to pervade and reign in the earthly realm. Humanity's continuing inherited moral sin and evil actions have infected the cursed earth mercilessly, and made it a suppurating hotbed of perpetual chaos, pain, and suffering.

God's original design brought protection of life without pain, sorrow, tragedy, misfortune, or suffering. It also brought God's goodness, peace, and happiness without sickness, disease, or poverty. Despite all these blessings, Adam and Eve rebelled against God, which resulted in Him expunging them from the perfect environment that He had created for them in Eden. As sin wrecked the world, humanity was forced to fight with his environment just to survive, while nature raged against this vile violation; it retaliated with sickness, diseases, poverty, deprivations, pain, natural disasters, and all sorts of other unexpected calamities.

The presence and perpetuation of chaos and destruction in the earth today is due solely to Adam's sin and the exponential accretion of sin from every other human being that followed him. That means all of us: you, me, and everyone else. We must all remember that humanity's disobedience destroyed God's perfectly created environment for humans to exist, interjecting into it their wretched sinfulness, evil, and wickedness. Humanity is responsible for opening this door. It is a seriously misguided mindset to harbor resentment, a caustic attitude, bitterness, or to get hung up with blaming God for being cruel and hard-hearted, as though He is responsible for the presence of suffering in the world. He isn't; we are. Ultimately, we, not God, are responsible for the presence of evil and suffering in the world. Child of God, this is where the entire mess of evil, suffering, and pain began for the human family. How arrogant of humanity to have opened the door to sin, evil, wickedness, and destruction in our lives, and then turned around and tried to instruct God on how to get rid of it all, thus eliminating or at least mitigating the consequences of our sin! God is not impressed with our faulty thinking.

Originally, God's intent was for humanity to thrive in a scatheless environment without sickness, disease, poverty, pain, hardship, death, destruction, or detriments of any kind. Sin destroyed the bliss of this paradise and catastrophically altered the whole spectrum of life. The fall resulted in disunion between God and humanity as well as causing a breach between them and their physical environment—a disunion that had not previously existed. At the same time, it gave birth to an innately continual corruption of both the nature of humanity and their natural environment. The harmonious relationship that originally existed between God and humans, between human and human, and between humans and nature was now totally destroyed. Sin shattered the whole of creation and ushered in a diabolical system that was full of chaos, calamity, destruction, and death. God had warned Adam and Eve of the consequences of their disobedience; eating the prohibited fruit of the tree of the knowledge of good and evil would bring the bondage of both natural and spiritual death to them, and into the earth realm. Despite this warning, they decided to disobey anyway, and in judgment God announced the consequences of their choice for them, which also fell upon the rest of humanity. He wrote:

> *"To the woman he said, 'I will greatly increase your pains in childbearing; with pain you will give birth to children. Your desire will be for your husband, and he will rule over you.' To Adam he said, 'Because you listened to your wife and ate from the tree about which I commanded you, 'You must not eat of it,' 'Cursed is the ground because of you; through painful toil you will eat of it all the days of your life. It will produce thorns and thistles for you and you will eat the plants of the field. By the sweat of your brow you will eat your food until you return to the ground, since from it you were taken; for dust you are and to dust you will return.'" (Gen.3:16–19 NIV)*

Consequently, because of their sin, Adam and Eve were driven out of the perfect environment God had created for them. They were now subject to a curse that brought sickness, disease, suffering, rejection, calamity, disappointment, violence, misfortune, pain, and eventually physical death. Their disobedience became the primary **root cause** of all human suffering in the world—past, present, and future.

Even worse, the moment they disobeyed, they also died spiritually. In one terrible, tragic moment they went from obedience to disobedience, and from innocence to intimate knowledge of good and evil. They went from life, happiness, and peace to sorrow, suffering, and death. God's original design was for sweatless and effortless enjoyment of their environment, but now they had to produce from stubborn ground, cursed by their disobedience. Only by the painful, arduous labor of their own hands and the sweat of their own brows would the earth grudgingly yield to them even a hint of its vast potential for abundance. In disobeying God, they traded effervescent life for the drudgery of a drab existence marked by suffering, pain, and death. From the sin of

Adam proceeded all the suffering, pain, tragedy, and misfortune that has characterized human life ever since. Humanity's fall brought total defeat and ruin. As a result, all human beings are born into sin; evil and corruption, without exception, characterize our fallen nature. Apart from salvation in Jesus Christ, all are doomed.

The whole world is fallen and is currently under Satan's power, influence, and dominion. Friend, this is the secondary *root cause* and origin of why so much suffering and evil pervades our world. Satan is the "*god*" of this age—the enforcer of evil. He and the kingdom of darkness constantly promote and spur on all the evil in human society. It was the apostle John who made this word explicit at the end of his first epistle:

> We know that we are of God, and the whole world lies under the sway [control] of the wicked one. (1 Jn. 5:19 NKJV)

Yes, tragically, humanity is fallen; the world is helplessly in Satan's grip and generally does his bidding. *But, praise be unto God, that is not the end of the story! There is hope—Glory to God!*

Restoration from the Fall of Humanity

The fall of humanity did not catch God by surprise. Omniscient as He is, God knew even before He created Adam and Eve that they would disobey Him, fall from the high place of authority and honor for which He had created them, and become enslaved to their newly corrosive and corrupted sinful human nature. And, knowing this would be the case, God made plans from the very beginning to undo the cataclysmic effects of inherited sin in the world and in the lives of humanity. Far too often, many humans abhor the thought of evil, suffering, pain, depravity, and wickedness in humanity and in the earth, but they don't give a second thought about the real condition of their own sin, disobedience, stubbornness, and rebellion, which has its *root cause* in the same source.

God announced His plan even as He dealt with the disaster in the Garden of Eden. While He pronounced judgment on the serpent (Satan) for his lies and deception of Eve, God also issued a mighty promise when He said, "'And I will put enmity between you and the woman, and between your offspring and hers; he will crush your head, and you will strike his heel'" (Gen. 3:15 NIV). Bible scholars and commentators are virtually unanimous in identifying this verse as a messianic prophecy of the coming of Jesus Christ, the Savior who would "destroy the works of the devil" (1 Jn. 3:8 NKJV). As Jn. 1:29 identifies Jesus as "'the Lamb of God, who takes away the sin of the world!'" (NIV), Revelation 13:8 refers to Him as "the Lamb [that] who was slain from the creation of the world" (NIV). From the creation of the world, even before Adam and Eve were on the earth, God foreordained that His Son would die for their sins—and ours.

G. K. Chesterton said, "**One thing is certain: man is not what he was meant to be.**" In the fall, humankind lost not only their place of authority and honor in the earth realm, but also their purpose and identity. Spiritually separated from God and from the life of God who created them, they also were separated from the knowledge of their divine destiny and God's intended purpose for them. Humans disregarded who they were. This is the dilemma that we all find ourselves in. Apart from Christ, we don't know who we really are or who Christ is within us. And apart from Christ, we cannot fulfill our destiny or God's intended purpose for our lives. It's only *in Christ* that we can regain the knowledge of our true purpose and identity.

The renowned pastor and theologian Donald Grey Barnhouse told the story of a young man who had suffered from amnesia. For 10 years the man had lived a new life in the midst of his old surroundings with no memory whatsoever of his life before the accident. At the age of 18, the man had fallen off a hay wagon. Witnesses observed that as he fell, he said, "Hand me that pitchfork and I will. . ." At that moment, his head struck the ground, and he left the sentence unfinished. Upon rising, the man could remember nothing of what had gone on before, and he had no choice but to try to build a new life. One day, 10 years later, he had gotten into a fight and received a sharp blow that knocked him to the ground. His head struck a rock and immediately he spoke—completing the sentence he had left unfinished 10 years earlier, ". . . spread the hay." This time when the man rose, his memory had been restored, and he had no recollection of the intervening 10 years; he thought that he was 18 years old and still with the hay wagon.

Similarly, the devastating blow struck by Adam and Eve made all their descendants, in every generation, unconscious of the true-life nature of God, being spiritually dead, and unconscious of their own identity as sons of God. Like the young man who had forgotten who he was for 10 years, we are all born into that same unconsciousness about God and ourselves, and we remain unconscious until the knowledge of our true identity is restored *in Christ*. That is what Christ came to do: restore us to the knowledge that we are sons of God, precious to and beloved of Him, and bring us back to that original place of open fellowship with Him which Adam and Eve enjoyed in the Garden of Eden prior to the fall.

Adam's sin brought death, both physical and spiritual, to all humanity. In contrast, Christ's sinless life and substitutionary death on the cross destroys the power of spiritual death and restores life to everyone who believes and trusts in Him; this is a certainty confirmed by His resurrection from the dead. Paul the apostle put it this way: "For as in Adam all die, so *in Christ* all will be made alive" (1 Cor. 15:22, NIV). Another way of looking at this is to say that everything Adam lost for the human race through his sin, Christ has restored through His victory. Everything Satan stole from humanity through his lies, deceit, and treachery, Christ bought back at the price of His own blood. Every evil work that Satan erected in the world, Christ tore down. There is perfect balance here—a beautifully symmetric characteristic which is in every plan and design of God. The symmetry is so perfect, in fact, that Paul referred to Jesus as the "*last Adam*" when he said, "The first man, Adam, became a living person. But the last Adam—that is, Christ—is a life-giving Spirit" (1 Cor. 15:45 NLT). Jesus Christ was and is the perfect man: Adam as he *should* have been, walking in perfect obedience and fellowship with His Father. This is not only perfect balance, but it is also perfect restoration. The Son of God became like us so we could become like Him.

Paul said in 1 Corinthians 6:20 that we "*were bought at a price*" (NIV). The purchaser was God Himself. We, the entire human race, were lost from Him without hope, and the price He paid was the lifeblood of His only begotten Son. To put it in simpler terms: God made us, Adam lost us, and then God brought us back from the precipice of destruction. Perhaps you have heard some version of the following story, which illustrates this truth.

32

Tom carried his new boat to the edge of the river. He carefully placed it in the water and slowly let out the string. How smoothly the boat sailed! Tom sat in the warm sunshine as he admired the little boat that he had built. Suddenly, an unexpectedly strong current caught the boat. Tom tried to pull it back to shore, but the string had broken. The little boat cascaded downstream. Tom ran along the sandy shore as fast as he could, but his boat soon slipped out of sight. All afternoon, he searched untiringly for the boat. Finally, when it was too dark to look any longer, Tom sadly went home. A few days later, on the way home from school, Tom spotted a boat just like his in a store window. When he had gotten closer, he could see—sure enough—that it was his! Tom hurried to the store manager and said, "Sir, that's my boat in your window! I made it!" The manager said, "Sorry, son, but someone else brought it in this morning. If you want it, you'll have to buy it for one dollar." Tom ran home and counted all his money—exactly one dollar! When he reached the store, he rushed to the counter and said, "Here's the money for my boat." As he left the store, Tom hugged his boat and said, "Now you're twice mine. First, I made you, and now I bought you."

Whether this story is new to you or familiar, it paints a beautifully vivid picture of what God has done for us. First, He created us. Like the boat that belonged to the little boy who made it, we belonged to God by right of creation. Then, through the evil devices and deceptions of Satan, we were lost from God just like the boat was lost when its string had broken and it had disappeared downstream. Finally, just as the little boy paid the highest price—all the money he had—to buy back his boat, God paid the ultimate price—the life of His Son—to buy us back from the kingdom of sin and darkness. Why did God do this? Because He wanted to! "God decided in advance to adopt us into his own family by bringing us to himself through Jesus Christ. *This is what he wanted to do, and it gave him great pleasure*" (Eph. 1:5 NLT, emphasis added).

The Bible has a wonderful word for this transaction: "*redemption*." In the Greek, the word is "*apolutrosis*," which literally means "to ransom in full," "to release on payment of a ransom," and "ransom paid for the deliverance from the power and results of sin." Romans 6:23 explains that the wages of sin is death. By His death on the cross, Christ *redeemed* us; He paid the full price to ransom us from sin and condemnation. There is not one, single righteous individual that has ever lived, except Christ. God, through His everlasting mercy, has provided a way for humanity to escape our eternal sentence of death. Through His death on the cross, Jesus Christ paid for our redemption. Ephesians 1:7 reveals that God "purchased our freedom with the blood of his Son" (NLT). Paul reiterated the same thought in Colossians 1:13–14, "For he [God] has rescued us from the kingdom of darkness and transferred us into the Kingdom of his dear Son, who purchased our freedom and forgave our sins" (NLT). And God did this because He wanted to! He did it because He loves us! He did it because we are precious to Him! What a great God we serve! What a wonderful Savior He is!

Subsequently, the fall of humanity drastically corrupted the world and handicapped humans in every dimension of life. It disrupted our relationship with the loving Father who created us. It destroyed our right standing with the righteous King who rules over a holy kingdom. It dispelled our peace of mind and heart by cutting us off from the gracious God who is our Provider and Protector. It disrupted our joy in life by separating us from the Life-Giver who alone can impart meaning to our lives. It destroyed our eternal destiny by enslaving us to the compulsory power and perversions of a pompous, false god who is a pretender, a flagrant extortioner, and a fallen angel with bizarre delusions of grandeur. Every human being is born a fallen being in whom the image of God has become distorted. The fallen state of our human nature is absolutely and totally unregenerate. This means that we are, in Paul's words, "dead in your [our] transgressions and sins" (Eph. 2:1 NIV). We talk a lot about "*good*" and "*bad*," but in truth, no one is truly good—except God. He alone is the moral standard of "*goodness*"—not people, world systems of governments, or any human ideas, efforts, or philosophies—and His standard is absolute. You can bank on this!

In our fallen state and limitations, if left to our own devices, we are incapable of producing a world without sin, evil, suffering, pain, decay, and death. Apart from redemption through Christ, we are hopeless and helpless. Every one of us, without exception, needs the salvation of Jesus Christ. Nothing else can restore us. Nothing else can remake us into the sons of God that He originally created us to be. Jesus Christ is the only way back to God from the fall we took in Adam. Salvation cannot be found in any other form, person, or thing. There is no other name that has been given to men and women, whereby they can be saved from that disastrous fall (Acts 4:12). When we reject Jesus Christ, we reject our only means of redemptive hope in this earthly fallen state and thereafter (Jn. 14:6).

In redemption, the restoration of the fall of humanity is not just a renovation project; the entire *house* must be gutted and rebuilt from the ground up. Christ didn't come to earth to make bad people better; He came to make spiritually dead people spiritually alive to God. Restoration *in Christ* means being raised from the dead and born into a brand-new life. This is what Paul meant when he wrote, "Therefore, if anyone is *in Christ, he is a new creation*; the old has gone, *the new has come!*" (2 Cor. 5:17 NIV, emphasis added). When God restores us by making us new creations *in Christ*, He doesn't make us the way we were before the fall; He makes us better! The nature and life of God that is resident in the born-again, newly created human spirit not only communicates and fellowships with the Almighty God, but also through the Spirit of God gives illumination, direction, light, life, and information on how to navigate through and overcome evil, suffering, pain, tragedy, and misfortune in this present world. First Corinthians 2:9 concludes, "'No eye has seen, no ear has heard, and no mind has imagined what God has prepared for those who love him'" (NLT). In our restoration, everything we lost in the fall is restored through Christ. And through our redemption *in Christ*, we become more than just the image of God; we become sons and heirs of God! When God restores us, He makes us more than we were before! C. S. Lewis expressed this truth beautifully:

> *For God is not merely mending, not simply restoring a status quo. Redeemed humanity is to be something more glorious than unfallen humanity would have been.*

Believers *in Christ* especially should possess a very deep and sincere gratitude toward God for Christ's redemptive work on the cross. "Thanks be to God— through Jesus Christ our Lord!" (Rom. 7:25 NIV).

Reflections of Humanity's Restoration—Through Jesus Christ

Obviously, there are many blessings that are ours due to the restoration of humanity since the fall. God has given every believer life-sustaining benefits to equip and encourage the faithful through every one of life's challenges. God restores our communication with Him in order to ensure our access to every possible and available benefit. When certain things in our lives are unbenefi-cial or are not useful to our walk with God, they cause us to have less than a full experience of the benefits of restoration. As a result, our relationship with Him and with other people falls short of what it could be. Although not a comprehensive list, here are five important areas related to humanity's restora-tion that are only found in Jesus Christ, and which can be experienced daily and throughout eternity:

1. **Relationship with God Restored:** *In Christ*, our relationship with God is restored. God created humanity to live in intimate, loving fellowship with Him forever. Adam's sin broke that relationship so completely that no human power, will, or effort could restore it. If that lost relationship was to be restored, then God would have to do it. And He did. Paul wrote to the Christian believers in Corinth, "God was *in Christ*, reconciling the world to himself, no longer counting people's sins against them. . . . For God made Christ, who never sinned, to be the offering for our sin, so that we could be made right with God through Christ" (2 Cor. 5:19-21 NLT). Reconciliation means a restored relationship! Your relationship with God should be the first and most significant personal relationship you have as a believer. It is God's design that you have a successful relationship with Him, so that your relationships with others can prosper as well. Our relationship with Christ requires that we have trust and faith in God and that we depend on His Word. When our relationship with God becomes Christ-centered, our chief aim and desire should be to serve and please Him. Christ paid the ultimate price so that our relationship with God could be restored. That's fantastic!

2. **Right Standing with God:** *In Christ*, our right standing with God is rees-tablished. The fall of humanity rendered all of us guilty sinners under the curse and judgment of a righteous and holy God. We had been caught red-handed, with our guilt exposed; we had no defense and no way to make amends for our mortal offense against God. Then Christ took our place. He bore the guilt of our sin on His own shoulders, carried it to the cross, and crucified it there just so that God could declare us "*not*

guilty." The Bible calls this "*justification*" (declared righteous), which is a legal term for guiltlessness. In the eyes of the law, someone who is justified has never been guilty. That is how God sees us when we are restored *in Christ*. "He [Jesus] was delivered over to death for our sins and was raised to life for our justification" (Rom. 4:25 NIV); "Therefore, there is now no condemnation for those who are *in Christ* Jesus," (Rom. 8:1 NIV). Since we are justified *in Christ* and without condemnation, our right standing— our righteousness—before God is restored. Our righteous standing with God *in Christ* has been approved. Wow—what an awesome thought! We don't need to spend any more time or energy deliberating out of a nagging sense of guilt, shame, or inferiority for a right position with Him. He has already made us righteous *in Christ*! Glory to the Lamb of God!

3. **Peace with God:** *In Christ*, our peace with God becomes a living reality. Adam and Eve enjoyed perfect peace with God in the Garden of Eden. Sin dispelled their peace; it disappeared, and humankind has been trying to recover it ever since: However, there is no peace with God apart from Christ. As St. Augustine said, "The human heart can find no rest until it rests in God." Justification, the restoration of our right standing with God through Christ, also restores our peace—*shalom*. "Therefore, since we have been justified through faith, we have peace with God through our Lord Jesus Christ" (Rom. 5:1 NIV). This peace does not mean the absence of conflict, because conflict is an inescapable reality in a fallen world. Peace with God is a sense of unshakable equilibrium, a rock-solid balance in life, and unassailable calmness in the midst of and in spite of outward, chaotic, and unflinching disturbance. It is the unwavering assurance *in Christ* that all is well with our spirits—no matter what is going on around us or what unusual difficulties we may be facing in life.

4. **Joy of Living:** *In Christ*, we enjoy the benefits of a life that's worth living. Joy is a spiritual force that keeps you strong in the midst of it all. The Westminster Shorter Catechism, a classic statement of faith, begins with the statement that the chief end of man is to "glorify God, and to enjoy Him forever." To enjoy something or someone means to take joy in that something or someone. It is the heavenly Father's desire that His children have an abundance of joy in Him and the life He has provided (Jn. 16:24

NLT). When we are restored *in Christ*, we discover that our greatest joy in living is found in Christ and obeying the Word of the Lord and following His will—His way. Psalm 19:8 reminds us, "The commandments of the Lord are right, bringing joy to the heart" (NLT). In Psalm 16:5–6, David said, "LORD, you alone are [have assigned me] my portion and my cup; you make [have made] my lot secure. The boundary lines have fallen for me in pleasant places; surely I have a delightful inheritance" (NIV). Nehemiah 8:10 states, "The joy of the LORD is your [our] strength." Joy's spiritual force breeds strength for living. Paul the apostle said, the kingdom of God is not about natural things such as eating and drinking, "but of living a life of goodness and peace and joy in the Holy Spirit" (Rom. 14:17 NLT). *In Christ*, joyfulness can rise up in our hearts and we can be joyful at all times regardless of our outward circumstances, because the joy of the Lord neither originates in nor depends on our temporary conditions. The joy that we have in Christ—the world didn't give it and the world can't take it away!

5. **Eternal Destiny:** *In Christ*, our eternal destiny is secured. Most people wonder what the future holds; many of them worry about it and live in paralyzing terror every day. *In Christ*, we don't have to wonder. There is no reason to worry, and the perfect love of God drives out all fear (1 Jn. 4:18). The Bible makes it absolutely clear that *in* Christ our eternal destiny is sure and certain, *if we remain in Him* (Jn. 15:2, 6). God never decisively overrides or violates human choice (free-will). Life in this material-physical world is temporary, but *in Christ* your life is secured for an eternal destination with God and His holy angels into His Everlasting kingdom. Jesus said: "For God so loved the world that he gave his one and only Son, that whoever believes (a placing of continual trust) in him shall not perish but have eternal life" (Jn. 3:16 NIV) and "'I tell you the truth, those who listen to my message and believe in God who sent me have eternal life. They will never be condemned for their sins, but they have already passed from death into life'" (Jn. 5:24 NLT). You must have the *"real stuff"* inside of you if you're to see Jesus' face in peace. When we are restored *in Christ*, we have the promise of eternal life as a present, ongoing reality. We have confidence *in Christ* even through the minor and major screwsups, mess-ups, and hiccups of life because of His great grace extended

to us. However, God's promises are only fulfilled in those who remain *in Christ*, follow, serve, and live for Him. God never promises eternal life for individuals who initially experience salvation with good-intentions, but then knowingly reject His grace and willfully walk away, choosing to turn back to a life of sin, hard-hearted rebellion, and rejection of the Lordship of Jesus Christ. Our faith-walk *in Christ* must be purposely deliberate in persevering, enduring, and remaining *in Christ*; anything other than this is a false assurance and a false hope (Mk. 8:34–38). Don't be deceived by the contemporary hyped-rhetoric. Stay on the road that ultimately leads to the fulfilled promise of eternal life with God—don't get off, and take no detours (Matt. 7:13–14, 24:13; Mk. 13:13; Rom. 6:22–23 NLT). The *promise* of eternal life with God does not wait for us way out there somewhere or at the end of this life; it is *right here, right now in Christ*, and it is *ours. That's* a secure destiny!

"To the glories of Jesus Christ, be honor, dominion, majesty, and power both now and forever."

3
GOD'S GOODNESS

"How great is the goodness you have stored up for those who fear you. You lavish it on those who come to you for protection, blessing them before the watching world."

— Psalm 31:19 (NLT)

"God is not merely good, but goodness; goodness is not merely divine, but God."

— C. S. Lewis, *Christian Reflections*

God is the Source of All Goodness

IF GOD IS ALL–POWERFUL AND HIS NATURE IS GOODNESS, THEN why do so many good people, including many children of God, continue to suffer bad things? God permits suffering, pain, evil, and misfortune to exist in the earth realm for His eternal pursuits and purposes. Sometimes, suffering, pain, and misfortune expose what's in the heart of people and what they truly believe. Suffering becomes a way of seeing authentic faith in the lives of some believers. It's one thing to shout from the mountaintop when things are well; it's a whole different experience to walk it out in your daily life of faith. However, the fact that God allows suffering and evil to exist does not negate the basic goodness of His character and nature. Psalm 25:8 concludes, "The

LORD is good and does what is right; he shows the proper path to those who go astray" (NLT). The Hebrew word for "*good*" refers not only to goodness but also to beauty and moral uprightness. God's entire nature is goodness—absolute, perfect goodness. This means that in God there is not even the faintest whisper of evil or the tiniest whiff of corruption. God is essentially, morally, eternally, spiritually, and immutably good. Such perfection of goodness is beyond our full comprehension as humans, because in our fallen world and everything around us, including ourselves, is tainted with the corruption of sin, decay and rebellion. Because God is perfectly good and infinitely wise, evil, destruction, misfortune, and calamity have no place, neither in Him nor in His eternal kingdom. God is the supreme standard of goodness. Originally, God made His goodness aesthetically attractive in the perfection of nature and the created order of things. As Genesis 1:31 informs us, "God saw everything that He had made, and indeed *it was* very good" (NKJV). For these reasons— the essential goodness of God and His creation—God abhors the presence of sin, evil, and the works of darkness in the earth. Darkness is completely foreign to God's character and nature. No lack or deficiency of any kind exists in Him at all. We should never take lightly God's goodness or the riches of His grace—He has so freely given to us. God's goodness and kindness are visible in His benevolence, tolerance, generosity, compassion, pity, forgiveness, mercy, love, grace, favor, patience, and longsuffering toward us—often granting blessing and withholding cursing. All of humanity embraces these blessings every day whether or not they recognize them. God is the ultimate source of all goodness (light). First Jn. 1:5 sums it up for us:

> *This is the message which we have heard from Him and declare to you, that God is light and in Him is no darkness at all. (NKJV)*

Understanding God's disposition and His attitude toward evil will help us to determine the proper perspective regarding ourselves and our suffering. The uncompromised goodness of God certainly cannot be measured in the balance of grievous human suffering, pain, tragedy, and misfortune. God does not and, indeed, cannot create evil, calamity, or disaster because these are diametrically opposed to His very nature, and God cannot act contrary to His inherent nature. In other words, God is absolutely good, and the capacity to do evil is not in Him. God absolutely detests evil, suffering, pain, and misfortune in the earth. God will never purposely use evil to violate His holy and moral character. Why does God permit it? The reason is because Satan has a lease in the earth to perpetuate sin, suffering, pain, and to enact evil.

One day, God will bring into judgment every act of evil and retribution. We must be extra careful when interpreting scripture not to think or suggest that God is in any way the creator or perpetrator of evil. Just because God sometimes allows evil actions to take place does not mean that they were produced out of His moral character. God does not and will not endorse evil—ever! God has no evil to disperse because there is no evil in Him. Absolutely None! To call God good is to define Him concretely, regardless of the things that happen independent of His endorsement. Because God is good and has no part in evil, we must take caution to never carelessly attribute to Him the evil acts, sicknesses, diseases, pain, deprivations, sorrow, or any other miseries of life that exist in this dysfunctional world. God's nature and character never change; He always remains wholly and eternally good. All the goodness in the world derives from God Himself. Not only was everything that God made good in its original intent, but also everything that is good comes from God. The apostle James said:

> Whatever is good and perfect comes down to us from God our Father, who created all the lights in the heavens. He never changes or casts a shifting shadow. (Jas. 1:17 NLT)

Everything about God is good: His character, His heart, His mind, His thought processes, His motivations, His purposes, His general disposition, and His spiritual inclination; the very core of His being is goodness. Whatever God does is always righteous, just, good, and perfect. How good is God? Take the sum total of everything good that we humans can conceive in our hearts and minds, even to the farthest possible extent of our imagination; God is all of that and infinitely more. It is no mystery, then, that we can count on God to be consistently good 24 hours a day, 7 days a week, and 365 days a year. Furthermore, this always-good God is always working on behalf of His children; He is always working for the good of all those who have believed on the name of His Son, Jesus Christ. This same Jesus, who is good like our heavenly Father, also works on our behalf by representing us before the Father as someone who has been where we are and knows what it is to be human in a sin-ridden world. As the writer of Hebrews explains:

> *So then, since we have a great High Priest who has entered heaven, Jesus the Son of God, let us hold firmly to what we believe. This High Priest of ours understands our weaknesses, for he faced all of the same testings we do, yet he did not sin. So let us come boldly to the throne of our gracious God. There we will receive his mercy, and we will find grace to help us when we need it most. (Heb. 4:14–16 NLT)*

Jesus already knows what we have experienced in this earthly body and everything that comes with it. God, in His goodness, established His Beloved Son as our High Priest, who presses our petition before the Father, sympathizes with our weaknesses, knows our every trouble, and gives us mercy and grace. Wow! Think about that, child of God!

God is good all the time, and all the time God is good. Yet throughout history and continuing into our own day, many have tried and do try to blame God for the continuing evil and suffering that dominate every culture in the world. This is absolutely false. The devil and human sin are responsible for human suffering—directly or indirectly. We have brought many of these miseries upon ourselves. God's nature is unalterably good, and we must never misidentify or misrepresent Him as being anything less. Time after time, we have seen when a friend or loved one has died unexpectedly, or some other colossal tragedy has happened, or intense suffering has occurred, it is difficult to fathom the goodness of God. Some people's claim to *"faith"* in God and His goodness lasts only as long as things are going well in life. All they want is God's *"goody-bag"*; they are not interested in trusting God when bad things happen in life. God is neither a puppet with strings for you to pull nor a magic genie in an Aladdin's lamp for you to rub. We must trust Him at all times and in all circumstances of life. All authority, power, might, dominion, and majesty are within His command. We must never make the mistake of applying to God the inescapable negative events and experiences that happen in life, as though they define the attributes of His nature or character. Absolutely nothing happens in the universe or in the earth realm that takes God by surprise. Nothing in either time or eternity is beyond His control. God is fully aware of everything that occurs within and around His creation. Although He cares deeply about the sufferings we endure, He is independent of humanity's choices and everything He has created.

In order to better understand this truth, let us examine the natural example of parents and children. The nature and character of a mother and father are independent of the nature and character of their children, even though the children exist as a direct result of their parents' procreation. While the actions of the children, whether good or bad, may reflect something of the values, genetic traits, and parenting philosophy of their parents, those actions do not define the identity of their parents. In plain terms, the good actions of children do not make their parents good nor do the bad actions of children make their parents bad. Any attempt to draw conclusions concerning the nature of parents based strictly on the actions of their children will fail. Parents and children alike are independent agents who consciously choose their own behavior, even though each has influence on the other. A parent's identity is a stand-alone attribute that does not draw its definition from what his or her child, as an independent agent, decides to do. Children make choices, and their actions based on those decisions absolutely cannot be used to assess the character of their parents. Children have their own character, just as parents have their own character.

Just as there is a distinction from person to person, we must also make the distinction between God's goodness and the goodness of humankind. They don't equate to the same thing. There are certain things which humankind has no foresight of and cannot discern. Humanity's judgment and goodness is limited. God's goodness and judgment supersede all of humanity's perfection, wisdom, courage, intellect, and maturity. Because the goodness of God is infinite, He is able to bring good out of evil, relief out of suffering, peace out of pain, and prosperity out of misfortune. We must always remember that God doesn't owe us anything; He is good to us out of the kindness of His nature because He chooses to be good to us. It's not that we are in and of ourselves so deserving of His goodness.

God is good by nature, and the bad that happens in our broken world does not change that fact. He wants the best for His human creation. Everything that God created was GOOD in the beginning. As author Lee Strobel has stated, "God did not create evil and suffering. Now, it's true that he *did* create the *potential* for evil to enter the world because that was the only way to create the potential for genuine goodness and love." He never intended to create humans only to destroy them later or to make their life on earth miserable. God's original intent was for all people to have a life of purpose and to fulfill their potential in joyful fellowship with their Creator. Since the fall of humanity, however, such a life of wholeness and security can now be found only in Jesus Christ.

King David of Israel understood that God is the source of all true goodness and joy:

> *Taste and see that the LORD is good. Oh, the joys of those who take refuge in him! (Ps. 34:8 NLT)*

God's Workings Are Often Invisible and Behind the Scenes

In the face of the immense suffering, evil, pain, and misfortune abroad in the world, it seems only natural that many people, believers and nonbelievers alike, ask God why He allows it to continue and, especially for Christians, why He continues to delay His justice and judgment upon sin, evil, and wickedness. Like the psalmist, we cry, "LORD, how long will the wicked . . . triumph?" (Ps. 94:3 NKJV). Our hearts yearn for peace, justice, and righteousness to prevail in our collapsed world, yet evil and suffering continue. Far too often, God is working His pursuits and own plan behind the scenes, which is not revealed and open to the naked eye.

Questioning God in this way reveals our failure to understand that, although God is always at work fulfilling His purposes in the earth for His glory and for the good of His people, much of the time He works quietly and invisibly behind the scenes rather than openly in spectacularly visible fashion. Miracles, in the minds of most people, are flashy, ostentatious things designed to reveal the presence and power of God in a way that is undeniable. Special miracles that are obvious and visible, while certainly real, are the exception rather than the rule—and always have been. That is why they are called miracles; they are a direct, divine override of the natural law and order of things. However, we need to continually release our faith, have expectancy, and believe God for the miraculous. In the normal, everyday flow of life, many people regard drastic changes in certain circumstances as merely coincidental. However, all too often, it is God's handiwork behind the scenes through ordinary people, inconspicuous promptings, and through natural processes which communicates His favor, grace, power, and com-passion to make provision for their deliverance, relief, and restoration.

The Old Testament story of Esther is an exemplary illustration of this. Inside the simple, but masterful narrative is a clear-cut picture of the choice she faced of whether or not to cooperate with God as He worked behind the scenes to turn a potentially catastrophic and unspeakable tragedy into an occasion for celebration and praise. It shows how He uses brave, faithful men and women to expose and destroy an insidious and genocidal plot in order to protect and preserve His people for His glory, for our sakes, and for the good of humanity.

Esther was a young, exceptionally beautiful Jewish orphan who became Queen of Persia at a critical time in the history of her people, and she was instrumental in delivering them from annihilation. Unique among all the books of the Bible, the Book of Esther neither mentions God by name nor invokes His name in prayer. No reference to God is found anywhere in its 10 chapters. The Book of Esther records no miracles, no great signs, and no wonders. Although never explicitly stated, God's providential care and sovereign protection are implicit in the background, overruling the lurid malaise of a nation, exerting His wisdom, power and influence, preserving and protecting His people from destruction as He "works all things according to the counsel of His divine will" (Eph. 1:11 NKJV).

King Ahasuerus (also known as Xerxes) of Persia, a man of great power, prominence, military strength, and vast wealth, was looking for a new queen. After a long and careful search, a young and beautiful Jewish maiden named Esther was chosen. Esther, whose Hebrew name was Hadassah, which means *"Star of peace and divine blessing,"* abiding by the counsel of her cousin Mordechai, who had raised her after her parents died, kept her Jewish ethnicity hidden from the king, at least for the time being. This was a wise move by her and Mordechai, because revealing her nationality too soon could have had potentially disastrous, retaliatory, or deadly repercussions for both of them and for all the Jews in the kingdom. The Jews in Persia, including Esther, were descendants of Jews carried into captivity in Babylon over a century earlier. And while many of the Jews chose to return to their own land at the end of their 70-year exile, many others chose to remain in Persia, perhaps for business or family reasons.

Not long after Esther became queen, Haman, one of King Xerxes' most trusted advisers and an implacably cruel and ruthless enemy of the Jews, concocted a scheme to exterminate them throughout the kingdom. Going against God's people was a fool's errand from the start, but Haman, hugely ambitious and egotistical, was too blatantly driven by bitter hatred, jealous rage, perverted humility, and intolerance to recognize the danger he had brought upon himself. Haman harbored a particular hatred for Mordechai, who, in Haman's eyes at least, refused to bow to his authority and failed to extend to Haman the respect and honor he was due. Craftily, Haman maneuvered the king into issuing a decree authorizing the eradication of all the Jews, with the date of the pogrom set for one year later. Haman's audacious plans for Mordechai were conspicuously more personal; he intended, with the king's permission, to hang Mordechai publicly on gallows specially built for the occasion. Unknown to the bloodthirsty and vengeful Haman, Mordechai had once been instrumental in exposing an assassination plot against the king.

Once Mordechai learned of the king's atrocious decree, he secretly approached Esther for help, persistently asking her to appeal their case before the king. Esther told Mordechai that anyone, including herself, who approached the king unsummoned would be instantly executed, unless the king held out his scepter to indicate that he would allow the audience. By going to the king on her own, Esther would be taking her life into her own hands.

To this, Mordechai responded:

> *Do not think that because you are in the king's house you alone of all the Jews will escape. For if you remain silent at this time, relief and deliverance for the Jews will arise from another place, but you and your father's family will perish. And who knows but that you have come to your royal position for such a time as this? (Esther 4:13–14 NIV)*

Inexplicably, as we unpack this story, we need to pay close attention to three things Mordechai said to Esther. First, he warned Esther that her being in the king's house would not protect her from the wrath of the decree. Second, if she refused to help, then deliverance for the Jews would come from somewhere else. Third, he implied that Esther becoming queen was no accident; it was purposely and divinely orchestrated by God, and she had "come to [a] royal position for such a time as this." Although not directly stated, implied in Mordechai's words was the confidence that God was the background force in the unfolding process of events to protect His people from extinction and to bring about His ultimate will.

After much prayer and fasting, Esther accepted her responsibility and, on her own initiative, approached the king, who welcomed her with pleasure and asked what she wanted. In reply, Esther asked the king to attend a private dinner in her chambers and asked him to bring Haman. Though unstated, the favor of God on Esther's life overrode the treacherous designs Haman intended for all the Jews in Persia. At that dinner, she asked both of them to return the next night for another private meal. During the second dinner, Esther exposed Haman's treachery and deception as she vehemently denounced his hateful and genocidal plot. The infuriated king ordered that Haman be hanged on the gallows intended for Mordechai. With Haman dead and out of the picture, King Xerxes issued a second decree to counteract the first one, which he had signed at Haman's behest. Since under Persian law no decree of the king could be rescinded, even by the king himself, Xerxes' second decree authorized the Jews in his kingdom the right to assemble and to defend themselves, by any manner necessary, from their enemies, who would try to eradicate them on the appointed day. When that day came, the Jews prevailed heroically and valiantly, and it was their enemies who were destroyed instead. There was great joy and celebration. The annual two-day Jewish festival of Purim was instituted to commemorate this great victory and God's deliverance of His people.

No miracles or any other obvious or visible actions of God are found in this story, but He was steadily active in the background orchestrating preferential treatment. And at the same time, He allowed extreme, negative events, including permitting political ambition, oppression, discrimination, prejudice, injustice, and insidious racial-hatred, while also turning them to bring about His own desired righteous end and purpose. Esther and Mordechai maintained a conscientious, positive attitude and an optimistic spirit in the face of adverse and dangerous circumstances. Remember, God is never on the sidelines wishing that He could intervene in our suffering and pain. He is also never plotting against humanity by working evil or engaging in demonic activity. However, God sometimes hides Himself behind the veil of evil and waits for the most opportune moment to manifest Himself and inundate the earth with His goodness, justice, and righteousness. Glory to God!

Even when He is not plainly visible, God always works deliberately behind the scenes in many other ways. We can see His goodness in the created order itself: in nature, cycles of the seasons, and in planting and harvesting. A farmer tills the soil, plants seeds, and waters it, but God is the one who brings the growth. As Psalm 104:14 points out, "He makes grass grow for the cattle, and plants for people to cultivate—bringing forth food from the earth" (NIV). We see God's goodness even in the cycles of the weather: "He gives his sunlight to both the evil and the good, and he sends rain on the just and the unjust alike" (Matt. 5:45 NLT).

Even answers to prayer most often come through everyday means, and sometimes in completely unexpected ways. For example, when was the last time you thanked God and gave Him praise in your adversarial circumstances? God is always working in the realm of the Spirit that is invisible to our natural sight. He is able to use anything to accomplish His goodness—even fleas!

In the fall of 1944, Christian Dutch watchmaker Corrie ten Boom and her sister Betsie were sent to the Ravensbruck concentration camp by the Nazis for the "*crime*" of hiding Jews in their home to protect them from the Gestapo. Their faith in God sustained them through months of horror amidst shattered lives, hopes, and dreams. Even though Betsie died in the camp before the end of the year, Corrie was released early in 1945 and devoted the rest of her long life to speaking to audiences around the world about the goodness and faithfulness of God.

Through answered prayer, Corrie was able to smuggle a very small Bible into the camp and past the guards, who physically inspected each woman thoroughly as she passed by. The woman immediately in front of Corrie was inspected, as was Betsie, who was right behind Corrie. But in this frightening, dehumanizing, tightly-controlled, tense, and panic-driven environment, Corrie somehow passed through untouched. It was as though she was invisible to the guards.

Like all the other inmates, Corrie and Betsie were assigned to gigantic barracks that were overcrowded, filthy, odious, and, worst of all, infested with fleas. Latching onto 1 Thessalonians 5:18 which states, "**in** everything give thanks; for this is the will of God in Christ Jesus for you" (NKJV; emphasis added), Betsie insisted that they give thanks to God in everything for their current circumstances, even though they were in an intolerable environment that could accurately be described as hell on earth. Betsie even thanked and gave praise to God as the fleas swarmed around her continually. When Corrie protested, asking how anyone could be thankful in a flea-infested hellhole, Betsie reminded her that the Scripture said to give thanks in everything.

Through constant prayer and the use of their Bible, Corrie and Betsie faithfully ministered to the other women in their barracks, and the light of God's loving presence began to shine in a place where spiritual darkness and human misery had prevailed. Every night, they read from the Scriptures and prayed with the women; they were gratified to see God working powerfully in their lives. But they were mystified as to why, in a place where their lives were so rigidly controlled and monitored, their nightly meetings were never interrupted or broken up by the guards. One day, they learned the answer: none of the camp guards would enter the barracks because of the fleas! In the least likely place on earth, many of those women found Christ. God, in His goodness, used something as mundane and minuscule (although annoying) as a flea, and made it possible for the light of His love to shine through two of His faithful daughters in a dark and hellish place.

God is at work reconciling the world to Himself, but His usual manner is to operate quietly and behind the scenes, using ordinary people in normal circumstances. We live in a fallen world that clamors for the camaraderie of social justice and equal rights transformation, primarily through government activism that will bring about sudden, radical, and coercive change. God, however, brings about genuine transformation of human life and destiny on a person-by-person, heart-by-heart basis. God is always at work for the good of His people. To the praise of His glory!

Falsely Accusing God

If God is absolutely good, or as C. S. Lewis puts it, "not merely good, but goodness," then there is no badness of any kind in Him. God is not the author of evil, suffering, sickness, disease, or any of the other bad things that happen to people. He is not the cruel *"big-bad-guy"* of the world. God is not a brutal, malicious, sadistic bully who delights in inflicting pain and suffering, but a loving Father who delights in giving good things to His children. After all, God is the one "who satisfies your mouth with good *things, so that* your youth is renewed like the eagle's" (Ps. 103:5 NKJV). He is the one who said, "'For I know the plans I have for you. . . . They are plans for good and not for disaster, to give you a future and a hope'" (Jer. 29:11 NLT). Jesus said, "'So if you sinful people know how to give good gifts to your children, how much more will your heavenly Father give good gifts to those who ask him'" (Matt. 7:11, NLT), and "'Do not fear, little flock, for it is your Father's good pleasure to give you the kingdom'" (Lk. 12:32 NKJV).

Yet, in spite of the overwhelming evidence of God's goodness both in the Scriptures and in everyday life, there are many people today who falsely accuse God of evil and are deeply angry, bitter, and resentfully rebellious toward Him because they believe that He is unconcerned about their suffering. Some have gone so far as to blaspheme and curse God, while others suffer silently, and seething with antipathy. They either accuse Him of causing humanity's pain and suffering or they accuse Him of not caring enough to do anything about them. Either way, they make God out to be the indifferent, uncompassionate villain.

William was a very altruistic, middle-aged laborer and devout Christian who loved his family and would give the shirt off his back to assist others. He never turned down an opportunity to help someone in need. Everyone who knew Bill loved his gentle touch, his kind-heartedness, and his genuine spirit of humility. He also loved the Lord with all of his heart; he was devoted to his relationship with God and his local church.

As a teenager, Bill had developed a chronic smoking habit. Although he had tried vigorously on many occasions to kick-the-habit, he had been unsuccessful. In the prime of his life, Bill was diagnosed with lung cancer, which was a direct result of his many years of smoking cigarettes. Although many prayers were prayed in faith for his healing to be released in his physical body and his life to be extended, Bill died shortly after receiving the terminal diagnosis.

At Bill's gravesite, many gave effusive thanks to God for the many years they had shared in Bill's life. With Bill's father, however, it was a different story. As we were leaving the gravesite, Bill's father, to my great surprise, unleashed a reckless, venomous stream of vitriolic hatred directed at God. In front of all the other attendees at Bill's graveside service, his father, consumed by blinding rage and sizzling with antipathy, spewed-out curses at God, damning Him for taking his son's life. I was profoundly shocked at what I had witnessed! Never before had I ever seen anyone literally point their finger at God, railing at Him as though He were some good-for-nothing, two-bit tyrant and trickster. Such a public display of ragged-rage and raw emotion was almost beyond belief. Bill's father accused God of somehow being responsible and the **root cause** for creating his son's smoking habit, which resulted in his terminal illness. I couldn't wrap my mind around that. Nothing could be more stupid and idiotic—plain and simple!

What Bill's father failed to understand is that God is not responsible for humanity's decisions and choices nor for the cancer that took his son's life. All too often, people become fiercely angry and resentful toward God because of an irreparable, irreversible tragedy or a catastrophic event that has taken place in their lives or in the lives of others. We may never know in this life why Bill couldn't overcome his smoking habit, and thereby avoid cancer, or why his body was never healed so that his life could be extended. However, we still give thanks to God for Bill's wonderful life and for the great memories of him that we will cherish for a lifetime. We simply were not given answers to all our questions.

Paul Reasoner, a university professor, addressing humanity's blame-game, said, "A sense of un-fairness, of injustice, seems to lurk behind much of life as we observe it and as we experience it. This sense of un-fairness can easily be directed towards God, resulting in blaming God for suffering experienced or doubts about God's justice."

Many people today are so self-absorbed and self-centered that it never enters their heads to seek God or to trust that He knows what He is doing. Their myopic nearsightedness blinds them to their real enemy—the devil. None of us are immune. If we're not careful, we can become so preoccupied with our own suffering and pain that we begin to view God as our enemy. Blaming God is the wide and easy road, and millions follow it every day. Unfortunately, this includes many otherwise good-hearted Christians who are angry at God because they simply can't make it over the hurdle of asking *"why?"* They compulsively want to know and are obsessed with demanding exact and detailed answers to the *"why"* of human suffering—their own as well as others'. Why does God permit babies to starve to death in third-world countries? Why does He allow innocent people to be slaughtered, and every conceivable evil to be displayed? Why doesn't He move more quickly to stop evil and wickedness? Why does God seemingly hide His face, become distant, and look like He disappears from so much suffering, pain, and misfortune in the world, often letting us deal with it the best way that we can? Why does He—either actively or passively—allow so much grief, torment, misery, maliciousness, cruelty, brutality, sadism, viciousness, and anguish? There is an answer and a reason for everything that happens in the universe, whether it is revealed in time or in eternity. Friend, it pays to know Jesus!

Ironically, the one caveat is a sign when an incredibly frustrated person has accused God erroneously or falsely. People who blame God for their suffering, pain, and misfortunes as well as make bombastic accusations toward Him, yet brazenly ignore His Word, betray the fact that they have either forgotten or do not yet understand the fullness of God's goodness, grace, and power. This mindset has become so prevalent and ingrained in the dominant culture that many people dismiss God during the good times, good health, great provision and pleasure, thus abusing His kindness and becoming so comfortable with His tender-mercies, generosity, and graciousness to the point of thinking that they have earned it themselves or they are entitled to it and have been exempted from the consequences of their wrong actions. Tragic or painful events occur all the time in this fallen earthly realm, and they are often created by our own or someone else's poor decision making and hard-heartedness, whether conscious and deliberate or otherwise. And we must never forget or underestimate the satanic forces that are always working actively against humanity by exploiting our weaknesses of the flesh, such as sin, rebellion against God, jealousy, unbridled anger, lust, and just plain stubbornness and foolishness. All of these can blind us to the reality that God's goodness is often working behind the scenes, restraining evil, showing mercy, extending blessing, granting favor, and withholding His judgment as He purposefully seeks to draw the hearts and minds of people to repent, change, and turn to Him. Tragically, the reason so many don't know, don't care, or can't discern God's goodness is because they are too engrossed in their own suffering, pain, and misfortune to listen for His voice, seek His wisdom—His Word, or open their eyes to really see Him!

This propensity to blame God has been around almost as long as humanity itself. Too many people view the suffering, pain, and evil that plague humanity as God's fault. Consequently, they accuse Him falsely, attribute evil to Him falsely, and live in continuous anger toward Him. The truth is exactly the opposite. Evil does not come from God; it never has and it never will. Evil comes from the devil and from within the hearts of humankind. If there is still any question of this, the apostle James' plainspoken words should remove all doubt:

> And remember, when you are being tempted, do not say, 'God is tempting me.' God is never tempted to do wrong, and he never tempts anyone else. Temptation comes from our own desires, which entice us and drag us away. These desires give birth to sinful actions. And when sin is allowed to grow, it gives birth to death. (Jas. 1:13–15 NLT)

God never tests us or tempts us for the sake of being evil to us, so that we fail in life, or because He grants Satan's every capricious desire to do whatever he wishes with us. God is not in bed with the devil. The devil and his cohorts have practiced wickedness and evil from the beginning. They attempt to inflict suffering, pain, and to bring bad things upon as many people as they can, motivated by their ferocious lust to destroy God's creation. God has no need or interest to see where we break, fall down, or miss it. He's God: He already knows everything.

Nevertheless, God often permits testing, suffering, and pain to come into our lives for a myriad of reasons. Ultimately, however, Satan is the primary catalyst for our suffering, although our personal choices before and after any given situation are always a factor in the intensity of our suffering and in how successfully we deal with it. It is Satan who delights in our suffering, pain, and misfortune, not God. Faith will always be tested. At the same time, if we allow it, God uses hardships to purify our hearts and minds to refine our attitude and character. Testing in life never comes without some kind of merit. The inescapable pressure from the suffering often reveals what is really working within us. More often than not, our perspective is limited or skewed because we don't always know specifically what's working behind the scenes against us in the spirit world, until (or unless) God reveals it.

God's goodness is seen even in the degree of pressure that comes with testing and suffering (1 Cor. 10:13). He actively restrains the amount of evil and suffering we face so that our plight is not more than we can handle. Oftentimes, people are intensely grieved and perplexed by the evil and wickedness that they observe, but they never even think about Satan's attempts to inflict massively greater degrees of evil, suffering, collateral destruction, and wickedness. But God, in His grace and mercy, never permits the full extent of Satan's plots and strategies to touch us.

God is completely trustworthy, and He is completely good without even the faintest shadow of evil. You can trust God because He loves you, and He will never do anything to harm you. The goodness of God is love, and all love has its origin in Him. In Jeremiah 31:3, God says, 'I have loved you, my people, with an everlasting love. With unfailing love I have drawn you to myself' (NLT). And because God loves you, He cares about you and everything that is going on in your life. So, instead of doubting God, questioning His motives, criticizing by mocking Him, or blaming Him in anger, turn to Him for help in the midst of your trials, pain, and suffering. Pay heed to the words of the apostle Peter:

> *"God opposes the proud but favors the humble." So humble yourselves under the mighty power of God, and at the right time he will lift you up in honor. Give all your worries and cares to God, for he cares about you. (1 Pet. 5:5–7 NLT)*

God's nature encompasses goodness, compassion, mercy, beauty, joy, love, and many other similar traits. From the very beginning, His desire has been to bring goodness to humanity—not pain, sorrow, misfortune, and death. Once we truly understand God's nature, we won't accuse Him falsely or believe false words of derision about Him being the cause of our personal pain, misfortune, and suffering. Instead, we will take comfort in the knowledge that He is with us in the midst of those things, and eventually will lead us out. God is able to take any pain, suffering, misfortune, or calamity in our lives and bring something glorious out of it, and He delights to do so. Praise be to the Most High God!

Turning Bad Things Around for Humanity's Good is God's Objective

God is sovereign, which means that He is the owner and the ruler of everything that exists, both natural and supernatural. He possesses and exercises absolute power and authority over it all and is accountable to no one except Himself. Everything in the entire universe is subject to Him—even evil, sin, suffering, and pain. Nothing happens without His permission. And because God is sovereign, His plans and purposes for the earth and those who dwell on it will be accomplished. No power on earth or in the spiritual realm can thwart God's ultimate will or defeat His purpose. God has bound himself to His Word. Again, I want to emphasize that even though God is sovereign and the universe is under His authority, and power is at his command, there are many painful and unpleasant things that happen in this broken, fallen, and sinful world that are independent of His endorsement.

When we observe the world around us, however, it appears that the opposite is true. Everywhere we look, the forces of evil, sin, and godlessness seem to be in the ascendancy. To even the casual observer, it seems that implacable, evil forces advance practically unopposed. Wickedness abounds; it goes unchecked and unpunished while God ostensibly continues to delay His judgment. The church of Jesus Christ is battered from all sides, and those who love and serve the cause of righteousness are ridiculed, criticized, marginalized, and often forced into retreat. By all appearances, our enemy seems to be winning, but appearances can be tricky and deceiving. Don't fear, child of God.

This problem of the apparent ascendancy of evil is not new; people of good heart and righteous spirit have pondered this question for centuries. If God is good, then why does evil prosper? Psalm 73 addresses this very question. Asaph, worship leader of Israel and the writer of the psalm, is open and brutally honest about his epic struggle to make sense of the apparent injustices which afflict the righteous and the outwardly thriving lifestyles of the ungodly, which seems so unfair and unjust:

> *Truly God is good to Israel, to those whose hearts are pure. But as for me, I almost lost my footing. My feet were slipping, and I was almost gone. For I envied the proud when I saw them prosper despite their wickedness. (Ps. 73:1–3 NLT)*

He goes on to describe how the openly wicked seem to enjoy idyllic, happy, trouble-free lives of ease, abundance, material prosperity, and power, even as they kick God out of their lives, boast of oppressing others, committing acts of evil, and mock God for His inaction: "'What does God know?' they ask. 'Does the Most High even know what's happening?'" (Ps. 73:11 NLT). Comparing the easy life of the wicked and their sins apparently going unpunished to his own litany of troubles and sufferings bothers him, and almost causes Asaph to lose his faith:

> *Look at these wicked people—enjoying a life of ease while their riches multiply. Did I keep my heart pure for nothing? Did I keep myself inno-cent for no reason? I get nothing but trouble all day long; every morning brings me pain. (Ps. 73:12–14 NLT)*

Then, Asaph has an epiphany that alters his entire perspective:

> *So I tried to understand why the wicked prosper. But what a difficult task it is! Then I went into your sanctuary, O God, and I finally under-stood the destiny of the wicked. Truly, you put them on a slippery path and send them sliding over the cliff to destruction. In an instant they are destroyed, completely swept away by terrors. When you arise, O Lord, you will laugh at their silly ideas as a person laughs at dreams in the morning. (Ps. 73:16–20 NLT)*

Asaph could not understand the apparent success of evil in the world until he shifted his misguided thinking by turning it away from material wealth and began seeing things from God's point of view. Then he realized that the apparent prosperity and success of evil is only an illusion; God has set the wicked on a path of destruction. God's wheels of judgment may appear to turn ever so slowly in bringing forth justice, but that day will soon arrive. There is a final and eternal judgment and destiny that awaits the wicked and those who practice evil; their end is everlasting punishment. God will not tolerate evil and wickedness forever, and it has no place in His eternal kingdom. God is good, and He is steadily at work turning the evil things of the world—suffering, pain, sickness, oppression, injustice, loss, misfortune, etc.—for the good of His people and for His ultimate purpose.

Like Asaph, we need a paradigm shift in our neurotic thinking so that we start seeing our world and its evils from God's perspective. Trouble is an inescapable part of life in a sin-sick world, but that is not the end of the story. Jesus said, "'Here on earth you will have many trials and sorrows. But take heart, because I have overcome the world'" (Jn. 16:33 NLT). And the apostle Paul assures us: "And we know that God causes everything to work together for the good of those who love God and are called according to his purpose for them" (Rom. 8:28 NLT).

The Greek word translated "*work together*" is "*sunergeo*" (from which we get our English word "*synergy*"), and it literally means "*to be a fellow worker,*" to "*cause to work,*" or to "*cooperate.*" Synergy is a "*mutually advantageous combining of resources or efforts that produces an end result that is greater than the sum of its parts.*" The Greek word for "*good*" also means "*benefit.*" Rephrasing the verse, we could say that God permits all things to be woven together—the good, the bad, and the ugly—to ultimately produce good out of it all, and causes these things to cooperate for the enrichment of those who love Him. And speaking synergistically, that benefit will exceed the sum total of "*all things*" that combine to produce it. The good that God will bring out of even the bad things in our lives will be greater than we can imagine. Compared to what lies ahead, we haven't seen anything yet! Just wait and see!

Genesis 50:20 states, "You intended to harm me, but God intended it for good to accomplish what is now being done, the saving of many lives" (NIV). The speaker is Joseph; he is explaining to his brothers how God completely turned his life's situation around from a cascading series of negative circumstances into a position of prominence in which he could bless many people and fulfill God's purpose for his life. Years earlier, while still a youth, Joseph had received two prophetic dreams which indicated that he would one day be a person of great power and influence. However, to Joseph, they must have seemed idle dreams on the day his pompous, jealous, and backstabbing brothers sold him into slavery. He spent a number of years as a slave in the household of Potiphar, Pharaoh's captain of the guard. Later, after being falsely accused by Potiphar's lustful wife, who had unsuccessfully tried to seduce him, was put in prison. To all outward appearances, Joseph's life seemed like a tragic fiasco. But during those 20 years as a slave in Egypt, God was working in the background preparing Joseph for his divine purpose. In Potiphar's house, as well as in prison, Joseph earned respect and positions of responsibility because of his integrity and leadership qualities; through it all, Joseph never lost his faith in God.

Eventually, Joseph's high character, diligent work ethic, and capabilities came to the knowledge of Pharaoh, who elevated Joseph to second in command over all Egypt. This positioned him to take charge of the preparations to protect the people from a great famine that was coming, which God had revealed to Pharaoh in a dream which interpreted by Joseph. The famine was so severe that Joseph's brothers, who probably assumed that Joseph was dead by now, came down from their home in Canaan to buy grain. When they learned that Joseph was Pharaoh's right-hand man and possessed great power, they were awestruck at his position and greatly afraid that he would seek spiteful revenge on them for what they had done to him. Instead, Joseph set their hearts at ease with the words quoted above: "'You intended to harm me, but God intended it for good.'"

Throughout the history of humankind, God has been doing good work, often behind the scenes, to bring good out of evil and out of the negative circumstances of life that are caused by the evil, sin, and rebellion of people working against Him. Through faith, our own experiences as believers, and in the pages of Scripture, we can see the goodness of God in His character, His nature, His compassion, and His counter-responses to the pain and suffering of humankind. Most of all, we see His goodness in the sending of His Son, Jesus Christ, to destroy the works of the devil and to reconcile a lost and dying world to Himself. To the only wise God, be Glory!

God's goodness extends to all people—even those who do not believe in Him, honor Him, or acknowledge Him in any way. Instead of persistently questioning and falsely accusing the Almighty God over why good people suffer bad things, why bad things happen to good people, or even why bad people don't get what they really deserve, we should be analyzing why so many good things still happen to many people in spite of their proclivities, disobedience, failures, mistakes, poor judgment, or simple refusal to listen. Look at all the frivolity of debauchery and sinful actions humankind has brought upon the earth. Yet, God keeps extending His mercy, patience, love, and grace to all of humanity. This is the epitome of the goodness of God because all of us rightfully deserve something else entirely. Don't keep taking advantage of God's goodness as if He will wait forever for you to accept His grace to change your ways. No, no, no! Never ever get it twisted. This God has power you can't even conceive or imagine in your brain; it would blow your circuit! For all who are willing to look close enough, even though some elements of it are shrouded in mystery, God's uncompromised goodness can be seen in the earth as well as in many of the creative and artistic developments and accomplishments of humanity despite all the evil, suffering, misfortune, and pain that characterize human life.

Reflections on the Goodness of God Without Reservation

Who can completely fathom the incomprehensible benefits of the goodness of God? They are clearly seen throughout the whole earth, consistently and faithfully being exercised by His nature in showing "**kindness**," favor, mercy, grace, compassion, and generosity toward all humanity, even though we are completely undeserving. God's greater goodness is often displayed in the works of His hands that He imparts through many different channels. Many take the goodness and kindness of God for granted. Below are five different areas where the goodness of God is evident, and all humanity is the beneficiary:

1. **The Beauty of Nature:** God's matchless creativity, spectacular grandeur, stunning artistry, and aesthetics are evident in everything He has made— His undeniable fingerprints. Just think for a moment of the beauty, variety, and abundance of life in both the plant and the animal kingdoms.

George Washington Carver said, "I love to think of nature as an unlimited broadcasting station, through which God speaks to us every hour, if we will only tune in." Consider the vast diversity of species: trees that provide shelter from the heat, fruits to nourish our bodies, wood to build our houses, other green plants that produce vegetables for our nourishment, and the astonishing variety of flowers whose brilliant colors and captivating scents bathe our senses of sight and smell. The earth has been graced with the wealth of His generous and rewarding deposits. God created the ideal world as a dwelling place for the people He created in His own image. The whole earth is filled with His glory. Let us rejoice and be glad in celebration of the awesome God of nature!

2. **Medicine:** It was only a few generations ago that people usually died from infectious diseases that today are easily cured with medicine; in some cases, diseases such as smallpox have been virtually eradicated from the face of the earth. The advancements in medical knowledge, research, discovery, and treatment of the sick just over the last 50 years alone is nothing short of astonishing. Every disease that has been cured, alleviated, or eradicated by modern medicine is due ultimately to the goodness of God. Think, for example, of the many millions of people who would still be suffering today, and even millions more of premature deaths that would occur if it were not for the many vaccines that have been developed to keep people alive. Glory to His name forever! God testifies to His goodness in that He has gifted men and women of all backgrounds and nationalities, Christians and non-Christians alike, with the ability to understand the workings of the human body, determine the causes of all sorts of illnesses, develop effective treatments and, in more and more cases, discover cures that would have otherwise cut people's lives short—doing God's goodness in the earth. All of these advancements help immensely to relieve human misery and make life better. Medical science is nothing short of the goodness of God as a gift to humanity.

3. **Divine Healing and Deliverance:** Although God has endowed humanity with the ability to accomplish amazing things in the field of medicine and healing, He also causes healings and deliverances to manifest after all medical science is applied. God is simply amazing! He has not relegated

healing capacity to humankind exclusively. In many of these miraculous cases, the power of prayer and faith are released for healing. He is always at work! God has always been in the healing business and He always will be, until all things have been consummated in the new heavens and the new earth. Psalm 103:3 describes God as the one who "heals all [our] diseases" (NLT). That certainly refers to our physical sicknesses and diseases, but it also refers to all other healing, both mental and, especially, spiritual. Even with modern medicine, all healing ultimately comes from God. And in our own day and age, He still heals people from diseases and conditions that remain beyond the reach of medical science. Just as Jesus healed the sick, restored sight to the blind, made the crippled walk, and cast demons out of the oppressed and possessed, so He continues to do today. All miracles, whether divine or human intervention, great or small, visible or invisible, come from God, and this, too, demonstrates His goodness.

4. **Modern Conveniences:** Some people decry modern technology and warn of its dehumanizing and desensitizing tendencies. While there is some justification for this concern, at the same time, modern-technological advances such as automobiles, airplanes, refrigeration, air conditioning, computers, cell phones, mechanized-farming equipment, automated-industrial equipment, household appliances, and medical-diagnostic equipment all serve to make human life more efficient, effective, and comfortable. The key is to remember that technology should exist to serve us, not the other way around. All of these technological advances have come about because of the creativity and imagination of human ingenuity using the gifts that God, the giver of every good and perfect gift, has given them. It's a blessing from God!

5. **The Human Intellect:** Genesis 1:27 explains explicitly that God created humankind in His own image, and Psalm 8:5 reveals that He created humankind a little lower than Himself. God created us to be like Him, and since He is a Creator by nature, so are we. The human brain unarguably represents the height of God's marvelous creativity. In many ways, the makeup and function of the human brain are still only partially understood, but our knowledge and understanding are growing every day. We know enough, however, to recognize that the power and capacity

of the human brain are truly prodigious; no one knows how far we can go or the full extent of what we can do. God created humanity with the capability to solve some of the world's most complex and difficult problems, including the ingenuity to invent new things and create solutions to intractable problems. It is said that even the greatest geniuses that have ever lived have been able to harness and utilize no more than 7-8 percent of their brain's total capacity. In this fallen world, none of us can reach the full dimensions (in the flesh) of who God has created us to be, but the day is coming when that will change. What a glorious day that will be!

"The kingdoms of this world will become the kingdoms of our Lord and of His Christ!"

4

GOD'S SOVEREIGNTY VS. HUMAN CHOICE

"'Wealth and honor come from you alone, for you rule over everything. Power and might are in your hand, and at your discretion people are made great and given strength.'"

— 1 Chronicles 29:12 (NLT)

"God is too kind to do anything cruel . . . Too wise to make a mistake . . . Too deep to explain Himself."

— William Peterson

Understanding God's Sovereign Rule

A STARTLING STORY ERUPTED ONE THURSDAY NIGHT IN EARLY January 2012. Mr. Ben Witherington received a phone call with terrible news from Sarangan, his daughter Christy's boyfriend, who was extremely frantic. The young man cried hysterically, which made it difficult for Ben to understand him. But it was clear that something awful had transpired. As Sarangan calmed down enough to be coherent, he explained that he had just talked to the Durham, NC police department, which had advised him that Christy had been found dead inside her home.

Her boyfriend, who was in Philadelphia at the time and getting ready to board a flight to Durham, had very few details to give Ben, who was at home in Kentucky with his wife, Ann. After hanging up the phone, Ben soberly informed Ann of the tragic news. They cried together and held each other tightly, each leaning on the other for strength. Amidst their despair, Ann kept repeating that for several days she had known in her heart that something terribly wrong had happened to their daughter; she had a premonition that something was not right. Adding to her concern was a voicemail that she had received a couple of days earlier from Christy's boss informing her that Christy had called off from work because she was not feeling well, but when he tried calling her back, he was unable to reach her.

According to Sarangan, Christy had seemed fine on Monday evening when he had last talked to her, but she failed to show up for a regular Tuesday night meeting with friends that she usually attended. Frazzled with concern, Sarangan sent a friend over to Christy's house on Wednesday to check on her, and instructed him to break into the house if necessary. After he climbed in through a first-floor window, the friend found Christy lying on the floor upstairs and unresponsive. He immediately dialed 911, even though he knew she was already gone.

At the height of their crushing grief, Christy's parents had to confront the harsh and bewildering question of why their daughter had expired so suddenly in the prime of her life; she was a vibrant young woman full of life and love who brimmed over with great beauty, promise and potential. Her father stated later that, from the first moment he received the devastating news, he determined to be open to the reality of what had happened to Christy and to look for any positive results that might come out of this terrible family tragedy. "Within myself," he said, "I made Romans 8:28 my refuge, believing that, somehow, good would result from Christy's death."

Christy's autopsy revealed that she had died abruptly from a pulmonary embolism—a blood clot in the arteries of the lungs. Her parents refused to blame God for her unfortunate and unexpected premature death. Instead, they rightly attributed their daughter's tragedy to the bent nature of this fallen and broken world; for whatever reason unknown to them, God, in His sovereign will, chose not to intervene to prevent her death or reverse her condition. Their unwavering stance was, "God is never the problem. He is always the solution." They refused to try to box God into a corner over their daughter's choices and decisions. God makes His own choices out of the counsel of His Word and His sovereign will. He's always right, and He never makes a mistake!

God's goodness is independent of the things that happen in this world. He is good because His nature is goodness. Whether or not we fully understand why bad things happen to apparently good people, God's unchanging character always remains the same—good. Ben remembered that as they rolled Christy in on the gurney, he stared at her lifeless body and, instead of venting anger and bitter rage, he began to thank God for having a better plan for her. He concluded that God's perfect will has never been death, disease, pain, suffering, sorrow, or even sin. God's promise of eternal life always trumps the evils of this world. He believes that despite the often unanswered and seemingly pointless tragedies of this world, it is possible to grieve for our loved ones and still retain hope beyond the grave, and the cruel sufferings of this world that we so often do not understand. God is sovereign in the midst of human choices.

For the purposes of this book, our reason for seeking to understand God's sovereign majestic rule and human free will (decision-making-power) is to bring us closer to comprehending why good people as well as bad people suffer, have pain, experience loss and encounter misfortune. Our objective is not to engage in a long theologically or philosophically acrimonious debate or dispute, but it is to gain practical insights into the supreme authority of God's command in the universe in relation to human suffering. The sovereign rule of God is that God possesses all power and is the ruler over all things in this world. Nothing happens within the universe that is outside of His foreknowledge and permission. Satan, demons, evil, wickedness, pain, suffering, and even human choices are all subject to His absolute rule. All things work according to His eternal purpose, even when certain life events, humankind's power of choice, and personal free will all challenge God's Word, His will, and even His awesome goodness. God's sovereignty is incomprehensible and inconceivable to the finite mind. Obviously, God neither crafts nor endorses everything that happens in the world. Despite human beings' choices, God's sovereignty often works things silently, invisibly, and often unexplainably after the counsel of His own plans. God allows us to make our own decisions, but He also chooses whether or not to intervene. Human choice coexists side-by-side with God's sovereignty, but it will never thwart God's eternal purposes. Every situation, good or bad, serves God, who always works all things out for the good of humanity and for His ultimate purpose in eternity. God Himself says, "'Remember the things I have done in the past. For I alone am God! I am God, and there is none like me. Only I can tell you the future before it even happens. Everything I plan will come to pass, for I do whatever I wish'" (Isa. 46:9–10, NLT). (See also Ps. 50:1; 66:7; 93:1; Isa. 41:4; 43:10–11; 44:6; 45:5; Jn. 6:44; 1 Tim. 6:15).

To be sure, there are some things in this life that God does not express a discernible interest in, and He leaves those matters to our own common sense and hopefully good judgment. There are also some other matters in which He chooses not to intervene because He already knows the outcome. Nevertheless, there are instances when God will intervene independently when either His own glory or the welfare of His people is at stake. Better still, there are times when God intervenes in a matter precisely because we ask Him to do so. For whatever His reason, God's intervention in the affairs of humankind is always for our good and for His ultimate glory. Never underestimate the power of your faith, hope, love and your prayers to open up the avenue for God to intercede for righteousness and justice in the earth realm. God is absolutely supreme. From eternity past to eternity future, He alone is God. His Word is true. His Word is just. His Word is for sure, and God will never break it.

The sovereignty of God means that God is the one and only sovereign being in the universe, and He alone is the Most High—the Almighty God. He is the ultimate God, the all-supreme governing power, and the possessor of all inherent, eternal power in heaven and on the earth. God has the unquestionable right to rule the universe after the counsel of His own will. God has the last say-so, and He calls the final shots without any limitations or reservations. There is no being in existence who can match or defeat God's power, oppose His counsel, circumvent His purpose, or successfully thwart His ultimate will—His way. Also, God is God among all the nations; His eternal kingdom will reign forever and supersede all other kingdoms. The kingdom of God is an everlasting kingdom, and He is the everlasting King: King of Kings and Lord of Lords, Great Jehovah, Mighty God, Everlasting Father, and Prince of Peace (Isa. 9:6).

God is many things and can be defined in many ways—after all, He is infinite and eternal! However, for our current discussion, there are four particular characteristics of God we need to consider in understanding His sovereign rule:

1. **God is OMNI-potent:** This means that He is the All-powerful One to infinity, and there is no creature in the universe that can match His power. God has limitless, governing authority over all creation. Nature, humankind, the spirit world, and everything that exists anywhere are under His divine rule. God rules and super-rules. God will prevail and have final victory over Satan, over all sin, and evil. Whatever God does is just and righteous altogether. All human logic and reasoning are subject to His power. Dominion, wisdom, might, and power all belong to Him. "For nothing is impossible with God" (Luke 1:37 NLT).

2. **God is OMNI-scient:** This means that He is all-knowing, and that He knows all things (Isa. 46:10). His knowledge is infinite. There is not one, single thing in existence that God is not intensely aware of. No one anywhere can hide anything from Him. God knows all things past, present, and future. He knows every possibility and every potentiality of every conceivable scenario anywhere at any given time. God's foreknowledge is incomprehensible for the finite mind; He already knows *what* we will choose even *before* we choose it. Accordingly, 1 John 3:20 declares, "God is greater than our heart, and knows all things" (NKJV).

3. **God is OMNI-present:** This means that God is fully present everywhere at the same time. There is nowhere He is not. He is readily available everywhere, and it is not possible to hide or escape from His presence. King David, the psalmist, put it this way: "Where can I go from Your Spirit? Or where can I flee from Your presence? If I ascend into heaven, You are there; If I make my bed in hell, behold, You are there. If I take the wings of the morning, And dwell in the uttermost parts of the sea, Even

there Your hand shall lead me, And Your right hand shall hold me" (Ps. 139:7–10 NKJV).

4. **God is Immutable:** This means it's impossible for Him to lie or change. Everything that changes is temporal. God cannot change; He lives in His eternal state. He is the self-existing One (Ex. 3:14). Humanity changes in relation to God, but God never changes in relation to humans. It is impossible for God to change His nature, His character, or His Word (Heb. 13:8). God is never potential; He is always actual at all times. God is sovereign over creation, human history, the universe, redemption, and every knee will bow to His majestic rule. "'I am the Lord, and I do not change'" (Mal. 3:6 NLT). (See also Ps. 102: 26–27).

God's Sovereignty Coexisting with the Free Will of Humanity

How, then, does this all-powerful, all-knowing, ever-present, and never-changing God work with human free will? The dynamics of this relationship can be illustrated with the example by A. W. Tozer of a large ocean vessel in the middle of the Atlantic Ocean pursuing a specific destination. Let's say hypothetically, a cruise ship leaves the port of south Florida, bound for Morocco in northwestern Africa. Cruise line officials have already predetermined Morocco as the destination, and nothing can change that fact. In a similar (but far greater) way, God, even before the foundation of the world, had already predetermined the course of human life, nature, and history in its entirety, as well as the final destiny of every human spirit as the result of their choices. God already knows the end from the beginning; He already knew what humans would and would not choose. Nothing in eternity is able to change the destiny of any person once his or her life is completed on earth. The cruise ship carries many passengers on board, and none of them are subject to any kind of bondage or restraint from their personal choices and decision making while the ship is cruising the ocean. Nothing has been predetermined by the cruise ship authorities regarding the passengers or their activities on board; they are free to lounge, gamble, read, party, sleep, talk, eat, shop, swim, and engage in other activities on the deck and all over the ship, each as they please. While all these activities are happening, the cruise ship is steadily moving them onward toward their predetermined and final destination. Likewise, all human beings are free to make their own decisions and choices while on the earth, even as human life as a whole moves steadily toward its predetermined end—the port of call known as eternity.

From this cruise ship scenario, we can readily visualize the principle of the cruise line authority ruling over the ship alongside every passenger's freedom to make individual decisions and choices. Both are in full synchronization with each other, but do not contradict nor interfere with each other. So, it is with God's sovereign rule right beside humanity's free will and choice. God's sovereign rule keeps the universe steady; it keeps the world, life, and history moving along, while at the same time gives permission for some choices to proceed from the devil or from humanity that cause or permit evil, suffering, pain, and misfortune to occur. These decisions, while permitted by God, are yet independent of God's initiation or endorsement. Whatever, whenever, and however God chooses to intervene or not, whether in the devil's plots or in human choices, the outcome still serves His eternal purposes. By sovereignty, we understand that God's ultimate purpose prevails—*always*. None of the decisions or choices by either the devil or human beings threatens God's fulfillment of His eternal plans, pursuits, and purposes. He is God, and He has already seen the end from the beginning, and knows the choices made by humans, every spirit being, and the Evil One.

Human Free Will and Moral Choices

Paradoxically, right beside God's majestic rule, humanity has a free will and chooses daily between good and evil. The origin of all human suffering, pain, evil, and misfortune can be traced back to humans' choices. Of course, Satan always has his hand in humanity's ills as well. When the first humans in the beginning made a decision because of their free will to disobey God's commands, evil, suffering, pain, and misfortune were the inescapable result. In order for humans to make moral choices and have the free will to do so, they must also have the freedom to choose evil; otherwise, the idea of free choice is an illusion. For evil and wickedness to reign in the earth realm, humans must have the freedom to choose. If there is free will, then there has to be freedom to choose good or evil. Freedom is good in and of itself, but it also entails our ability to deliberately choose the opposite of good. Parallel to water (H_2O), the wetness always comes with the water. You can't have moisture without having the water any more than you can have freedom without having the ability to choose either good or evil. Human free will and our sinful choices have brought much grievous suffering, sorrow, and pain on the earth. The rebellious exercise of our free will is the major source of the bad things that happen in the earth. God cannot eradicate all of humanity's evils on the earth at this time, without eliminating humanity's free will.

Humans are free moral agents in that they make willing decisions that have actual consequences. The philosopher Immanuel Kant, said, "A free will and a will subject to moral laws are one and the same." In other words, human free will is not morally neutral; we do not make our choices in a moral vacuum. Despite what we tell ourselves, our personal choices *do* affect others as well as this world we live in. Again, human suffering, pain, misfortune, and tragedy are either directly or indirectly the result of humanity's choices and are part of the **root causes** that bring these conditions. This is one important caveat for us to realize, because ever since the fall, humanity's free will has been in bondage to the devil, sin, and evil. Without God's divine grace and a recreated, born-again human spirit, humanity's choice will be to freely and consistently disobey God's moral law and His Word. This is perhaps the most significant consequence of the colossal fall of humanity. Our human will is less free than in the beginning because our unredeemed, sinful nature blinds us to the truth and inclines us toward evil choices.

Martin Luther believed that humanity's sinful nature restricts his free will almost to the point of non-existence, at least in regard to spiritual matters:

> *For, first, free-will led us into original sin, and brought death upon us: afterwards, upon sin followed not only death, but all manner of mischiefs, as we daily find in the world, murder, lying, deceiving, stealing, and other evils. . . This is my absolute opinion: he that will maintain that man's free-will is able to do or work anything in spiritual cases, be they never so small, denies Christ. . . Faith is far another thing than free-will; . . . . faith is all in all.*

Although the fall has damaged our full ability to choose freely, the Bible nevertheless affirms both God's sovereignty and humanity's free choice existing together. If we want to discover the reason for the presence of sin, evil, death, and general misery in the world, then we need look no further than the sin-corrupted nature and the will of humankind. God does not and never has used the devil, evil, suffering, or pain to teach His creation by purposely sending bad things upon them, nor has God's sovereignty ruled against them to pronounce evil or darkness on them. To explain it in very simple terms: this is not God's nature. Satan and his demonic hordes have access through Adam's fall and the sins of humanity to infect God's creation and the systems of this world with their evil and moral corruption. The devil has a lease on the earth through Adam's sin and disobedience. Jesus Christ appeared in the flesh so that He might destroy the works of the devil and alleviate evil, pain, and suffering in the earth. It is the Father's will that believers know and live under the New Covenant He has provided, which gives a higher level of living and protection against these powers of darkness. I am not advocating that believers won't be zealously attacked. However, there is a contract agreement (the New Covenant), and we need to know and understand what it is and how it works (Heb. 8:6).

As children of God, we have the responsibility to minimize the devil's influence in our lives. God expects us to live faithfully according to His will and Word, but He doesn't expect us to do so in our own power or with our own resources. That is why He gave us the Holy Spirit and His Word. When we submit ourselves humbly to God in the power of the Spirit, we can resist the devil and evil, and he will flee from us (Jas. 4:7). This is a battle we must fight every day through spiritual means.

The "*why*" of human suffering in the presence of a sovereign and loving God is the perennial question of the ages. Every new tragedy or disaster intensifies humanity's cry of: Why? Why? Why? The Christian author Phillip Yancey calls it "the question that never goes away." And to be sure, the question poses a dilemma for Christians. On the one hand, the Bible makes it absolutely clear that God is not the author of evil. Sin, suffering, evil, pain, tragedy, and misfortune did not originate with Him nor have any part in His character or nature. On the other hand, is the equally obvious fact that, for some reason, God in

His sovereign rule gives Satan's and his demons limited access to the earthly realm and allows evil to take place. We know that at the root of this lies Satan's and Adam's sin, but why? The Bible never fully explains why God allows evil, nor does it give explicit details about the relationship between God, the devil, and evil. More often than not, many have attempted to give detailed hypotheses, theories, and theological and philosophical arguments, but that is all they are. It is notably presumptuous to believe that God has revealed all His cards to humanity. The most we can say under present revelation is that God, for some purpose, allows evil to exist in the earth realm, although only within certain limits and boundaries and for a specific span of time. Things could be a whole lot worse than they presently are. Let's thank the Lord that they are not!

Undeniably, yet contrary to outward appearances at times, God does not give evil completely free license to wreak untrammeled havoc throughout the earth. We find in the Book of Job that Satan had to receive permission from God before he could inflict Job with sickness and suffering. What the Book of Job does *not* tell us, however, is *why* God allowed Job to suffer like he did. Likewise, we do not fully understand how or why suffering comes in every instance nor do we always understand why some bad things happen to people—especially righteous people. We do know from our own and others' experiences that Satan, whenever he can, will viciously attack righteous people and anyone else that he thinks he can destroy. While Scripture clearly teaches that God hates evil, He also permits it to continue for some reason or purpose of His own volition that has not yet been revealed. Even so, He restrains its power and limits its destruction. He also judges it and uses it for the good of His children, as well as using it for the fulfillment of His ultimate purposes. In Paul's words, "And we know that God causes everything to work together for the good of those who love God and are called according to his purpose for them'" (Rom. 8:28 NLT).

Understanding how God's absolute sovereignty and humanity's free choice coexist can be difficult to grasp, but we can get a glimmer of an idea when we liken it to some of life's coexisting elements or circumstances. As an example, in America we live in a democracy, a nation that is governed by the rule of law. The laws of our "*sovereign*" government establish the standards for acceptable behavior, which work to the greater good of society as a whole. Within the parameters of the law, citizens are free to do as they please. They are also free to choose to break the law, but if they do, they will suffer the consequences determined by the "*sovereign*" government as punishment for law breaking. The power of a sovereign state and the freedom of people to act coexist, and actions in violation of a state's sovereignty will only be tolerated for so long before consequences fall. The relationship is similar between God's sovereignty and humanity's free will. People are *free* to live as they please—even to violate God's laws and do evil—but God's sovereign rule guarantees that someday that *bill* will be called in for payment in full. You can bank on this!

We must be immensely careful not to attempt to draw a conclusion about God's purpose in allowing evil to have a course in the world. Because the Bible limits our insight regarding this, we should also limit our own speculation. Even so, we can still refine our understanding that God can work in such a way that evil, the devil, and humanity's freedom to choose all cooperate with the inevitability of His ultimate predestined purpose. Since God's purpose supersedes all things, His manifold wisdom is such that humanity's choices, as well as evil and the devil play right into His hands. God is always in control, even when things appear to be out of control. God's insight is infinite; ours is finite.

Yet the stupendous wisdom of God allowed humankind to retain his freedom of choice, even to the point of rejecting Christ, which was evident when God allowed Satan to work through Judas to betray Christ. Again, let us understand clearly that God did not have to use evil in order to bring His will to pass. Quite the contrary is true. God fulfills His sovereign will *in spite of* human and satanic opposition. God set His will in motion first, and it carries forth regardless of any obstacles erected in its trajectory by the sinful, free choices of humanity or the devil's agenda. Their opposition to Christ actually becomes immobilized by the supremacy of His will, even as they remain ignorant to the fact that His will comes to pass despite their resistance and defiance. God's sovereignty is so absolute that He turns even the opposition of His enemies to His own purposes.

God is Not Responsible for the Bad Choices of Humans

Some people believe that we live in an entirely deterministic universe. They believe that there is no such thing as free will, and that every action taken and every thought we think is predetermined by God, by the laws of physics, or by the laws of nature. There are even some professing Christians who believe in divine determinism or fatalism to some degree or another. Every choice and decision of humans follows a preordained or preconceived plan that God predetermines and makes, only giving humans the illusion of choosing. This is absurd and nutty thinking! The biggest problem with the idea of a deterministic system is that it reduces human beings to the level of robots or biological automatons who do not and cannot truly think, act, and choose for themselves, but who only carry out the predetermined "*programming*" of their creator.

More often than not, many idolize God's sovereignty as if He is meticulously and exclusively controlling every conscious decision and choice in the universe. This is not the case. Such a deterministic concept of humanity and God's relationship to us does not line up with the clear teaching of Scripture. God neither interferes with nor manipulates humanity's free will; on the contrary, He allows it. This was part of His original design and plan. The power of free will and choice is partly due to humanity having been created in the image of Almighty God (Gen. 1:27). Humanity has always had the ability to choose and to respond to God's commands. When God created humankind, He was not looking for mindless robots that would obey Him, having only irresistible instincts; He was looking for His creation to share His nature and to love Him by their own free decision. If Adam and Eve had no free will, then God's prohibition of their eating of the fruit of the tree of the knowledge of good and evil would be meaningless. What is the point of forbidding human beings who have no choice but to obey?

God wanted His children to love Him, but love is not love unless it is freely given. Giving humanity freedom of choice was risky for God because it meant that humans were free to choose either to obey or to disobey. However, free choice was necessary if humanity was truly to be created in God's image. God is a free agent. He is accountable only to Himself, so everyone created in His image also had to be a free moral agent.

Since humans are free moral agents, and since God does not interfere with or manipulate humanity's free will, it follows, then, that God is not responsible for humanity's wrong moral choices. Wrong choices are also a part of the **root causes** for human suffering and pain in this world. As human beings, every one of us bears responsibility for the use and misuse of our free will and our moral choices. The sin, evil, and suffering in the world are the result of our wrong human choices; God did not create such a world originally. Because of our universal sin nature inherited from Adam and Eve, all human beings consciously and deliberately choose to do wrong. We choose to sin against God. Romans 3:23 explains, "For everyone has sinned; we all fall short of God's glorious standard" (NLT).

Not only has every one of us sinned, but we have all done so voluntarily and of our own volition. In Romans Chapter 1, Paul the apostle said that no one has any excuse for not knowing and worshiping God because the evidence for God is plain to see in the things He has made (Rom. 1:18–20 NLT). Despite this evidence, however, many people still do not believe—not because they cannot but because they choose not to. As Paul explains, "Yes, they knew God, but they wouldn't worship him as God or even give him thanks. And they began to think up foolish ideas of what God was like. As a result, Paul said their minds became dark and confused" (v. 21). Paul then describes the depraved minds and debauched lives of those who reject God (vv. 22–31). On the Day of Judgment, there will be no acceptable excuses or plausible exemptions for rejecting God, His Word, or Christ's redemption plan. God's love and goodness are perfect to all. He gives everyone a free will to choose. Everyone has the ability to accept Christ's sacrifice for their sins or to reject it. Finally, Paul concluded, "They know God's justice requires that those who do these things deserve to die, yet they do them anyway. Worse yet, they encourage others to do them, too" (v. 32).

Paul's words make it clear that sin and evil in the world are the direct result of the exercise of the human free will and the conscious, deliberate choices of people acting as free moral agents. Humanity's sin nature has trapped all people in a downward spiral of choices that lead them farther and farther away from God, which in turn leads only to more sin, worldliness, immorality, depravity, and false belief systems. It is popular today to blame God for the litany of ills and troubles of humankind. This is merely blame-shifting, a game that we humans have been playing ever since Adam and Eve started it in the Garden of Eden, and we have gotten very good at it. We cannot escape the fact, however, that humanity has only itself to blame for the presence and continuation of evil and suffering in the world.

God is not responsible for our wrong choices, but He has provided a solution—and He is the only one who can: "God did not send his Son into the world to judge the world guilty, but to save the world through Him." (Jn. 3:17 NCV); "If we say that we have no sin, we deceive ourselves, and the truth is not in us. If we confess our sins, He is faithful and just to forgive us our sins and to cleanse us from all unrighteousness" (1 Jn. 1:8–9 NKJV). Until we *confess* our sins to God (agree with God concerning our sins), *repent* of our sins (renounce and turn away from our sins), and *embrace* faith in Christ as Lord and Savior (giving our lives to Him and continuing to remain in Him), the only one who can take away our sins, we will be *enslaved* to sin and eventually condemned to eternal damnation. Christ came to set us free. After we become believers, the susceptibility to temptation to sin remains an inescapable part of life in the earth realm, but even in this, God has provided a way to escape our *surrender* to temptation: "The temptations in your life are no different from what others experience. And God is faithful. He will not allow the temptation to be more than you can stand. When you are tempted, he will show you a way out so that you can endure" (1 Cor. 10:13 NLT). To the praise of His Glory!

Where is God When Humans Make Wrong Decisions?

One of the accusations most frequently flung at God by unbelievers regarding the human condition is that He seems indifferent to the reality and depth of human suffering; He is silent, detached, and distant. Why is He seemingly hidden from evil and human suffering? If God is real, declare His accusers, then apparently He doesn't care about the human beings He created, because if He did, then He would do something immediately about the pain and misery they live with every day. It is easy to draw this conclusion if all we look at is the depressing and frightening plethora of evils that seem to dominate our world: illness, poverty, disease, hunger, hatred, violence, rape, murder, war, terrorism, ethnic cleansing, and genocide. We stand witness to all the hurt, the horror, and the insanity of suffering in our world and sometimes we cry out: Where is God?

God is right where He has always been: on His throne. And, contrary to the many accusations made against Him, God is not indifferent to the plight of humanity in our suffering. He cares—deeply—about the human condition, the pain, the misery, and the death that sin has wrought in our lives. He is wholeheartedly engaged in His divine plan to destroy sin's curse on humanity and to reconcile us to Himself—a plan He established long before the world began—and He has been working out His plan since humankind's initial rebellion in the Garden of Eden.

Rather than being distant, God is always close at hand. However, God doesn't always stop everything from happening in the earth realm. All too often, there are other laws and circumstances that are at work. All humans are vulnerable to evil and suffering. Ironically, most people do not see God's hand, because they are not really looking for it. They complain about His absence, but they don't expect His presence or deliverance. They don't realize that God is only a prayer away; all they have to do is call out to Him, and He will answer. God truly is a loving Father to all who believe in His name and to all who become His sons by adoption into His family through faith in Christ. As Creator, God has a loving compassion and concern for all people, including those who do not have His Spirit, acknowledge, or follow Him. Even in the face of humanity's rebellion, God consistently demonstrates His care. Apart from Christ, we are all enemies of God, but He still loves us. Jesus taught us to love our enemies and, using His Father's love as an example, He said, "'But I say, love your enemies! Pray for those who persecute you! In that way, you will be acting as true children of your Father in heaven. For He gives His sunlight to both the evil and the good, and He sends rain on the just and the unjust alike'" (Matt. 5:44–45 NLT). Christians especially have the ability to reflect the character and love of God to those who don't know or understand. They are God's representatives in the earth. We must all remember that the earth is broken, and every person is in need of God's help to alleviate and fix the damage done through our bad decisions and wrong choices.

Preventing and Limiting Suffering and
Evil through Better Choices

More evidence of God's fatherly love and care for rebellious humanity is that He established law and government among humankind for the purpose of restraining the spread of sin and evil in the earth. No human government is perfect, and some systems have been far worse than others; however, any system of government is better than anarchy, in which every person would be completely free to indulge in and pursue his or her every capricious desire and ambition without restraint, regardless of how sordid, perverse, or violent it may be. Paul gives us the proper perspective:

> *Everyone must submit to governing authorities. For all authority comes from God, and those in positions of authority have been placed there by God. So anyone who rebels against authority is rebelling against what God has instituted, and they will be punished. For the authorities do not strike fear in people who are doing right, but in those who are doing wrong. Would you like to live without fear of the authorities? Do what is right, and they will honor you. The authorities are God's servants, sent for your good. But if you are doing wrong, of course you should be afraid, for they have the power to punish you. They are God's servants, sent for the very purpose of punishing those who do what is wrong. So you must submit to them, not only to avoid punishment, but also to keep a clear conscience. (Rom. 13:1–5 NLT)*

After Adam and Eve rebelled against God in the Garden of Eden, God could have written off the entire human race, destroyed us, and started over. But He didn't. Why not? Because He loved us. He created us in His image because He wanted a family of sons, and He was not about to abandon us. His love is stronger than our rebellion and can overcome all our sin. Romans 5:8 concludes, "But God showed his great love for us by sending Christ to die for us while we were still sinners" (NLT). God is patient about judging humanity's sinfulness because He wants to allow time for everyone to have the opportunity to choose Him. "The Lord isn't really being slow about his promise, as some people think. No, [H]e is being patient for your sake. He does not want anyone to be destroyed, but wants everyone to repent" (2 Pet. 3:9 NLT). He "desires all men to be saved and to come to the knowledge of the truth" (1 Tim. 2:4 NKJV).

Unquestionably, whether we see it or not, God is at work breaking sin's curse in the world and alleviating many of its immediate consequences regarding human suffering, pain, tragedy, and misfortune. Human beings (believers and nonbelievers alike) who still bear the image of God are cooperating with God in these efforts. We become co-workers with God when we respond in various ways to such conspicuous suffering in the world that personally motivates us to stand against and combat sin, suffering, and evil as much as we are able. The evidence is all around us. We see it in men and women who use their God-given spirit-ingenuity, intelligence, creativity, and compassion as doctors, nurses, other healthcare providers, and medical researchers, all working constantly to improve humankind's knowledge and treatment, and the curing, and the prevention of illness and injury. We see it in the thousands of charities and foundations established to assist people in need, whether financial aid for education, financial assistance for single mothers, or any other type of human need. We see it in the many ongoing political, religious, and humanitarian efforts in pursuit of social justice, both at home and around the world. We see it in the multitude of nonprofit organizations dedicated to disaster or hunger relief. We see it in the Christian church's commitment to worldwide evangelism, ministry, and missions, in order to fulfill Christ's Great Commission to "make disciples of all the nations" (Matt. 28:19–20 NKJV), teaching men and women around the world to turn from sin and evil and to live for Christ. God is at work even through the hearts, actions, and conscious decisions of humanity.

Right now, the world is under the sway of the prince of darkness, but God is sovereign, and His plan for the redemption of humankind and the restoration of all things to His original design and purpose *will be fulfilled*! Nothing can stop it. Glory to God forever!

Reflections on How to Use Your Free Will for the Better

Successful living in a fallen world doesn't happen inadvertently. If you want to achieve your greatest dimension in life, then you must become proactive in making quality decisions. You must first understand that there are consequential effects that stem from free will. Free will is the God-given ability to make decisions and to exercise voluntary choice according to your own mind, inclination, or personal bias among numerous options and potentialities, without compulsion or prior restraint from any external force, whether human or divine. In a nutshell, free will is your capacity to choose as you see fit within the parameters of human limitation and natural laws.

Some degree of suffering and hardship is part of every life, but don't make yours worse than it needs to be because you lack diligence in learning how to make good decisions (see chap. 11). If you leave it to chance, then you will default into following only your sinful, fleshly desires and worldliness, thus setting yourself up to fall under Satan's deception and influence. Despite its potential risks for both God and humanity, free will is a practical necessity for creatures made in the image of God to experience a full and meaningful life. As C.S. Lewis notes, "Because free will, though it makes evil possible, is also the only thing that makes possible any love or goodness or joy worth having." With these thoughts in mind, here are five practical principles you can embrace to help you become proactive in using your free will to affect your life for the better.

1. **Accept and seek a balance between God's sovereignty and your free will.** God is sovereign, but He has given you a free will. On one hand, we submit to His authority to rule over all of creation. On the other hand, we recognize the privilege and power that God has entrusted to us with the limited latitude to operate our lives through the power of decision making. Even though He is sovereign, this doesn't mean that things will automatically work in your favor if you choose to do something that is diametrically opposed to what He has spoken. Humankind is free to resist God's will and His Word. Keep in mind, however, that even if your spirit has been redeemed, you still have an unredeemed, fleshly nature. Your mind, body, and free will, if unrestrained by discipline and unresponsive to the internal reproofs, proddings, and promptings of the Spirit of God and His Word, along with your on-again-off-again bad habits, then your fleshy nature will eventually creep in leading you back into a life of bondage, difficult situations, dangerous circumstances, depraved

behavior, damaged relationships, and, ultimately, destruction of your life here on the earth. Maintaining a healthy balance should be front and center in your daily decisions.

The only way to properly "*balance*" your free will with God's sovereignty is to cultivate a humble spirit, and place your free will under the control and authority of the Spirit of God and His Word. Take off the table the mindset that whatever happens in life happens or what will be—will be. That kind of thinking will only lead to disaster and perpetual suffering. Everything matters in life, even the way you respond when bad things happen to you. Resist the insidious tendency to go to one extreme or the other—seek and value a balanced mindset. Know that God's sovereign will chooses some things that are beyond your control, but, at the same time, He has given you great freedom to make choices that are within your sphere of control. You may not be able to control everything that happens to you, but you *can* always control what *comes* from you.

2. **Take full responsibility for your free will actions and your decision making.** Don't leave things up to God when He has placed the power of free choice and responsibility in your hands. Don't weaken your personal responsibility by automatically writing off the consequences of your actions and decision making, whether good or bad, as "*God's will.*" Thomas H. Huxley said of humankind's freedom, "A man's worst difficulties begin when he is able to do as he likes." God is never responsible for your personal proclivities, mistakes, impaired judgment, or wrong decisions. Don't minimize them or spiritualize them, but own up to them. Passing the buck is a favorite human activity, but it never gets you anywhere. Refusing to accept responsibility for your own decisions, particularly the wrong and damaging ones, may make you feel better in the short run, but, ultimately, it will stunt your growth, hinder your path to success in life, voiding you of any real purpose and spiritual potential.

Resist the perverse tendency to blame others for your own mistakes or failures. Everybody has failed at one time or another. Stop trying to hide! Start by taking responsibility for your actions, and begin moving toward better ones. Stop painting yourself as the victim, and start seeing and thinking of yourself as the victor—an overcomer. The only way to grow is by accepting personal responsibility for your actions and choices, right or wrong, learning from the experience, and building on that knowledge. People of integrity and solid character are never afraid or ashamed to own up to their failures, mishaps, and actions or own the consequences of those actions.

3. **Exercise your free will to choose a life of continual edification rather than one of continual self-gratification.** In other words, dedicate your life, time, and energy to edifying or building yourself up in the disciplines and practices of righteousness and self-giving, as well as edifying others by helping and encouraging them in their journey toward wholeness in Christ and the fulfillment of their divine call and purpose. A life devoted to self-gratification is a losing ticket because you will never be satisfied. The more you get, the more you will desire, in an ever-escalating and, eventually, an all-consuming passion of much wontedness, greed, and lust. Don't gamble with your life—playing the *"lottery"*; it will only destroy you and take a tremendous toll on your life. Jesus said, "'If any of you wants to be my follower, you must [turn from your selfish ways], take up your cross, and follow me. If you try to hang on to your life, you will lose it. But if you give up your life for my sake, you will save it. And what do you benefit if you gain the whole world but lose your own soul? Is anything worth more than your soul?'" (Matt. 16:24–26 NLT). Absolutely nothing!

A much better approach is to make it your daily practice "to do what is right, to love mercy, and to walk humbly with your God" (Mic. 6:8 NLT). This means, among other things, putting the good and the welfare of others ahead of your own, and seeking always to lift others up in the name and love of Jesus. It is easy to theorize, criticize, and tear down, and most of us are experts at it. Much harder, but much more profitable for every-one, is to be a builder, an edifier, and an encourager of others as they also try to deal with the personal struggles, pain, and suffering of life. Even as you seek, with the help of God's Spirit, to build yourself up in your faith and walk with God, strive also to be an encourager—not a discourager. As my pastor used to always say, *"Be an asset—not a liability."* This involves both your words and your actions. You must learn to crucify the flesh, its passions, and desires. Be diligent to "make every effort to do what leads to peace and to mutual edification" (Rom. 14:19 NIV). And, "Don't use foul or abusive language; [this is an ugly stain—keep your cool]. Let everything you say be good and helpful, so that your words will be an encouragement to those who hear them" (Eph. 4:29 NLT).

4. **Decide never to misuse or abuse your free will to indulge in your fallen human nature.** In the physical world, falling is easier than climbing. Climbing takes effort; to fall, all you have to do is let go. Because of the law of gravity, the natural state of any object is to seek the lowest place; it requires no thought and no effort. The same is true in your life. It's very easy to *fall* in with the crowd. Raising your life to a higher plane requires work and constant attention. As a sin-fallen creature, your *natural* state is to indulge your corrupt and depraved, fallen nature (the flesh). Even as a Christian, that fallen nature remains your *default* state, the *"lowest place"* you can always slip into unless you take a conscious and deliberate action to do otherwise. Your free will can be misused and abused—even at the expense of others. Christians' spiritual freedom is being abused in epidemic proportions today because God's undeserved grace is being misrepresented and misinterpreted, and many have fallen prey to many fancy-foot-loose talking preachers. Don't be fooled! The ultimate consequences and implications are more far-reaching than what they are preaching—rotting the hearts of the hearers. God does not and will never lower His standard so you can feel better about living in your mess. Free will is not a license to sin or have a continual heyday in wrongful behavior. The will of the heavenly Father is that your new nature dominates you, through the power of the Holy Spirit and His Word, to rise above sin, and live a life of righteousness that pleases God. As a believer, your free will gives you the ability to deny your fallen fleshly nature and pursue the higher road of holiness, purity, integrity, righteous living, and obedience to God instead of filling your life up with a bunch of junk and trash. Don't give into uncontrolled and wrong behaviors, wrong thinking, and wrong actions, which contaminate your mind and spirit. Stay on the right road and renew your mind with God's Word. However, this takes time and effort; it requires diligence, determination, and deliberate intent. It

always pays rich dividends to follow God's laws and His ways. Serving and obeying the Lord always pays off!

When dealing with any problem, the simplest approach is usually the best. In your spiritual life as a believer, work to train yourself (spirit and mind) not to misuse your free will or indulge in the ungodly demands and urges of the nature of the flesh—which often appear to be more attractive. At the same time, recognize that your will-power alone is not enough to achieve consistent success. You must also call on the power of God's Spirit to help you make healthy and holy decisions that will keep your mind and behavior on that higher road which is that "narrow . . . road that leads to life" (Matt. 7:14 NIV). Satan will always try to drag you down, to get you to cater to your old sinful nature. Don't let him do it. But also, don't try to resist him in your own strength; stand up to him in the power of the Holy Spirit. That's what Paul was getting at when he wrote, "Neither give place to the devil" (Eph. 4:27 ASV). In other words, if the devil doesn't have a foothold in your life, then he cannot gain the opportunity to work severe havoc and it will be impossible for him to defeat you. Humble submission to God gives you access to the divine power to resist and prevail in every situation. Enjoy your Christian freedom and salvation without misuse and abuse!

5. **Avoid tricks, gimmickry, and all other kinds of manipulation of your free will for personal gain.** God did not endow you with a free will so that you could overindulge in it for selfish purposes, but rather so you could employ it to accomplish His purposes in the earth. Just as He freely and unselfishly chose to give His Son for you on the cross, so He also wants you to freely give of yourself for the good of others. As a believer, you are free in Christ, but it is not the freedom to claw, clamber, or connive your way to the top by employing trickery, gimmicks, ruthlessness, or deceit along the way to cheat your *rivals* or *competitors* or anyone else, or to hold them back unfairly. Free will, or freedom in Christ does not mean that you are at liberty to use others as expendable stepping-stones in your own rise to success, power and achievements. You are not free to pervert, injure, or take advantage of others. To live that way is to become trapped in another kind of slavery, prison, and bondage to gratify your own fleshly

nature with all its deception, corruption, and craven lusts—willfully using the ends-to-justify-the-means.

George Santayana said, "Real unselfishness consists in sharing the interests of others," while an anonymous sage said, "Self-preservation is the first law of nature, but self-sacrifice is the highest rule of grace." You are never freer than when you freely use your freedom to help free others and to serve their interests more than your own. And you should do it out of love. Lust enslaves, but love liberates. Consider the apostle Paul's counsel, "For you have been called to live in freedom, my brothers and sisters. But don't use your freedom to [tolerate and] satisfy your sinful nature. Instead, use your freedom to serve one another in love" (Gal. 5:13 NLT). If you commit to live that way every day—openly, honestly, transparently, free of all deceit and flattery, false humility, posturing, and self-serving motives—then God will be glorified, your life will be extensively enriched beyond measure, and you will experience satisfaction, fulfillment, victory, and joy in your walk with the Lord. Yes, and amen!

"To the everlasting grace of Christ and the love of God for His own people!"

5

THE LIFE AND TIMES OF JOB

"I consider that our present sufferings are not worth comparing with the glory that will be revealed in us."

— Romans 8:18 (NIV)

"Anyone who has gone through great suffering is bound to have a greater sympathy and understanding of the problems of mankind."

— Eleanor Roosevelt

The Misery of Extreme Suffering and Recovery

SOMETIMES TRAGEDY STRIKES WITH SUCH FEROCITY THAT IT seems miraculous that anyone survives, let alone rises from the ashes to rebuild a successful and productive life. Celebrity chef Matthew Golinski is such a person. Until a few years ago, Matt Golinski seemed to have it all: a lovely wife, three beautiful young daughters, plenty of money in the bank, a very successful career, and a palatial home in Queensland, Australia—not bad for a man who was only 39 years old.

Then disaster struck.

On December 26, 2011 (the day after Christmas), Matt's beautiful house caught fire and burned to the ground. Unfortunately, his wife and three daughters perished in the blaze, because they were unable to escape from the flames and the heavily toxic smoke. Fire investigators later found that the deadly fire originated when the family's Christmas tree ignited, either by the overheated electrical equipment which was too closely positioned to the tree or possibly by the Christmas lights on the tree. In addition, the house's smoke detectors had malfunctioned, thus delaying the family's response to move away more quickly from the blaze.

During an unsuccessful attempt to save them, Matt suffered severe burns on over 40 percent of his body. The burns were so severe that doctors feared he was unlikely to survive, or if he did, would never again enjoy a quality, productive life. To increase his chances as much as possible, they placed him in a medically-induced coma. When he woke up two months later, he was out of danger physically, even though he faced months of rehabilitation. What was the condition of his mental and emotional states? In one terrifying incident, Matt Golinski lost everyone and everything that made his life worth living. Many people who experienced similar situations, having lost everything that was precious and dear to them, have never recovered. They simply gave up. Life had beaten them, robbed them, and degraded them. Tragically, some of those traumatized individuals, unable to handle their despair, took their own lives, concluding that they no longer had any purpose for living—fortunately, not Matt Golinski.

Contrary to all expectations, he survived his devastating injuries. He credits the love and support he received from his extended family, friends, fans, and others for stirring up in him a stubborn, determined spirit and the will to live. In the wake of immense personal loss, and after months of painful rehabilitation and therapy, Matt said, "I am grateful to be alive. I am now trying to look to the future and live a life that would make them [his wife and daughters] proud."

By all accounts, he has done this and continues to do it. Less than two years after the tragedy, he was running again with a new dimension to his life. He trains and competes in half and full marathon races. He is back to cooking regularly and is also working on a cookbook. Through his tragedy, pain, and loss, he added other burn victims to his personal charity. In 2012, he donated $100,000 of the money that he was given for his own recovery to help other burn survivors.

Helen Keller, who certainly was no stranger to misfortune, said, "Although the world is full of suffering, it is full also of the overcoming of it." Matt Golinski exemplifies this truth. Out of the ashes of his tragedy and loss has arisen a new life of purpose and significance.

The Life and Times of Job

Matt Golinski's story possesses many parallels to that of one of the most familiar figures in biblical history; a man who indubitably qualifies as the "*poster child*" of suffering and tragedy, yet who ultimately triumphed: Job. The Old Testament book of Job, one of the *wisdom* writings, is a profound, yet comprehensible, examination of the human experience of and response to extreme suffering, and of God's relationship to the reality of human suffering. Job, through no fault of his own, suffered an avalanche of disastrous and tragic events that tested him to the very limits of his endurance. Yet, through his steadfast and unshakable faith in God, he held on tenaciously through it all and, in the end, experienced complete restoration that left him better off than when he started. His was truly a "*riches-to-rags-to-riches*" story in, which the latter riches were much greater than the former riches.

The moral *takeaway* of Job's story is that no tragedy, grievous suffering, or any other misfortune that may strike us, no matter how severe, should be able to persuade us to abandon our faith in Almighty God and His ability to restore us completely, even after the worst tragedies imaginable. Even though God neither creates evil nor inflicts tragedy and suffering into the lives of His children (remember that God is absolutely good), nevertheless, He uses those events for His glory and for the good purpose of redeeming from their troubles all who place their total faith and trust in Him. Job's story doesn't answer every question regarding the prevalence and proliferation of suffering in the world, such as why evil, seemingly, is permitted to run amuck. It does, however, explain from the spiritual dimension, at least to some degree, *how* senseless tragedy, calamities, pain, grief, and misery may happen, and how we should respond to keep our faith in God strong while going through them. It also helps us to understand how to pick up the pieces in the aftermath, and how to position ourselves to move forward into a brighter future. There is always hope in God.

Job, according to Scripture, "lived in the land of Uz, was a man of complete integrity . . . [and] was . . . the richest person in that entire region" (Job 1:1–3 NLT). His wealth consisted of enormous flocks and herds, land, and a multitude of servants. His greatest treasures by far, however, were his 10 children: 7 sons and 3 daughters. In the culture of that ancient day, Job's goodness, prosperity, and status undoubtedly gave him a great deal of respect and influence among the people with whom he lived. Everyone looked up to Job, because he was a great man of high moral standard, sterling character, scandal-free life, wielded influence, and vast wealth; most important of all, he feared God, loved Him deeply, and always tried to do what was right. However, all of these superb qualities made Job a prime target for Satan to hit.

One day, when the angels presented themselves before God, Satan was among them. Job became the epicenter of discussion and debate between God and Satan. God directed Satan's attention to Job by characterizing Job's faith, obedience, and righteous life as a man whose heart was pure and perfect toward God; he was a man who desired to please God and serve Him alone. God asked Satan the following:

> "Have you noticed my servant Job? He is the finest man in all the earth. He is blameless—a man of complete integrity. He fears God and stays away from evil." (Job 1:8 NLT)

First Challenge of Job's Faith

Satan then challenges God with insinuating accusations that Job doesn't genuinely love Him freely and that he serves Him only for selfish motives, his own self-interest, and is only faithful to Him because of the material blessings which allow him to experience just the *good things* in the temporal world:

> *"Does Job fear God for nothing?" The only reason Job serves God, Satan insists, is because God has made him wealthy and constantly protects him. Then Satan throws out his challenge: "But now stretch out your hand and strike everything he has, and he will surely curse you to your face." God accepts Satan's brash challenge: "Very well, then, everything he has is in your hands, but on the man himself do not lay a finger." (Job 1:9–12 NIV)*

Satan becomes the driving force behind Job's suffering and pain. Along with his demonic initiatives, we also learn that Job opens the door to his own tragedy, suffering, and misfortune through his secret fear of the unpredictable, thus giving the spirit world power for his fears to become a reality (Job 3:25; 9:28). Fear is a spiritual force, as is faith. Fear is the opposite of faith, and works in the reverse. Our personal actions always impose a dynamic element to opening up the spirit world to cause a reaction and permission. All fears that are undealt with can easily become magnified and, if misappropriated, carry the colossal potential for disastrous and dangerous probabilities and possibilities.

Perceivably, this story depends on viewing it in the light of God's sovereign rule, which permits certain things in the earth to transpire, both good and evil. The earth is flawed and imperfect. In Job's case, we see Satan's pretentions to inflict evil and suffering on God's creation, as well as the capacity of Job's free will and fear to open a door to his own tragic situation. These are some of the given factors. God is not in the business of purposely sending havoc, evil, or destruction into anyone's life unnecessarily. Neither does He abrogate anything that is good, allow innocent people to be killed for no reason, or inflict unbearable and often unexplainable human misery and grief upon them. This is especially true with regard to His most devoted and righteous servants. Yet God sometimes permits some of these things to happen, as Job's experiences demonstrate, although some of His reasoning and answers to the root question of "*why*" remain undisclosed.

God doesn't need to prove a point or settle any scores with Satan. Think about it! God already knows everything while Satan's knowledge, though vast, is limited. It should always be understood that Satan is not working for God.

However, we do perceive that Satan has to get permission from God before he does anything. One thing is certain: God is implacably at war with Satan—completely at odds with evil and the kingdom of darkness. However, Job was completely unaware of the spiritual warfare that was at work against him. Not everything that happens in this world is an endorsement of His desire or the divine expression of His perfect will. What may appear on the surface to be God's uncaring acquiescence to Job's tragedy, grievous suffering, and injustice may simply hide an unknown plethora of divine reasons and purposes that God has chosen not to reveal as of yet. In our efforts to answer all our questions and console our heart-stabbing wounds while lacking substantial proof, we cannot accuse God of lacking the power and the will to defend His children, or falsely accuse Him of being unfair and unjust. We don't have all the answers behind this story or others like it, so we must be careful not to ignorantly ascribe to God motivations and reasons for His actions or for allowing the actions of others that He has not yet revealed. If anyone believes that God shows his entire hand, and has given humankind all the answers to the suffering of humans and evil, then that person is flat-out wrong—deceived. God has not done so and has never promised to do so. With this in mind, let us recalibrate ourselves to thanking the Lord for what He *has* revealed and for what we *do* know, both of which are substantial!

Having received God's permission to act, Satan wastes no time attacking Job and bringing pure agony into his life. Over the course of one terribly horrifying day, Job loses all his livestock to raiders who also kill all his servants, except a few who survive to bring Job the horrific news. Job has lost all his material wealth and is now destitute, but the worst is yet to come. Another servant brings him the news that all 10 of his children are dead; they were killed by a windstorm from the desert that collapsed the roof of the eldest son's house, where they had all gathered for a dinner party. Understandably, Job is utterly stunned to the very core of his being by this unimaginable and catastrophic sequence of events. He goes from having everything anyone could ever dream of having in life to being totally destitute—stripped of everything except the clothes on his back. Everything he owned and everything he called his had disappeared before his very eyes as fleetingly and ephemerally as the early morning mist that vanishes in the dawning daylight.

Job's first response to these devastating tidings is to tear his robe and shave his head, both of which were customary signs of mourning (for suffering and tragedy) in ancient times in that culture. Then Job does something that, while unexpected, nevertheless, is in keeping with his character: he stoically and courageously worships the Lord, thus revealing the remarkable strength of his trust in God. "'I came naked from my mother's womb,'" he said, 'and I shall have nothing when I die. The Lord gave me everything I had, and they were his to take away. Blessed be the name of the Lord'" (Job 1:21 TLB). Job, apparently, is unaware of Satan's role in his heart-wrenching misery, but he clearly believes that God's sovereignty has permitted the events to come to pass and is at the forefront of his excruciating suffering.

Because of Job's resilient, unshakeable faith in God and his recognition of God's ownership over all things, Satan fails in his first attempt to turn Job against God. So, he tries a different strategy. In Job chapter 2, when God pointed out that Job had maintained his faith and integrity even in the face of losing everything, Satan said, "'Skin for skin! A man will give up everything he has to save his life. But reach out and take away his health, and he will surely curse you to your face!'" (vv. 4–5 NLT).

Second Challenge of Job's Faith

God accepts the second challenge and permits Satan to viciously attack Job's physical and mental health, but not to kill him.

Satan leaves God's presence and immediately afflicts Job with gruesome-looking boils from head to toe. Not only are they very painful, but they also make Job repulsive to look at. Destitute, desolate, hurting, and oozing pus from all over his body, Job sits in the ashes and scrapes his blistering sores with a broken piece of pottery—a poor, pathetic shell of the man that he once was. His wife—her own raw emotions and nerves shot and shattered, no doubt— gives him dangerously bad advice and admonishes him "'to curse God and die'" (v. 9). But Job, giving no place to her "*foolish nonsense*" of a suggestion, refuses to relinquish his faith, and trusts in God regardless of his crushing grief, humbling misfortune, and unrelenting suffering. Job's faith was stronger than the crushing blows that he received from Satan. The Bible says that in all that happened to him, Job did not sin against God (v. 10).

Hearing of Job's travails, brokenness, and anguish, three of his friends, Eliphaz, Bildad, and Zophar, agree to travel together to Job's side to comfort and encourage him. Upon seeing him, however, they are shocked beyond belief by his terrible appearance, which has made him almost unrecognizable. Stunned and speechless by the magnitude of his suffering, they sit in silence with him for seven days.

Finally, out of the depths of his agonizing heartache, lacerations, and internal scarring, Job capitulates to his suffering and breaks his silence. Speaking for the first time since his friends had arrived, Job begins by cursing the day of his birth. Job's spirit is deeply wounded, and he struggles to comprehend his tragedy and suffering while still affirming his steadfast faith in God. Job is in a conundrum, profoundly puzzled about his loss—not to mention God's perceived unfairness—and seeks satisfactory answers for his turmoil. He is acutely aware that he is unable to force God's hand to end his suffering immediately. He is also confused about righteous living and its rewards. He tries to reconcile, in his heart, God's uncompromising goodness with his experienced reality of being attacked mercilessly with evil. He wonders why he was even born, if all he was headed for was a series of unexplainable and egregious losses, misery, and unremitting suffering. In our modern parlance, it is as though Job says, "I wish I were dead!"

The Mental Assault of Job's Friends

Speculatively, Job's three friends illustrate the impossibility of trying to solve spiritual problems through human efforts alone. In the beginning, Job's three friends make a sincere attempt to comfort Job with pure empathy, and encourage him not to lose his faith; it is an attempt that fails completely. One by one, beginning with Eliphaz, Job's friends offer increasingly accusatory, but formulaic counsel in an effort to mitigate Job's pain by persuading him to confess his sins before God, which are obviously (in their minds) why he is suffering. Eliphaz speaks, and Job responds. Then Bildad speaks, and Job answers. Finally, Zophar says his piece. Back and forth they go: challenge, response, challenge, response. The problem is that they are not talking to each other, but instead at each other, or even past each other; each friend is believing that he has all the pieces to the puzzle and understands the entirety of Job's personal trial while Job consistently insists on his innocence. The useless counsel of his friends only exacerbates Job's inward pain through prejudiced opinions, false accusations, criticism, and misinterpretation of the reason for his suffering.

Unsympathetically, from the position of their own narrow perspectives, Job's friends eventually lose patience with him and begin to taunt him and arrogantly accuse him of being the cause of his own tragedy and the subsequent suffering in his life. It is obsessively easy to nit-pick at someone else's short-comings and weaknesses, and even to ostracize them in order to avoid facing up to our own deficiencies. Job's three friends are locked into a rigid and simplistic mindset of cause and effect, suggesting that Job has sinned against God, and his guilt which, ironically, is revealed by the fiercely adamant manner in which Job insists on his innocence. In their minds, Job's unconfessed sins, arrogant impatience, and self-righteous demeanor are the causes that have brought about the effect of God's judgment in his life in the form of disaster, loss, and sickness. Job, on the other hand, consistently and stubbornly insists that he has not sinned against God and has not done anything deserving of God's apparent punishment in this way.

Like Job, his three friends are unaware of Satan's significant role in the traumatic disaster that has befallen him; this fallen angel is behind the sudden onslaught of tragedy and grievous suffering in his life. Job's friends find it conceivably difficult to believe in his integrity because they cannot understand why God, in His goodness and justice, would not immediately reward Job's uprightness and eliminate his terrible pain and suffering. Consequently, they continue to try to convince him to come clean and confess his sins to God, but Job continues to declare that he has nothing to confess, and only wants the chance to present his case to God directly, and ask Him why He has allowed these atrocities to come to pass in his life. This is the same argument people throughout history have used to brazenly deny God, because they cannot understand how a good, moral, and loving God would allow the perpetuation of human pain, suffering, disease, and injustice. This is the basic mindset of people who deny the fundamental reality of the curse in the earth, sin, the fall of humanity, and Satan's interjection—believing that all people are basically good.

Throughout the numerous chapters of back-and-forth dialogue and response, Job's three friends consistently argue that nothing happens without the permission of the all-powerful, all-wise, all-knowing, all-righteous, and all-just God. He would only permit blessing and honor upon the righteous, and only judgment and punishment upon the wicked. People, basically, only get what they deserve—from an outward appearance. In the end, God deems the latter part of this argument to be totally false.

After a while, the four men reach an impasse. Job maintains his innocence one last time, and then stops speaking. His three friends, equally intransigent and convinced that they cannot persuade Job to accede to their viewpoint, also fall silent.

At this point, an intriguing young man named Elihu appears in the story suddenly and mysteriously. Berating the three friends for failing to perceive God's present wisdom in the earth, Elihu, with no holds barred, takes his shot and, for several chapters, presumes, despite his own youth, to *teach* the wisdom of God.

The Superior Wisdom of Elihu

It appears that the presence of Elihu in Job's dilemma serves three primary purposes in shedding light on human suffering and pain. His comprehensive knowledge of the provocations and particulars regarding Job's case is second to none. Firstly, Elihu represents God's "**witness of wisdom**" of those who speak forth His truth in the earth realm. At the end of the story, God never rebukes Elihu for his words of wisdom to Job. Down through the eons of history, God has never been without a witness to answer humanity's dilemmas in the earth; however, one has to be open to receive His wisdom. Although Elihu may not have had the full scope of Job's answer to his entire ordeal, he did possess a greater witness of wisdom than the others. No one individual possesses all the wisdom of God. God's wisdom may not always give an answer to every question in detail, but rather a broad-brush perspective of His revealed purpose, and the role of His justice in suffering on the earth.

Secondly, Elihu represents the wisdom of God that is available to us presently in the earth and in His Word concerning evil, suffering, and pain. It may not answer all our questions about our troubles, but it gives us insight both into God's thinking as well as show us how to move forward to gain deliverance, healing, and full restoration from our suffering. Humans only possess facts and limited knowledge; only God is able to give wisdom and clarity in a situation. Elihu did give Job some direction and godly counsel concerning his predicament.

Thirdly, Elihu's appearance in the story represents the truth that whenever God seems to be silent in certain situations, individuals seeking God's wisdom in their suffering and pain need to be open and ready to hear from the Lord through all other legitimate means, even if they struggle with the wisdom they receive.

At the end of his spiel, Elihu drops out of the story just as suddenly and mysteriously as he appeared, opening the way for the climax of the story of Job.

God's Answer to Job's Suffering and Travails

Finally, the story of Job ends in an earth-shaking crescendo when Job gets his chance to face God, which he has wanted since the beginning of his ordeal, but the encounter is not what he expects. Rather than boldly presenting his defense before the Almighty, Job can only stand in cowed silence as God peppers him with the following rapid-fire questions:

> *"Who is this that darkens my counsel [obscures my plans] with words without knowledge? . . . Where were you when I laid the earth's foundation? Tell me, if you understand. Who marked off its dimensions? Surely you know! Who stretched a measuring line across it? On what were its footings set, or who laid its cornerstone—while the morning stars sang together and all the angels shouted for joy?" (Job 38:2, 4–7 NIV)*

(Can you hear the sarcasm?)

"Have you comprehended the vast expanses of the earth? Tell me, if you know all this. What is the way to the abode of light? And where does darkness reside? Can you take them to their places? Do you know the paths to their dwellings? Surely you know, for you were already born! You have lived so many years!" (vv. 18–21) "Do you know when the mountain goats give birth? Do you watch when the doe bears her fawn? (39:1) . . . Does the hawk take flight by your wisdom and spread his wings toward the south? Does the eagle soar at your command and build his nest on high?" (vv. 26–27)

Unapologetically, God's interrogation and rebuke of Job goes on for four chapters of increasing intensity as God, through these questions, reveals His power, His glory, and His awesome majesty; He is truly a God to be revered and feared. One of the great ironies of this story occurs near the end of chapter 41 when God, referring to the two different great beasts, gives what could be an explanation to the fundamental question of why good people sometimes suffer bad things. He indicates that the universal human capacity of free will to make conscious, deliberate choices is directly connected to the origin and **root causes** of all human suffering and evil. Some choice or decision was made somewhere down the line that opened the door to it all. Our freedom to choose absolutely requires that good and evil coexist. We cannot have only one or the other and still have free will.

When it is all over, Job is repentant, apologetic, and has been reduced to a puddle of humility. His brash, repeated challenges to debate God have withered away into thin air in the face of His overpowering divine presence. Job realizes that he should have waited before he drew his conclusions about God and his suffering. All that is left for Job is his meek confession:

"I know that you can do all things; no plan of yours can be thwarted. [You asked,] 'Who is this that obscures my counsel without knowledge?' Surely I spoke of things I did not understand, things too wonderful for me to know. [You said,] 'Listen now, and I will speak; I will question you, and you shall answer me.' My ears had heard of you but now my eyes have seen you. Therefore I despise myself and repent in dust and ashes." (Job 42:2–6 NIV)

God's wisdom is often beyond human comprehension, and His insight is sometimes difficult for us to grasp completely. Job has ignorantly misinterpreted God's permission of his misfortune as an unjust indictment. He finally realizes, however, that God was not the driving force which brought suffering and evil upon him, and that there were other factors in the overall equation that made his suffering possible. He promptly releases his anger and frustration toward God and no longer holds God directly responsible for his dire circumstances. In Job's heart and mind, God is completely vindicated.

After Job's confession, God turns to the three friends, Eliphaz, Bildad, and Zophar, and chastises them for misrepresenting Him and His ways when they spoke to Job. He commands them to offer burnt offerings for their sins and tells them that Job will intercede for them: He "will accept his prayer, and not deal with [them] according to [their] folly" (Job 42:8 NIV).

In the end, Job's estate is bountifully rewarded, and his prosperity is fully returned. All of his suffering is dramatically turned around; all of his heartache, pain, misery, grief, and sorrow vanish like a fleeting wisp of smoke. His body and mind are made whole from the physical disease that has wracked his body from head to toe. All the outside anguish, desolation, and distractions that so thoroughly agitated his life are totally erased; peace and calm once again surround him like a blanket. God restores and heals Job's spirit, body, and mind. He causes him to prosper again by blessing the latter years of his life more than the former and gives him payback—twice as much as he had before—double for his trouble. He permitted Job to suffer for a season, but that season didn't last; it ended abruptly. God even gives him seven more sons and three more daughters. Finally, at the age of 140, Job dies after having lived a prosperous, abundant and full life again.

Reflections on the Strengths that Emerged from Job's Sufferings

Despite the terrible tragedies that befell him and the unjustified criticism from his friends, Job emerged from his great ordeal stronger and better than he was before; he was stronger in faith and had a better understanding of God. Suffering often has a redeeming and character-building quality when you release it to God in faith and seek to understand its purpose and learn from it. Job emerged from his trials stronger in at least five areas that can also be instructive for anyone who suffers today.

1. **Job increased in his knowledge and wisdom about God, life, and especially suffering.** Even before his own troubles began, Job understood that trials and suffering are realities of life, and that life is a mixture of good and bad experiences. Early on, he asked the question, "'Shall we accept good [abundance] from God, and not trouble?'" (Job 2:10 NIV). At that time, he may have held similar beliefs to those of his three friends: that the blessings of prosperity were God's reward for right living while adversity and God's justice were reserved only for the wicked. This may be part of the reason why he struggled to understand what had happened to him. Job knew that he had not sinned, and he was frustrated and confused when God would not immediately respond to his cries and groans for an answer. Job initially predicted that God would act and respond within a certain order and structure, but when He did not, God began to appear to Job as cruel and calloused toward him. When God finally did speak to him, Job received a newer, bigger view of God than ever before. He saw God's majesty, justice, purity, holiness, goodness, and greatness from a whole new perspective, and it paradigmatically transformed the way he thought about his own life and suffering. Job realized that God had purposes for what He did and for what He permitted. His ways go far beyond our individual lives, and we need to gain His perspective if we want to understand them.

We must remember that God is not accountable to us to always do things the way we want Him to do them, but we are always accountable to Him to accept His way of doing things. Satan's main strategy is to scorn God's character and discredit His goodness through human suffering. Once we comprehend this fact, it gives us a different lens through which to view our past and present sufferings and leads us to the eventual conclusion that God's way does not always follow a distinct or readily obvious chain of reasoning or logic. God initially allowed subtractions through Job's misfortunes, only to reverse and supplant them with enormous additions in the end. However, God will always remain faithful and accountable to His Word. It is our part to hold fast to our faith and trust Him completely.

2. **Job learned to avoid making assumptions about God.** At first, Job may have thought that he understood God—shocked and surprised by the events that showed up at his doorstep. His inflated ego-driven friends Eliphaz, Bildad, and Zophar apparently were the same way. Throughout their extended efforts to persuade Job to acknowledge his sins and faults, his three friends stated many assumptions about God. Most of them were correct to a certain extent, but they erred in their belief that God would always act in accordance with their silent assumptions, and they erred in their belief that people get what they deserve and that suffering is always linked to sin and wrongdoing. Sometimes good people, righteous people, suffer for no apparent or known reason. Their arguments were inadequate because they were ignorant of the background to Job's dilemma and could not see the full picture or fully know the mind of God. They certainly did not possess a revelation of Satan and the works of the kingdom of darkness. Job also made the foolish assumption that God had no right to permit his attack from Satan. But, whatever God chooses to do or not do, He always remains right and righteous altogether.

Many well-intentioned Christians are convinced they have God and life all figured out. This is both pathetically naïve and severely detrimental to their spiritual growth and development. No one on earth has life or God *"figured out,"* and no one ever will! The Christian life is all about the walk of faith and trusting God wholeheartedly. When God spoke to Job and his friends in the closing chapters of the book, He corrected them of their faulty ideas. They all learned not to make assumptions about God, and we must also be careful to do the same. God is always bigger, greater, and vastly different than every one of our assumptions about Him. We cannot always know why God chooses to respond the way He does. God is too awesome to be boxed into some humanistic framework. More often than not, events that appear inexplicable at the time become explainable later down the road. God will never contradict Himself, His nature, or His Word, but He will contradict our assumptions about Him every day of the week. Nothing that anyone does against you will ever be able to compare with or supersede what God has done for you. Life will continually move on even when we finally realize that we were wrong about our assumptions and things didn't go according to our plans. Don't ever get stuck!

3. **Job gained a deeper understanding of how to walk in humility before others and before God.** There was a certain tone of arrogance in Job's assessment of himself, his own righteousness, and his blamelessness. The Bible does indeed say that Job was blameless in the sense that he did not sin against God in any of his actions. But there are times when Job sounds like he is *"too big for his britches."* He believed he was grossly mistreated by God, and was itching to defend himself. In his impatience and self-righteousness, he thought too much of himself and not enough of God. That's the way many of us modern Christians respond to life and view ourselves; we think more highly of ourselves than we ought to think. We believe that because we practice certain things, we are entitled to endless earthly comforts, ease, wealth, and prosperity without ever having any winds of adversity. We feel that we should never be required to experience any intense hardship in life, and are quick to trot out our good works and righteous behavior before the Lord, as if they should guarantee our protection from any difficulty or attack. This is an unrealistic expectation. Such parading of our pride and arrogance stinks in the nostrils of God and in the presence of His grace. Humility and mercy should always be our approach.

Inextricably, Job's view of himself was too big because his view of God was too small. His encounter with God at the end of the story readjusted that balance. Seeing God in the right perspective always changes us. We are the ones who always need to change, not God. It resets our priorities and puts everything into proper relation with everything else. After any great tragedy, trauma, or loss, don't focus on what you have lost or don't have, but focus on what you have left and on the new horizons that are set before you. When God allows certain doors to close, He always opens up new doors of opportunity. Like Job, seeing God also permits us to be ruined for the ordinary, and moves our thinking and faith into the extraordinary. Job was never the same after he saw God in that awesome whirlwind. His faith was raised to a higher level. That encounter changed him forever.

4. **Job greatly expanded his capacity to empathize and sympathize with others who suffer.** No one is better at understanding and comforting

a sufferer than someone who has also suffered, especially in a similar manner. Nothing works more effectively than compassion and a sympathetic attitude toward understanding someone else's predicament. As the old axiom says, "Never criticize another until you have personally walked a mile in their shoes." Job suffered the extravagant loss of everything that most of us would consider dearest and of greatest importance. He knew the shock of financial reversal, the pain of estrangement in his marriage, the uninformed and hurtful criticism of his closest friends, and the heart-stabbing grief from the deaths of his children. Even though God gave him 10 more children in the end, certainly he never forgot the others, nor the grief he felt after they died. Suffering often humbles us, and humility gives us the capacity and the quality of character to empathize with others who internally hurt and suffer. This quality often brings out in us the great gift of Christ-like empathy—the ability to identify with, encourage, and help others who suffer in life. Suffering humanizes us by breaking through the false shell of invulnerability we erect around ourselves in order to avoid involving ourselves in the pain of others, and project to the world a false image that we have things more together than we really do.

5. **Job's relationship with God was catapulted to another dimension.** Life itself often becomes our education when we are willing to learn from it. The curriculum studied and the tests often given in the school of hard knocks are the subjects of adversity, suffering, and hardship. We must never forget that God will never permit us to be tested above the strength we are able to bear *with His help* (1 Cor. 10:13). Job came away from his suffering ordeal with an entirely new view of God. From then on and throughout the rest of his life, Job related to God on a higher, deeper, and more intimate level than ever before. Many people who experience intense suffering or hardship get so caught up in constantly rehearsing the grotesque injustices they have suffered that they become completely inward-focused, so that they never see the light at the end of the tunnel. Their lives become stalled on the tracks in the darkness. Paralyzed by pain, resentment, and bitterness, they never learn from their experiences, never grow to greater levels of maturity, and never move forward into a greater and brighter future. Depending on how you approach them, your trials will either break you or make you. It is very easy to allow yourself

to slip into a deep ditch over your hardships and surrender to seemingly insurmountable odds. Rather than focusing on the unfairness of life and continually devoting your complete energy to your deprivations and setbacks, try adopting a different viewpoint by learning to see your situation as an opportunity to catapult you to another dimension.

Conceivably, I imagine Job was wiser and more inclined to reflect on and savor the good things—the overall graces and richness of life. For believers, endurance of suffering adds a needed dimension to life's reality. The apostle James, in the New Testament, quotes Job's experience and gives credence to the spiritual dimension of endurance for those who suffer undeserved adversity when he says, "We give great honor to those who endure under suffering. For instance, you know about Job, a man of great endurance. You can see how the Lord was kind to him at the end, for the Lord is full of tenderness and mercy" (Jas. 5:11 NLT). Job *chose* to never lose his faith in God, even though he did not fully comprehend the reason behind his unfathomable suffering. His endurance brought about real purpose, and resulted in His seeing the rewards of God's kindness and goodness in the end. Persevering through suffering makes us more grateful; it increases our capacity for joy and for seeing the beauty of life, because no one appreciates the brightness, beauty, and the joy of life more than those who have seen firsthand its dark, bitter, ugly, and miserable side. Spending time in the depths of suffering conditions us to long for God's very best and prepares us to be exalted to heights of victory unknown to us before. Sometimes God allows us to be knocked down, which often reduces us to less than zero, even as He gets ready to lift us higher than we have ever been lifted before.

"To God who is our Savior forever, He alone is all wisdom, power and salvation!"

6

LIFE LESSONS FROM THE BOOK OF JOB

"Good people suffer many troubles, but the Lord saves them from them all."

— Psalm 34:19 (GNT)

"Although the world is very full of suffering, it is also full of the overcoming of it."

— Hellen Keller

A Lesson of Faith and Courage from Severe Trials of Suffering

LIKE JOB AND JOSEPH CENTURIES EARLIER, NELSON MANDELA endured years of brutal suffering, misery, and hardships, including decades of a long prison internment, while steadfastly pursuing his mission in life. From the very beginning of his life, Nelson Mandela was destined for greatness. If overcoming suffering and hardship is part of the standard resume of all great people (and it is), then Mandela certainly qualifies. Through it all, he never lost his faith in God or his vision for a better life of full equality and justice for all the people in his native land of South Africa.

Born July 18, 1918, Mandela studied law at the University of Witwatersrand, where he faced racism as the only black African student. He soon became involved in anti-colonial politics. In the early 1940s, he joined the African National Congress (ANC) and became a staunch advocate for complete independence and political self-determination for black Africans. He rose to national prominence during a 1952 anti-apartheid Defiance Campaign.

Apartheid is an organized system of racial segregation that gave whites expansive privileges while severely suppressing blacks. Specifically, apartheid is "the official name of the legalized program of segregation and political and economic discrimination against non-European groups in the Republic of South Africa," practiced and promoted as established government policy.

Mandela, a lawyer, was arrested numerous times (along with other ANC members) for active efforts to subvert the established apartheid government. In 1956, he was brought up on charges of "*high treason*" against the state. The formal Treason Trial began in 1958 and ended in 1961 with the acquittal of all the accused, including Mandela, much to the embarrassment of the South African government. That same year, he co-founded Umkhonto we Sizwe (or "Spear of the Nation") and led a campaign to overthrow the government. He was arrested again in 1962, and was this time convicted of conspiracy to overthrow the state; he received a sentence of life imprisonment.

For 27 interminable years, Nelson Mandela endured imprisonment: first on Robben Island, second in Pollsmoor Prison, and lastly in the Victor Verster Prison. It may have seemed as though his activist life and unrelenting campaign to win freedom for his people had come to a complete standstill. However, outside his prison walls, his efforts had taken on a life of their own. As Mandela's incarceration dragged on from one year to the next, the South African government faced growing public dissention over his imprisonment. Steadfastly resisting the pressure, the government doubled down on its position by outlawing public discussion of Mandela and his situation, and by severely restricting his privilege of receiving visitors. But the government was fighting an unstoppable swell-tide of public opinion. Over time, Mandela became the focal point of worldwide protests against apartheid.

In 1988 he was hospitalized with a sickness, but was sent back to prison after he recovered, though the prison conditions were less harsh and miserable than before. By this time, however, the South African government was under intense pressure and was the target of condemnation from every corner of the globe. Government leaders were becoming desperate, afraid that South Africa would become globally isolated because the world at large viewed the nation as a racist entity unto itself. Finally, South African president F. W. de Klerk surrendered to worldwide demands. On February 11, 1990, Nelson Mandela was freed from prison to the applause and celebration of an international audience. In 1991, he resumed his post as president of the ANC, which had finally been legally recognized by the government.

Almost immediately, Mandela entered into negotiations with President de Klerk to end apartheid, prevent civil war within South Africa, and quell the brewing unrest between races. Their dedicated work in these negotiations resulted in their being co-recipients in 1993 of the Nobel Peace Prize. The next year, President de Klerk abolished apartheid. On April 27 that same year, the first open elections were held, allowing all South African citizens to participate. The ANC won 62 percent of the vote and Nelson Mandela was elected president.

Like Job, who experienced a sudden, glorious turnaround of his harsh circumstances after a sustained ordeal of suffering and privation, and like Joseph, who in one day was elevated from a slave in prison to the second-most powerful person in Egypt, Nelson Mandela's lengthy and cruel but ultimately uplifting, inspiring, and triumphant suffering climaxed in astounding exaltation as he rose from seemingly obscure imprisonment to international superstardom. As the first-ever black African president of the nation, he skillfully and successfully guided South Africa through its transition into democracy and helped erase its *pariah* status in the eyes of the world. A true historic figure for the ages, he received well over 250 honors and has been the subject of hundreds of articles, books, documentaries, and movies. The life of Nelson Mandela proves that the world never outgrows its need for heroes.

Fifteen Life Lessons Drawn from Job's Suffering and Restoration

Mandela's life mirrors that of Job's life; we can extract and learn many life lessons from their suffering. The Book of Job is not simply a historical account of a wealthy man who had it all and lost it all, only to gain it all back in the end. Job's story contains much more. Within its 42 chapters lies profound knowledge, wisdom, and spiritual insights—priceless hidden treasures waiting for us to extrapolate them from the narrative of Job's extreme and agonizing experience. Consequently, there are many lessons we can draw from the Book of Job and apply to our own lives—lessons that will be of great benefit to us in our own efforts in dealing with perplexing times of hardship and suffering, however severe. Below are 15 significant life lessons that I have distilled from Job's example. Let's examine each of them briefly.

Lesson One
Everyone is vulnerable to sufferings and hardships; no one in the material world is exempt from trouble.

Job's number one revelatory lesson from his sufferings and hardships was that the righteous and unrighteous alike experience suffering. Many Bible-believing Christians are under the misguided belief that because they are now believers and in the family of God, they can expect smooth sailing in life, with no trials or troubles and a steady, easy road to success, comfort, and prosperity. Most who seek these deceptive teachings are searching for a life of comfort, happiness, and the endless nostalgic-wistful-bliss of pursuing pleasure with as little trouble as possible. This false teaching deceives many into living in a fantasyland that is completely divorced from reality and, if perpetuated, will eventually cause irreversible damage to their faith. This "*smooth-seas-and-bed-of-ease*" mentality is one of the biggest misconceptions and most dangerous deceptions regarding the Christian life in the contemporary church. No one on planet earth is immune to suffering, pain, or misfortune. To say it another way, none of us can prevent trouble from ever arriving at our doorsteps. If someone has convinced you of this false perception, then you have been tricked with one of the biggest lies that has ever been told on planet earth.

There is not enough faith in the universe to keep trouble from knocking at your door. Unfortunately, there are many churches, groups and ministers that espouse this erroneous teaching. Instead of proclaiming the truth, they teach that if you only "*have enough faith*," then you can accumulate incredible wealth, always enjoy perfect health without ever being attacked, experience one sweatless victory after another, suffer no real or steep adversity in life, and reach "*happy-forever-land*" on this earth. No sir—not so! The witness of both Scripture and history says otherwise. Yes, we need to develop and use our faith, but faith doesn't stop trouble from coming. While it is true that as Christians, we enjoy the bountiful largesse of God's grace and favor, His deliverance, His Spirit, His generosity, His Word, His blessings, protection and prosperity, and a great eternal inheritance in His everlasting kingdom, it is also true that in this life, we share a common human-thread with every other person on this planet without discrimination; therefore, we are subject to the same or similar challenges, dangers, illnesses, misfortunes, pain, sufferings, setbacks, sorrows, trials, and tragedies as anyone else. The rain never makes any distinction about who it falls on; everyone gets wet. God never promises any of us that we will live a trouble-free life while on the earth (Matt. 5:45).

Like everyone else in this world, believers can face the same unmerciful attacks as unbelievers: debilitating diseases such as cancer, diabetes, arthritis, heart disease, aging, and many other serious illnesses; suicides, loss of spouses, children or grandchildren through illness or accidental death; natural disasters such as volcanoes, hurricanes, earthquakes, tsunamis, tornadoes, etc., which result in loss of life, home, and other possessions; job loss, financial setbacks, business failures, and bankruptcy; and criminal activity, including assault, abuse, robbery, rape, murder, and other like things. It is not a negative statement to acknowledge that believers are attacked and do suffer—it's simply flat-out crazy to believe otherwise. So please don't go there! I am not saying that you should just roll over, succumb to these evil forces, and not fight back. It is not the decreed-will of God that Christians should suffer egregiously without deliverance, but many still do. Believers should use their faith and the Word of God to combat and overcome suffering and the wicked forces of this world. However, if you think that you will never be attacked by just simply using faith confessions, you are absurd and only fooling yourself—ignorance gone-to-seed. Yes, sir! Don't be caught off guard. By all means arm yourself and be prepared!

Trouble, evil, wickedness, suffering, and pain do not suddenly happen out of nowhere. People do not suffer for no reason. Suffering, deprivations, and pain are a part of the fallen material world. Humanity is born into trouble: the sin curse in the earth is the source of our troubles. Humanity will always have troubles, from the time of birth until the time of death. Though many may limit the influence of evil and suffering, there will certainly be some form or level of trouble and misery in their lives. Far too often, many people have created their own suffering, pain, and unhappiness. The human existence is very fragile and limited. Humanity has a brief life span and there is much turmoil to contend with while on the earth (Job 5:7; 14:1; Eccl. 2:23).

The trials of righteous people have always been around, but what seems to have seen a significant rise in recent years is Christian persecution. Nowhere in the Bible does God promise His people exemption from trouble and suffering in this life. Paul explicitly said that "everyone who wants to live a godly life in Christ Jesus will suffer persecution" (2 Tim. 3:12 NLT). Living godly and righteous lives in this present world often brings some form of suffering. As the psalmist said, "Many *are* the afflictions of the righteous, but the LORD delivers him out of them all" (Ps. 34:19 NKJV). Jesus Himself also made it clear to His followers that trials will come: "'Here on earth you will have many trials and sorrows'" (Jn. 16:33 NLT). Yes, trials will come, even for believers, but we have a source of strength, deliverance and support that unbelievers do not have: the peace, presence, and power of Christ and His Word. Consider this Scripture verse again in its entirety: "'I have told you all this so that you may have peace in me. Here on earth you will have many trials and sorrows. But take heart, because I have overcome the world'" (Jn. 16:33 NLT). There is hope for the believer! Through Christ, and by His great grace, believers are able to triumph over (not avoid) these forces of evil. The apostle John said, "For whatever is born of God overcomes the world. And this is the victory that has overcome the world—our faith" (1 Jn. 5:4 NKJV). Victory is available in our lives as believers when we receive God's Word, believe it, and then act upon it. Trials and struggles will come our way, but we can conquer the trouble with faith in His Word. Yes, there is much trouble in the material world, but faith in God can and will defeat it. You don't have to face your trouble and suffering alone; there is hope and deliverance. Faith in Christ and His Word overcomes the world. Thanks be to God!

Lesson Two

The pivotal key to survival and resilience is grounding your trust and faith in God, especially before times of suffering hit.

Superficiality is a substantially huge problem in the Christian world today. The message of following Christ and being committed to Him has been watered down to "**lollipop candy**." Superficial faith will not ground you or provide you with a firm foundation on how to deal with the complex issues of life. Authentic faith will always be tested, proven, and tried, but it will eventually rise to the top. Conversely, superficial faith that is never tested and tried, is a faith that can never be trusted and will be burned up, destroyed, and demonstrated to be false. Many modern believers have very little resistance to hardship or resilience to bounce back from it, because they live their lives in excessive shallowness, encumbered with temporal things, selfishness, delirious ambitions, and unhealthy relationships that they deem important. Their faith in God and spiritual matters in general is extremely lightweight, with no depth, and many aspire to nothing higher than an easy way of life. The Christian life and experience has become a mockery to many who are only mimicking true Christian faith. When the storms of life appear, many of them don't have enough roots in God's Word to withstand even the tiniest little rain shower, let alone a windstorm of trouble. Many well-intentioned Christians are dangerously unprepared for the hostile realities that await them in this life.

Job wasn't just afflicted for the sake of suffering for no reason. His faith in God was being tested. Yours will be tested too! It is only when we experience the furnace of tribulation that our faith has a chance to be further perfected and strengthened. Although Job repeatedly expressed his frustration and confusion over why God had subjected him to such enduring suffering, or at least permitted it, and although he called and waited on God to reveal His reasons for it, never once did Job curse God or threaten to abandon his faith in God. Rather than spurning or turning his back on God in the midst of his wretched suffering, Job appealed to God's justice and mercy. And even though God remained silent for a long period of time, Job never gave up on Him. In fact, early on in his affliction, when his wife encouraged him to 'curse God and die,' Job refused, saying, "'You are talking like a foolish woman. Shall we accept good from God, and not trouble?'" (Job 2:10 NIV).

Job's steadfast faith in God, even in the face of terrible suffering, was the result of his having thoroughly grounded his faith in God during good and pleasant times long before the time of his vexatious suffering. Job had to trust God without having all the answers or explanations to mitigate his cause. All too often, many Christians live their lives every day virtually ignoring God—until they get into severe trouble. Faced suddenly with a major crisis or disaster, they belatedly call on God for help, only to discover that they don't have a large enough *"faith account"* to sustain them. Having neglected to nurture their relationship with God and make regular *"deposits"* into their *"faith account"* during the easy times, they lack the faith, courage, confidence, patience, and spiritual maturity in God's Word to carry them through the hard times.

The Hebrew word for *"faith"* is *"emeth"* which means *"firmness," "faithfulness," "stability," "sureness," "integrity,"* and *"authentic,"* and is also defined as *"truth with certainty."* This word speaks of God's unquestionable covenant loyalty to His people, with steadfast goodness, mercy, and love, meaning that *"God is faithful in everything He does."* God never abuses His power and never acts out of any unjust reasons or purposes. God's justice reaches far beyond just rewarding the innocent and punishing the wicked. The meaning of this Hebrew word for *faith* is also carried through the New Testament. The Bible makes it distinctly clear that "without faith it is impossible to please God" (Heb. 11:6 NIV) and "'The righteous shall live by faith'" (Rom. 1:17; Gal. 3:11 NIV).

Don't wait until trouble comes before you learn how to use your faith to trust God. The time to build your faith relationship with God is now, before the tough times come—as they inevitably will. Tough times will certainly overwhelm the spiritually unprepared. Ground your faith through worship and regular prayer, faithful attendance at a Christ-centered, Bible-teaching and preaching church, and by consistently saturating your heart and mind with the divinely inspired Word of God. The faith you build in God today, while life is easy, will sustain you tomorrow when the chips are down. Without one doubt!

Lesson Three

Satan and the kingdom of darkness are the driving forces behind all the promotion of evil, suffering, pain, and misfortune in the world.

As a created being (although a fallen angel rather than a human), Satan acts with a certain degree of free will. The first two chapters of the book of Job depict Satan directly challenging God regarding the motivation behind Job's faithfulness. Satan seemed convinced that Job was driven to serve God purely by self-interest—by what he could get from God rather than by his genuine love for God. In effect, Satan said, "Take away Job's blessings and opulent-regal life, then you will find where his heart truly lies." In answer to the challenge, God gave Satan the authority to afflict Job with all the troubles and suffering that soon followed. Satan is the one who purposely set out to bring tragedy, suffering, and untimely destruction to Job's life. Not God! Remember, Satan is the one who stood up and openly dared God. God permitted it, but Satan was the driving force behind Job's destruction, suffering, and pain; he is the outside, influential force of evil and corruption in the world.

As children of God, we must be utterly cautious not to cross the line into Satan's territory; he is always busy trying every conceivable mechanism to inflict as much evil, pain, wickedness, and suffering on humanity as he possibly can. Human suffering and evil can all be traced back to the free will and conscious choices of humanity, and the influence of Satan's free will. This is a lesson we must embrace and keep at the forefront of our thinking and our entire decision-making process. Whenever we operate against God's Word, we increase our potential for greater suffering, pain, and misfortune; thus, we open a door to Satan's influence and free will in our lives.

When we think in terms of the impact of our free will in perpetuating suffering and pain in the world, we will begin to make different choices. Just as a farmer prepares the ground and then sows his seed, humanity is always planting seeds of some kind. We must be careful to note, however, that God did not give Satan a completely free hand in Job's predicament. Satan was free to act against Job, but only within the parameters that God set. And that is still the way Satan operates today. For reasons we may never understand, at least in this life, God allows Satan, for the time being, a broad latitude of flexibility to act in the world, increasing the magnitude of human suffering through direct spiritual attack, but even more so by frequently stirring up evil desires and ambitions in the already sin-ravaged hearts of fallen humanity. Humans are sinners by their fallen nature, and are quite capable of—and highly accomplished at—creating (in cooperation with Satan) a world full of evil, pain, hurt, and suffering all on their own. After all, Jeremiah 17:9 describes the fallen heart of humankind this way: "'The human heart is the most deceitful of all things, and desperately wicked. Who really knows how bad it is?'" (NLT). Like pouring gasoline onto an open fire, Satan's insidious, rancorous, and hateful spirit inflames the evil in fallen humanity, which he immensely helped to ignite in Adam and Eve so long ago. And his diabolical will keeps it blazing like a bonfire throughout the human history of the world (this is only for a span of time).

In the life of Job, Satan's works were often hidden under the guise that God was somehow behind the suffering and pain, and endorsing the evil that befell him. Job walked in the limited viewpoint that he had at the time. But it is Satan's free will and the powers of darkness that are bent on destruction and are causing havoc in the world. He often uses humans, when they give him a place to operate, to carry out his schemes and plots. However, in the New Testament, God reveals greater light and progressive wisdom found in Christ Jesus. Christ made an open show of the powers of darkness, and opened our understanding (Col. 2:15). Satan's free will was revealed and its intent when He said, "'The thief does not come except to steal, and to kill, and to destroy. I have come that they may have life, and that they may have it more abundantly'" (Jn. 10:10 NKJV). God, in Christ, also revealed and gave insight that Satan does not work for Him, and has nothing in Him (Jn. 14:30).

Christ defeated Satan at the cross and the empty tomb, which gave His children a new nature and victory over Satan's power, the flesh, sin, and all the forces of evil. One day He is coming back, and then the devil and all his works will be consigned to the lake of fire; all of God's people will be free of his influence forever. To the praise of His Glory!

Lesson Four

No one has the power to force God's hand to respond in a specific way or timing to their suffering, nor to anyone else's suffering.

One truth that the book of Job clearly reveals is that despite Satan's apparent *free will*, God is still sovereign. No one orders God around, and He exercises complete, ultimate control over all creation, both the natural and the supernatural; God rules and super-rules. Had Satan had his way, he would have destroyed Job completely, but God did not allow him to do so. At the same time, however, God did allow Satan to test Job with bitter sufferings, and then apparently allowed Job's traumatic suffering to generally run its course before bringing it to an end. We are not told how long Job's trials lasted, from beginning to end, but the story leaves the overall impression that many months, and perhaps even years, went by. One thing we do know is that God has set limits over Satan's free will. Over and over during that time, Job cried out to God with his complaint, seeking an answer as to why God would allow a righteous human to suffer so egregiously without cause. But the heavens were silent. God cared about Job, but the severity and longevity of Job's rigorous suffering did not move God or force His hand to end it before the right time, according to His sovereign purpose. Faith in God doesn't always move things or bring our suffering to a quicker end. This is one of the biggest misnomers taught by some in the Christian community.

Who can force God's hand to move when we think it should? Who can predict God's plans and then box Him into a corner? Who can make the ruler of the universe change if it doesn't appear the way we envision? Who can counsel or instruct the Almighty God that He has allowed things to go too far? No one! God is God! Job said of God, "'But He *is* unique, and who can make Him change? And *whatever* His soul desires, *that* He does'" (Job 23: 13 NKJV). Yes! Faith in God does work, but no human has the power to rush Him or push Him. God honors and keeps His Word and will never break or revoke it (Ps. 89:33–34), but who can force God's arm to make things happen and come forth when and how they desire or think they should? Not one soul—not a single one!

God's apparent, delayed action or inaction in the face of very real and painful suffering despite, releasing our faith in Him, repeated confessions of faith, standing on His Word, prayers, cries for answers of deliverance, and relief, is one of the thorniest and most difficult questions we have to deal with as believers. Sometimes there are no quick-and-easy answers. In such a situation, we have to *rest our faith* in the integrity of God, His Word, and His promises that He hears our prayers, answers them, and will come to our rescue. But He will do so in His own time and in His own way, although neither may be what we would prefer.

The critical key to relief is persistence on our part; keep pressing in and moving forward rather than giving up so easily and quickly at the first sign of adversity. In Luke 18:1–8, Jesus tells the story of a widow who appeared every day before an unrighteous and unsympathetic judge, pleading for relief in her righteous cause. Eventually, the judge granted her petition and gave her justice simply to get her out of his hair. Then, Jesus drives home the point of the story by saying, "'Learn a lesson from this unjust judge. Even he rendered a just decision in the end. So, don't you think God will surely give justice to his chosen people who cry out to him day and night? Will he keep putting them off? I tell you, he will grant justice to them quickly!'" (Lk. 18:6–8 NLT). God's *quickly* may not always fit into our mindset of quickly, but persistence will always pay off. Also, remember that Hebrews 11:6 says that God is a rewarder of those who diligently seek Him. Hang in there—don't give up!

We cannot second guess God's reasoning, nor try to fit His infinite wisdom into our finite, frivolous thinking. God is under no obligation to bend His ways to our immature thinking or ominous wishes so that they make sense to us. Child of God! We cannot manipulate God into doing what we want Him to do, and how we want it done. No one can force God's hand, but He will respond in His own timing when His people exercise prayer, patience, persistence, and faith in His Word.

Lesson Five

Fear is often a factor that opens up doors to the spirit world, causing the dimensions of suffering and evil to become a greater reality.

One of the most eye-opening lessons we can glean from the life of Job is the "**fear-factor**" that had such a dominant impact on his tragedy and traumatic suffering. His own secret fears triggered and opened up the spirit world, which gave the devil the opportunity to viciously attack him. At the conclusion of his first monologue, after being stricken with multiple travails, Job laments, "'Everything I feared and dreaded has happened to me. I have no peace or quietness. I have no rest, only trouble'" (Job 3:25–26 NCV). This statement reveals Job's inner struggles with fear and turmoil that were percolating inside and building up steam in the boiler room of his heart, long before tragedy finally struck him. Job had dreaded the reality of some devastation that might actually overtake his safety, security, entire life, and family. He lacked peace contemplating the possibility of the complete decimation of the monstrous empire he had built. His lack of a deep, inward, God-focused peace left room for fear to ignite in his heart, and torment to take control of his thoughts.

It is very apparent from this story that it is possible to have trust in and reverence toward God in our hearts, and yet have the spirit of fear lurking around at the same time or at least vacillating between the two. This apprehensive unrest was evident in Job's continual sacrificial offerings that he made to the Lord regularly on behalf of his children, in case they had sinned, or cursed God in their hearts. He also secretly feared that some misfortune might shatter the enormous wealth and prosperity that God had blessed him with (Job 30:15). By surrendering to his inner fear of looming disaster, he established the conditions for his fear to become a terrifying reality. One fear led to another. After Job's fear of devastating disaster became reality, he then feared that his present trauma and suffering would never cease (Job 9:28). Job's restless, fearful heart reveals for us a picture of Satan's primary goal in perpetrating fear: to destroy the peace and joy in the hearts of God's people so, they will find no rest in this earthly life.

The New Testament gives us greater insight into the powerful, devastating potential of fear to amplify in our minds our own weaknesses, insecurities, uncertainties, doubts, guilt, shame, pain, and suffering so that they seem far greater to us than they really are. Satan's primary weapon for whipping our spirits, destroying our confidence, and stealing our peace as Christians is to inject fear into our consciousness. The purpose of fear is to cheat us out of the life of God—the abundant life Jesus came to give us (Jn. 10:10)—and bring us to accept the inevitability of defeat, as with Job. Paul, the apostle of Christ made it explicitly clear that the spiritual force of fear is not a part of the nature of God. "For God has not given us a spirit of fear, but of power and of love and of a sound mind" (2 Tim. 1:7 NKJV). Fear comes in many guises: doubting, worrying, anxiety, meditating on the wrong things, lack of rest, lack of peace, etc. Satan's strategy is to get you so paralyzed by worry and fear that your faith cannot function, thus depriving you of the ability to enjoy and appropriate all the good gifts God has blessed you with as one of His beloved children. The only way to combat this evil is by putting it in God's hands (once and for all) and learning to focus your mind only on the right things (Phil. 4:6–8). The fears that you speak and yield to in life will have a direct impact on the outcome of your situation. No matter what you are facing in life, learn to resist fear, worry, and doubt.

Lesson Six
The earth realm is flawed and imperfect; no one should ever be surprised by evil, suffering, pain, and conflict when they show up.

Job was in total shock and disarray when suffering landed in his lap. Part of his problem was that he believed he was protected from attack, and from facing severe hardship or adversity. His ordeal is a further demonstration that the earth is fallen, cursed, and imperfect, and is a war zone. Suffering has been part of the human experience ever since Eve took her first bite of the forbidden fruit from the tree of the knowledge of good and evil in the Garden of Eden, and it will be with us until Christ makes a change in the order of things. This single act of Adam and Eve's disobedience opened the floodgates to every *root cause* of human suffering and evil in this world (Rom. 5:12). Yes, suffering, pain, deprivation, tragedy, and misfortune do happen even to good people—righteous people. This world is no longer the perfect world that God originally created. Obviously, no one alive is exempt; if you are a member of the human race, then suffering in some form is and will continue to be part of your lot in life. The sin of humanity corrupted every part of the created order so that the earth realm in which we live is now imperfect. All of creation is *"out of sync"* with God's original order, and that misalignment causes disorder, disharmony, dysfunction, and distress in all our relationships: with each other, with the natural world, and, most seriously, with God. The curse is still present in the earth; Christians must continually combat and stand against its effects using the consciousness of their good will, their authority, and faith in God's Word to overcome the powers of darkness (Matt. 11:12; Lk. 10:19; Eph. 6:11).

In the mid-1980s, when the oil industry was taking off like a rocket, an east-Texas businessman had a booming and lucrative oil business. Many of the oil entrepreneurs were finding large pockets of oil on rural and city plots in the southwestern part of the United States, but especially in Texas.

When the oil boom went bust in the late '80s, the east-Texas oilman lost his business due to incredibly low profits and dried up oil wells. He had invested his life savings, and all of his hopes, and dreams into his oil venture. When his profits evaporated, he was forced to sell his business; he and his wife moved to another city to start life all over again. Both of them found jobs: he as a convenience store clerk, and his wife as a waitress at a local diner. Their standard and status of living had plummeted, along with all of their hopes and dreams. In the course of time, the wife met another man at the diner where she worked, had an affair with him, and eventually divorced her husband.

Today, the former east-Texas oilman is still extremely angry and bitter at God. He is still asking why God allowed these unfortunate events to come into his life when he knew they would destroy his marriage, his family, and his business. He believes with all his heart that, had God prevented the price of oil from dropping so low, and allowed his business to stay afloat, his economic tragedy would have never occurred, and he would have never lost his wife and family. Just beneath the man's seething anger over his losses in life lies a root of bitterness and resentment toward God, because he did not anticipate and was surprised by the disastrous reversals that entered his life.

Considering the ubiquitous nature of suffering in the world, how could anyone have an honest expectation of escaping it? Nevertheless, there are some in certain

Christian circles who have embraced the sadly mistaken belief that one's Christian faith and commitment to Christ should shield them from all hardship and difficulty. This is a mendacious belief that has no support neither in the witness of Scripture nor the experience of history. No matter who we are, Christian or not, as humans, we all inhabit this imperfect, broken earth realm together and, therefore, share mutually in the suffering that comes with it. Let us not be caught off-guard, shocked, or even taken back when suffering touches our lives. It touched Jesus' life, and He told us that it would touch ours as well. Instead of becoming distressed and fretful over the vexing hardships we face, we must learn to trust God's Word, His promises, and the promise of His presence with us, and thank Him for the strength to stand and endure it.

Lesson Seven

Experiencing suffering should motivate you to combat the works of sin, suffering, and evil in this world as much as you are able.

Every single experience of suffering, pain, tragedy, and misfortune in life should remind us that our world is still under a curse and that we should all strive to make it a better and safer place to live. The pain and suffering we endure in our lives as believers in Christ should greatly motivate us to produce more acts of kindness and goodness in the earth.

There is nothing quite like going through personal suffering to make you more acutely aware of the suffering of others. Basically, there are two ways you can respond to suffering in your life. On the one hand, you can become inward-focused being, preoccupied with your own pain and misery from your grievous circumstances. It is easy to slip into this mindset, especially in the early stages of a period of suffering, when the suffering is quite severe. The danger of focusing inwardly on your suffering is that it can cause you to become selfish, bitter, angry, and resentful. On the other hand, you can choose to become outward-focused by allowing God to use your suffering to sensitize you to the pain and suffering of others, increasing your ability to empathize with their pain, and deepening your sense of authentic compassion. For example, it is not at all uncommon for cancer survivors to become more sensitive to other people who are going through their own cancer journey. Those who have lost family members and friends to drunk drivers have used their pain to become advocates against those who drink, drive, and kill. Advocacies for injustices, civil rights, safety hazards violations, abuses, discrimination, and inequitable policies oftentimes have become the driving force behind reducing, halting, and changing laws, regulations, and procedures that save lives and stop further suffering, pain, tragedy, and misfortune around the world. Those who have already walked the same roads can understand, encourage, and empathize with others who are currently on that road in a way that no one else can. Seek to be the answer and the solution in life for someone else's suffering and misery, not the problem or a headache. We should always make space to minister to those who are suffering and dealing with pain.

Suffering, if you will allow it, will help you get out of yourself, lay aside your self-interest, and engage more with other people. More often than not, there is a greater purpose at the root of suffering and pain. Your experiences in life are more than one-dimensional. They can be strong motivating factors in turning you to work at combating the evil that plagued you and in seeking to alleviate suffering and injustice wherever you find it, whether in your daily life at home, at work, or anywhere else you go. This does not necessarily mean devoting your time and energy to this as a full-time occupation (although that is certainly possible), but rather being sensitive to discern opportunities, and being quick to act as you come across them in the normal course of daily life. Your own heart, enlarged with the dimension of compassion birthed from your own suffering, should spring forth and motivate you to build a connection with another pain and affliction. Authentic compassion removes analytical probing and the critical and judgmental spirit, which only multiplies a greater magnitude of pain, grief, suffering, and misery that exist in the world. Christ is our supreme example, and He was full of compassion and mercy for others who faced suffering and hardship. In this way, we become more like Christ "who comforts us in all our troubles, so that we can comfort those in any trouble with the comfort we ourselves [have] received from God" (2 Cor. 1:4 NIV). Work to be a blessing!

Lesson Eight

It's not expedient to prejudge, falsely accuse, or misrepresent someone in their personal suffering and pain.

We don't always know the full story behind someone's personal suffering, pain, or hardship—except that individual and God. With sinful human nature being what it is, most of us are naturally inclined to jump to conclusions in judgment when we see someone in trouble. One of our first impulses is to ask: What did he do to cause himself such suffering? Like Job's three friends who didn't budge on their position, we assume that the person has committed some gross sin or wrong that has brought hardship into his or her life, either as a natural consequence of his actions or as judgment from God. When it comes to our own suffering, however, we tend to assume that we have done nothing wrong, concluding that our troubles must be due to Satan's attacks on us. The same things we attribute to God's judgment in others' lives we attribute to Satan's attack in our own. Either way, we assume there must be a specific, identifiable reason for the suffering—a clearly discernible cause-and-effect relationship. Perhaps this is due partly to the fact that we simply do not like to face up to the idea that suffering sometimes happens for no apparent reason— being victims of circumstances (unless, of course, it happens to us). We are quite prepared to arbitrarily attribute someone else's suffering to that person's weaknesses, failures, and sins while at the same time excusing or ignoring our own unscrupulous or disreputable behavior and blaming our personal hardships, challenges, difficulties, and disappointments on external sources. The continual pernicious attacks, premature judgments, and piercing insults of others can cause irreparable damage to the suffering individual, causing him or her to feel ashamed, confused, rejected, and isolated. That's the way sinful human nature works. Not God!

Assuming personal sin, guilt, or wrongdoing as the cause of suffering is almost as old as humanity itself. This kind of perception can be very destructive, dangerous, and deceptive. Sometimes it is true; our decisions and actions, good or bad, do bring consequences. What we need to understand, however, is that suffering is a part of life in a sinful world. People suffer whether they deserve it or not. It is wrong for us to assume, simply because a person is suffering hardship, that he or she has done something wrong, has some hidden sin in his or her life, or is being punished by God. Many times people prejudge, ridicule, or ostracize others falsely in an effort to distract attention from their own personal inner weaknesses and proclivities. Coldly closing their hearts to the sufferer, they open their mouths, spewing forth a deluge of abuse from a critical and crass spirit with a stabbing tongue. The proverb writer said, "Fools do not want to understand anything; they only want to tell others what they think" (Prov. 18:2 NCV).

This is the lesson that Job's three friends, Eliphaz, Bildad, and Zophar, had to learn, which we discovered in the previous chapter. Their entire debate with Job was based on their false assumptions, personal opinions, and ignorance believing, that Job had defiantly and maliciously sinned and brought God's judgment on himself. Although they spoke some truths, they were basically wrong in their assessments. In the end, they had to repent for their errors of overestimating what they thought to be true—after being chewed-out for mischaracterizing both God and Job. In addition, Job had to intercede with God on their behalf. For the first few days after they arrived to comfort their suffering friend, they did the right thing. They didn't theorize or philosophize with Job; they simply sat with him and wept quietly in sympathy. It would have been better for them to have kept their mouths closed (but then, of course, we would not have this wonderful story and the powerful lessons it teaches). We must always remember that the crowd is not always right in its analysis and assertions of another's suffering. God is always our final and greatest vindicator!

Paul the Great Apostle strongly admonished Christians to support one another when he said, "By helping each other with your troubles, you truly obey the law of Christ. If anyone thinks he is important when he really is not, he is only fooling himself" (Gal. 6:2–3 NCV). We must not be so quick to judge or to jump to conclusions over another's suffering; otherwise, we may pervert someone as Job's three friends did by falsely accusing, misrepresenting, sarcastically criticizing, or impugning the character of that person (not to mention God). Sometimes the best and most appropriate advice and support we can give to someone who is suffering is our quiet, sympathetic, nonjudgmental presence. So, keep your mouth SHUT. Yes, and amen!

Lesson Nine

The best counsel and advice in supporting others who suffer is to pray in faith and keep silent about any personal opinions or judgments.

The New Testament clearly charges us as fellow believers to pray and intercede for one another; we should uphold each other with our prayers, our faith, and our support, especially our brothers and sisters in Christ who are in great trials and sufferings. After all, someday we may find ourselves in the same or a very similar situation.

Unfortunately, one of the biggest nerve-racking issues that especially vulnerable people who are hurting often have to deal with is well-intentioned people who want to help but end up saying or doing the wrong thing. This only makes things worse for the sufferer, because each misguided word or act is a stab that brings more pain. Some people, for example, faced with the suffering of another don't know what to say, but instead of staying silent they say something anyway. The result is rarely positive. Disaster strikes, and some well-meaning but thoughtless friend says, "Well, it's probably for the best in the long run." A child dies, and sympathizers "*comfort*" the grieving parents with words like: "We have to accept it as God's will, and that He knows best," or "God must have wanted another little angel or flower in His garden in heaven." Most of these thoughtless and flippant responses have no real biblical basis at all. Meanwhile, those parents, at the height of their raw, burning pain, are still assaulting heaven with their bewildered, angry cries: "Why, God, why?" The shallow, empty aphorisms of their "*comforters*" only add salt to their open wounds.

Significantly, suffering, pain, tragedy, and misfortune may be much more than merely a physical or intellectual problem; oftentimes they reflect a spiritual problem as well. Nevertheless, the last thing people who are in pain or suffering need is to have judgmental accusations thrown at them. Seldom are there any simple or easy solutions to the real-life problems of suffering and pain. Be careful what you say—when you say it—and how you say it—to someone who is suffering. Saying the wrong thing or saying it at the wrong time is often worse than saying nothing at all. A far better approach is to remain quiet and try to connect with the heart of the sufferer without a lecture or speech. Give heed to the apostle

James' wise counsel: "Understand this, my dear brothers and sisters: You must all be quick to listen, slow to speak, and slow to get angry (or to judge). Human anger does not produce the righteousness God desires" (Jas. 1:19–20 NLT).

At all times, but especially during hard times, we need to rest in the assurance that God loves us unconditionally; He loves us regardless of the reason that precipitated our suffering. He cares about us and invites us to cast all our cares upon Him (1 Pet. 5:7). He is merciful, just, and loving to all who turn to Him. He is not only just, but also the champion of justice. Don't let the false accusations or empty assurances of insensitive people get you down when you're going through tough times. Instead, keep your eyes and your hope fixed on the God who loves you and has promised to bring you justice and relief in His good and perfect time.

The word translated *"Redeemer"* in Job 19:25 comes from the Hebrew word *"go'el,"* and it means *"Vindicator"* or *"Avenger."* In Job, *Redeemer* generally means that—*"God is the vindicator who becomes one's protector, defender, helper,"*—and more specifically,—*"the one who wins your case, the one who stands up for you in a court of law, and the one who proves to be on your side; defending your rights."* It is *"the act of a ransom or release, one who rescues someone else from loss, bondage, or even death; a deliverer."* Jesus Christ has redeemed us from the curse of the law through His own blood sacrifice on the cross of Calvary. Christ's payment was our ransom that ultimately rescued us from the life of sin, fear, and bondage that Satan held over us. In the end, God will champion your defense and deliver you; He will have the final word regarding your suffering, pain, tragedy, or misfortune.

Lesson Ten

Sowing and reaping is an operational spiritual law set forth in the earth realm; no one bypasses it.

There is an old axiom that defines insanity as doing the same thing over and over but expecting a different result. That is the way many people approach life. They repeat the same negative, hurtful, and self-destructive behaviors over and over, and then are frustrated and angry when they keep getting burned. This illustrates the unbreakable law of sowing and reaping, which is also demonstrated in Job's experiences.

One of the greatest lessons we learn from Job's life, and find enunciated throughout Scripture, is the spiritual law of sowing and reaping that has been built into the universe; thus, it transcending time, space, and every human belief system (Gen. 8:22; Job 4:8; Prov. 22:8; Hos. 8:7; Gal. 6:7–9). What often appears as someone not getting what they evidently deserve has to be weighed in the balance of our never knowing the full scope of every predicament or other spiritual laws that may be at work and run parallel with the law of sowing and reaping. The grace of God is certainly a factor in the believers' eternal salvation, thwarting and often limiting some of the most brutal suffering they would have had coming to them while on the earth, however, His grace does not wipe out every consequence of their actions, and He has not eradicated all of human suffering in the earth realm. At least, not yet!

Everything in the earth realm operates on the principle of seedtime and harvest which, makes certain elements of life predictable and/or probable (Gen. 8:22). Even though Job was living righteously at the time when his story was formulated, the earth still yielded misfortune against him because of the law of sin and death that already existed and was in force. The law of sowing and reaping can be applied to Job's life, both before his catastrophic experience and during his recovery and restoration. Although God never gives specific details as to exactly how the door of suffering came open and troubles relent-lessly attacked Job, the principle of sowing and reaping is still visible through-out his existence.

It is impossible to outwit, outmaneuver, or circumvent the law of sowing and reaping. Sowing and reaping is a universal spiritual law that touches all of humanity. Spiritual laws and natural laws are both affected by one another in the human experience while on the earth. The law of sowing and reaping works in the positive as well as in the negative. This law should be one of the first things that we teach our children when they come of age; they should have knowledge and understanding of spiritual laws as well as know how the earth realm works. The basic principle to embrace from this spiritual law in the story of Job is not to become sidetracked when suffering strikes, and not to convince yourself through nickel-and-dime thinking that doing the right thing doesn't pay-off; it always does in the long run. Take advantage of every opportunity to plant good seed in all facets of life, and always do what is right. When someone sows trouble, he harvests even more trouble, but when someone does well, the payback is that good things come in abundance. Sowing a field with seeds of injustice, evil, wickedness, or misery leads only to a harvest that multiplies the same.

Whatever is sown will eventually be reaped by the sower. The bill for the negative as well as the positive always comes due. However, many individuals (not just unbelievers) believe that life is all about being slick or smart, that it doesn't matter, or that somehow one can outthink or cheat the system. They believe that one can do the wrong thing and still get by or succeed without any repercussions or consequences. But for every action, good or bad, there is a payday someday. Many Christians treat spiritual laws that govern their lives and wellbeing with great contempt, because they believe the new covenant of grace protects them from any consequences of their actions, as though they will somehow not be affected by them. What absurdity! What dangerous foolishness! They are standing on shaky ground with this belief system. No one will ever be able to outsmart or outwit God, or bypass the spiritual laws which He has established within the earth realm. He's too great, and He's too smart for humans. Everything in the earth is a recipient of and/or a beneficiary to any spiritual law that interacts with it. It doesn't make a difference whether we know what we are planting or not. Anything that is planted in and on the field of the earth realm makes contact with the invisible, spiritual world and produces a harvest after the kind of seed that is sown. Period!

Lesson Eleven
Wait patiently until God answers before drawing any final conclusions as to the ultimate reasons for your suffering or others'.

Throughout his excruciating suffering and afflictions, Job grappled with God's failure to respond quickly to his despair. He grew increasingly impatient and wasn't above an occasional indulgence in a little self-pity. Who among us would not do the same when faced with difficult challenges similar to his? I dare say that most of us would capitulate to our pain much sooner and under far less pressure than what Job endured! Job never learned the "*why*" of his suffering. God never revealed it to him, and that was God's prerogative. God doesn't always reveal His plans, but He will always reveal Himself. In the end, it didn't matter anyway, because Job received something better. I'm not talking about having his wealth and prosperity restored at twice the level it was before, as wonderful as that was. I'm talking about the fact that Job gained new knowledge and experience of a God who was much bigger, much greater, much more loving, and much more awesome than he had ever imagined. At the end of the story, Job was a different man than he was when he began. He had been transformed, and his pernicious suffering was the catalyst. This was a part of God turning his captivity (Job 42:10). I believe it is fair to say that without his trials, Job would not have grown significantly in the way he did. The challenges, hardships, inevitable difficulties and disappointments of life cause us to become acutely and consciously aware of our need for God. We cannot equate our suffering, pain, tragedy, and misfortune with God trying to punish us. More often than not, He is trying to bring us into a new territory of blessing, favor, His purpose for our lives, and an understanding of His Word.

Implicitly, trust in God is the key to persevering through trials. You must learn to trust the God who loves you like no one else, and who has your very best welfare at heart. It can be extremely difficult, if not impossible, to know or understand the reason for suffering while you are in the midst of it. Enlightenment may come later . . . or it may not. Learn to say—and believe—that either way God is good. One of the greatest lessons taught in the history of Job's life experience is to wait for the conclusion or resolution of the matter before presuming harsh judgment against yourself or God. Ask God to give you understanding, or to give you peace in not understanding and not knowing all the facts. Prayer, patience, and faith in the midst of and in the aftermath of suffering is critical. You will never know the truth of your situation until you hear from God. Great suffering often proves to be the most valuable treasure and the richest blessing in disguise for God's mercy, justice, and vindication: "As you know, we consider blessed those who have persevered. You have heard of Job's perseverance and have seen what the Lord finally brought about. The Lord is full of compassion and mercy" (Jas. 5:11 NIV).

Lesson Twelve
God knows your limits and boundaries in your suffering much better than you do, so trust Him.

"I can't take this anymore!" *"This is more than I can bear!"* *"I am about to lose my mind!"* These are common sentiments expressed by many who are in severe suffering or anguish. When going through hard times, it is vitally important to believe with complete confidence that God knows where you are, that He knows what you're going through, and that He knows how much suffering you can endure, just as He knew Job's limits (Job 1:12). It may often feel like you can't survive another day, but your feelings of inferiority are not a reliable barometer of what you can and cannot endure. Just as important is to know that God loves you, cares about you, and will not allow your suffering to break you as long as you keep looking to Him. Because God created you and because He is omniscient or all-knowing, He knows you better than you know yourself. David had this to say about our all-knowing God:

> O LORD, you have examined my heart and know everything about me. You know when I sit down or stand up. You know my thoughts even when I'm far away. You see me when I travel and when I rest at home. You know everything I do. You know what I am going to say even before I say it, LORD. You go before me and follow me. You place your hand of blessing on my head. Such knowledge is too wonderful for me, too great for me to understand! (Ps. 139:1–6 NLT)

If God knows you that well, then He certainly knows how much hardship or suffering you can endure, and He will come to your relief before it destroys you. Perhaps you feel you have reached your breaking point and cannot endure beyond your present circumstances. Maybe you are baffled because you feel you have taken all you can possibly take, and God has not come to your rescue yet. You may be tempted to conclude that God has let you down and abandoned you to senseless, demonic misery. Regardless of how you may feel at the moment, this is simply not the case. Writing to the Christians in Corinth, the apostle Paul said, "The temptations in your life are no different from what others experience. And God is faithful. He will not allow the temptation [test] to be more than you can stand. When you are tempted, he will show you a way out so that you can endure" (1 Cor. 10:13 NLT).

Although Paul is specifically addressing temptation, the same truth holds true with suffering. It is often during times of suffering that we are at our most vulnerable because we are tempted to genuinely question God and His goodness. But just as God will show you a way out, to help you endure temptation, He will do the same when you are going through hard times. You may think you have reached the end of your rope, but keep trusting in God, and don't let go. He knows how much you can stand. God already knows your breaking point. He will not let you suffer beyond what you have the strength to endure, and He will carry you in difficult times from the inescapable pressure of the outside and inside. He knows exactly what you need, and He will be faithful to provide it. Even when we don't sense God in our suffering and pain, He is ever present. Remember that as a believer, you have a blood-bought right in Christ Jesus to come boldly before God to obtain whatever you need to overcome your hardship and suffering. He knows the limits and boundaries, and He also understands your pain and suffering at the same time. God identifies with all of our suffering and pain in His Son Jesus. We can always trust God and find grace, help, mercy, and compassion in a time of need (Heb. 4:14–16 NKJV).

Lesson Thirteen

The "Fear of the Lord" is the beginning of wisdom and knowledge, even in your suffering.

Proverbs 1:7 says, "Fear of the LORD is the foundation of true knowledge, but fools despise wisdom and discipline" (NLT). This is just as true in times of suffering as it is in times of ease. To fear the Lord means to acknowledge His absolute sovereignty as God and King and to humble ourselves by obeying Him in our thoughts, words, and behavior. The fear of the Lord is respect, honor, reverence, and awe toward God—trusting His wisdom to be far superior to our wisdom. It means, in other words, doing things God's way regardless of our own ideas and agendas. The fear of the Lord produces good judgment, peace, soundness, and wholesomeness, which are not found in any other place, but only in Him alone (Job 28:28). The *flip side* of fearing the Lord is that we are not just to reverence Him and His Word, but we are also to shun even the very appearance of evil.

Job persevered in his horrific suffering and saw victory at the other end because he had determined in his heart long before to fear the Lord. By the time Job's great sufferings began at Satan's hand, his heart and mind were already in the right place spiritually—a place of trust and surrender to the will of God. At one point, Job declared, "Though he slay me, yet will I hope in him; I will surely defend my ways to his face. Indeed, this will turn out for my deliverance, for no godless person would dare come before him!" (Job 13:15–16 NIV). Live or die, Job was committed to hoping or trusting in God, yet he had confidence that someday his deliverance would come. Even as his travails continued, he never lost faith: "'But as for me, I know that my Redeemer lives, and he will stand upon the earth at last. And after my body has decayed, yet in my body I will see God! I will see him for myself. Yes, I will see him with my own eyes. I am overwhelmed at the thought!'" (Job 19:25–27 NLT).

Today, many Christians with good intentions lack spiritual depth or maturity because their hearts and minds are absent of the fear of the Lord. They don't reverence God or His Word in their lives, never turning away from evil practices, and are unwilling to judge between right and wrong. They are too carnal, too careless, and too lax in abstaining from the defilements of the world; these and similar undisciplined mindsets and behaviors open the Pandora's Box of worldliness, which unleashes all manner of endless malignant and maleficent trials and tribulations into their lives. Job understood and practiced the fear of the Lord principle even through his most brutal sufferings. He never looked for an excuse to engage in wrongful behavior—then blame God for it.

Your highest priority regarding your personal relationship with God should be to develop a deep, pervasive, and all-encompassing fear of the Lord. Wealth and material things do not impart wisdom, neither can they buy it. Education may give you a great base of human knowledge and facts, but it alone will never make you wise, especially in spiritual things. Human ingenuity can be rewarding, but by itself it will never give you spiritual insight and illumination into God's thoughts. The fear of the Lord sets us in a posture that gives us access to receive the very best of God's spiritual knowledge and wisdom, which is often not available to the unbelieving world. And that wisdom and knowledge given to us is the foundation, character, courage, and strength to stand tall and to persevere in hard times and ultimately overcome all adversity. Some of the greatest wisdom you will ever gain in this life will be from the fear of the Lord!

Lesson Fourteen
Your suffering is often a direct result of decisions made in the spirit realm, which wages warfare that often affects things in the earth realm.

Your suffering is often a battle of spiritual warfare—not necessarily God settling a score with Satan, but waging great spiritual conflict in the spirit world (Eph. 6:12). We will never fully understand from this side of life what may be in jeopardy, because of our lack of determination to war or to pursue against the kingdom of darkness. Humanity is at the center of a great spiritual conquest between good and evil, and the kingdom of darkness is against God's creation. While there may be many reasons for this conflict, many suffering believers often attribute their troubles in life to some natural occurrence or to some people who oppose them and are "*out to get them.*" Some even blame God when severe and/or a plethora of difficulties arrive on their doorsteps—as did Job. Strangely enough, while quick to blame God or other people for their problems, they often seem totally clueless and unaware that spiritual warfare raging in the unseen realm more than likely is directly related to their present circumstances. There are supernatural forces that are always at work against the children of light. Lack of awareness and the lack of preparedness are two of the main reasons that so many believers suffer severe spiritual defeat in their lives and do not understand why. Your fight is a spiritual battle—a fight of faith!

In Job chapter 1, God asked, "'Have you considered my servant Job?'" Satan replied that the only reason Job served God was because God had blessed him with great wealth, and if that wealth was taken away, then Job would curse God. God allowed it, but even after losing everything, Job was unaware of this spiritual encounter, but always maintained his integrity and his faith in God. Trying a second time, Satan, battling in the heavenlies, accused Job again, declaring that if Job was afflicted in his own body, then he would certainly curse God. Once more, God allowed it, and again Job persevered. Job's suffering was obviously a direct assault from a spiritual force that was beyond his physical and mental perception.

Keeping the children of God ignorant of spiritual warfare is Satan's *modus operandi*. Sometimes, Satan is the catalyst for our trials and suffering, but even when he is not, he still uses those circumstances to fight against us and sow doubt and fear in our minds: "If God loves you, then He would not let you go through this. God is mad at you because of what you did, and that's why He is punishing you. You really messed up this time! You're supposed to be a 'child of God'? No wonder you're in trouble!"

Whenever you are going through a difficult time filled with trepidation because you are under attack, and negative warfare like this starts flooding your mind, remember, that as a child of God, the person you are ultimately accountable to is your heavenly Father. He allows or disallows suffering into your life; Satan can do nothing completely on his own. He is a defeated enemy, and his power was vanquished by Christ at the cross, so don't give him credit or influence in your life that he doesn't deserve. Satan may want to do battle with you, but he cannot unless God allows it, and if God allows it, then there's is a reason for it. However, it will eventually result in your good. And remember that God will never leave you to suffer alone; even if He seems to be silent at times, He is still with you and will never leave you. Why are you so important to the spirit world? Why are human beings so important that God and Satan have conversations about them, pay detailed attention to them, and war over them? Why does God set His mind upon humanity and put His eyes on them every morning? It is because, frequently, there is a cosmic battle between good and evil, between heaven and hell, and for the very souls of humanity that is directly related to warfare in the spirit world (Job 7:17; 22:2; Ps. 8:4).

Lesson Fifteen

It is extremely important to grasp God's perspective in your suffering, especially when He seems to be perplexingly silent.

Another life lesson that we learn from Job is that during the course of his story, he became so focused on rebutting his friends' false accusations and mischaracterizations, and on seeking the opportunity to defend his righteous cause before God Himself, that he didn't realize the limitations of his own perspective until God spoke to him in the final chapters. Job did his best not to say anything untrue or inaccurate with his limited knowledge. No matter how much pain, anguish, and confusion Job suffered, he never cursed or blasphemed, or spoke ill of God, nor did he ever purposely mischaracterize God in a demeaning way. However, unlike King David and King Hezekiah, who refused to blame God for their suffering, Job (in a sense) did become a fault-finder, and complained at certain times in the process of his suffering. Time after time, many of us are guilty of the same thing while experiencing difficult adversity. Job's affliction, however, eventually brought him into a deeper place of humility and purged him completely of any excuses, arrogance or pride that he may have had in the enormously wealthy empire he had built. Job's main problem was that his conception of God was too shallow and his understanding of how the spirit world operated was too limited. It took God's personal appearance in the story and His challenges to Job to expand Job's horizons, so that he could see his life, his circumstances, and indeed all of creation, from a much wider, broader, and more comprehensive point of view—God's point of view. Once Job began to see things from God's perspective, his own sufferings, as well as his intense desire to know the *why* of them, began to fade into insignificance and obscurity. Compared to knowing God in a newer, bigger, better, and deeper way than ever before, his earlier trials seemed much, much smaller in his eyes.

Paul the apostle had the same experience when he came to know Christ. Considering his earlier life as a strict and devout Jew who sought God's favor by his own good works, he wrote:

> I once thought these things were valuable, but now I consider them
> worthless because of what Christ has done. Yes, everything else is
> worthless when compared with the infinite value of knowing Christ

134

Jesus my Lord. For his sake I have discarded everything else, counting it all as garbage, so that I could gain Christ and become one with him. I no longer count on my own righteousness through obeying the law; rather, I become righteous through faith in Christ. For God's way of making us right with himself depends on faith. (Phil. 3:7–9 NLT)

As a devout Jew, Paul thought he knew and understood God, but when he met Christ, his whole perspective changed. God's knowledge about everything is much better and far surpasses anything we know about this life. God visualizes everything we can't see and knows things we have no knowledge of. Wait for God to reveal all things to you. Until you know and understand, allow yourself to be guided by your faith in God, and trust in His Word.

No matter where you are in life, whether in good times or bad times, set your mind and heart on seeking God's perspective for your life, and do not let your circumstances guide you. Let God broaden your horizons so that you can learn to see everything, even the peripheral things, from His point of view, even during those times when He seems to be silent in your life and to your prayers. Put your complete trust, faith, and confidence in His Word. (Job 13:15; Ps. 23:4; Isa. 43:2).

Reflections on Life Lessons Learned from the Book of Job

The overarching truth that we take away from the story of Job's monumental suffering is that God permits crises to come, and good people to suffer, but within limits. There may be a myriad of reasons why different individuals suffer what they suffer, but God always has a definite purpose behind why He has allowed evil to remain in the earth even though He has not fully disclosed that reason at this point in time. In the meantime, there are so many life lessons we can learn and apply from the sufferings of others, as well as our own. God often speaks to us about our suffering through many different vehicles: an inward witness, a personal witness, dreams, visions, impressions, images, etc. God always speaks to us specifically through His Word. However, our perception is often cloudy so that we are not always able to grasp it clearly. Some things in life are precisely avoidable if we follow the correct road signs, but other things must be dealt with more wisely by adapting to certain conditions, enduring the hardships, and overcoming every obstacle while believing God's Word and staying in faith.

135

Life can be very tough at times—extremely tough! However, all things are possible through Christ and faith in His Word. Like Job, some of the best wisdom and most valuable lessons that we can discover come from the devastating experiences of other individuals who have already lived. This is one of the reasons why God chose to plaster the story of Job's life and suffering right in front of the whole world, so we could visualize it. Hopefully, by studying the life and sufferings of Job with an open mind, you will grow as you learn not to capitulate to Satan's visceral attacks, or take the bait and become blindsided by the suffering itself. His goal is to turn the faithful against God and cause them to curse Him to His face. If your ambition in life is to minimize the vexatious suffering in your life and the lives of those around you, then it is important that no matter where you are in life, you continue to have a willingness to absorb life lessons that can be discovered and learned from humanity's common experiences. This means being humble enough to learn as though you know very little, open enough to unlearn what needs to be changed or forgotten, and a willingness to relearn and practice habitually what you need to embrace.

Through every relationship with family, friends, acquaintances, colleagues, and even strangers, we should seek to better understand suffering, pain, and hardship; we should learn through personal growth to make life work better for us and for others. Life can at times be complicated and unpredictable, and throw you many unwanted and unexpected curve balls. It is important that you don't concentrate on how hard you have been hit, but instead focus on how you can bounce back from the hit. The life of Job provides a backdrop for the resilience we can have in suffering that eventually leads to restoration. When we continue to think that God and/or the world owes us a certain kind of life that we are constantly expecting and anticipating to happen, we only position ourselves for huge disillusionment and disappointment. The world has created an optical illusion of an ideal life with very few hardships and endless happiness; it is a life that is totally separated from reality and is simply not possible on the earth at this point in time.

Everyone needs to find and know their own personal ordained purpose and assignment in life, so as not to chase after vain and silly imaginations that will only lead to further suffering, pain, sorrow, and hardship. Life itself can be shorter than what we think, and very fleeting; it can be interrupted by many momentary circumstances of life. As in Job's case, so will it be in the lives of many who pilgrim through the earth. There will be times in life when things will go really well and other times when the unexpected, unpredictable and sometimes the inconceivable will show up. Conversely, when you learn from the pernicious sufferings and hardships of others as well as your own, you will be better equipped to live out your God-given potential, and also to appreciate the good and wonderful things that God allows you to enjoy while living on the earth.

7
RESTORATION

"'Then shall your light break forth like the morning, and your healing (your restoration and the power of a new life) shall spring forth speedily; your righteousness (your rightness, your justice, and your right relationship with God) shall go before you [conducting you to peace and prosperity], and the glory of the Lord shall be your rear guard.'"

— Isaiah 58:8 (AMP)

"Restoration and hope is available each time you return to God."

— Jim George

Restoration Often Follows a Design or Formula

LEONARDO DA VINCI'S *THE LAST SUPPER* IS UNIVERSALLY RECOGNIZED as one of the greatest masterpieces of Western art. Leonardo himself, despite being the product of a broken home, rose up to prove himself as one of the greatest polymaths and creative geniuses of the fifteenth and sixteenth centuries and, indeed, of any century. He was not only a renowned artistic painter, but also an author, astronomer, researcher, and engineer. His ever-fertile giftedness led him also to produce great works of art such as the *Mona Lisa*, the *Virgin of the Rocks*, and The *Last Supper*.

Until recent years, *The Last Supper* mural was one of the most endangered paintings in the world. Adorning one wall of the refectory of the Convent of Santa Maria delle Grazie in Milan, Italy, the mural measures approximately 15′x 28.5′; it took the great artist over three meticulous years to paint and complete the flawless masterpiece in 1498. The famous painting depicts Jesus sitting at the center of a long table with His 12 disciples beside Him, 6 on either side. Behind them are three open windows that reveal a distant hillside. The disciples are obviously agitated, reacting strongly to Jesus' shocking statement that one of them is going to betray Him.

Rendered in tempera on plaster (an experimental medium at the time that proved to be disastrously flawed), the mural began to show unmistakable signs of deterioration even during Leonardo's lifetime. As it suffered the ravages of time and the elements, various attempts were made over the years to restore the painting. Most of those efforts, however, did more harm than good. By the mid-twentieth century, there were serious concerns that this priceless masterpiece might eventually be lost to humanity altogether.

In 1979, a new restoration effort to repair portions of the mural where paint had flaked away quickly turned into a full-scale restoration project of the entire painting as restorers discovered fragments of Leonardo's original that had been covered over by repainting during earlier *restoration* efforts. This massive restoration project was completed in May 1999 after 20 years of meticulous work, employing the latest techniques and processes to restore life to Leonardo's masterpiece.

The renowned restoration artist Pinin Brambilla Barcilon oversaw the project. Recognizing that the foremost task was to stop further deterioration, she and her team utilized chemical analysis to determine that the repainted sections were eating away at Leonardo's original paint, while areas that were flaking away took parts of Leonardo's original work away altogether. The solution was to carefully and laboriously remove everything that had been added to the painting—deliberately or otherwise—since its completion in 1498. This involved removing centuries-long accumulations of mold and smog that had collected on the painting, as well as removing glue and repaint from earlier restoration efforts. In addition, infrared reflectoscopy revealed Leonardo's original work that lay underneath layers of newer paint. Careful studies were made of the colors and materials that Leonardo used in creating the mural, as well as studies of the elasticity and structural characteristics of the masonry upon which he painted it. The restoration process was so slow and meticulous that it often took a full day to clean only a postage stamp-sized portion of the painting. All of this was done to ensure that the end result would restore the full luster, beauty, luminosity, and magnificence of Leonardo's original work. By all accounts, the effort succeeded. Once regarded as a "*sick patient*," Leonardo da Vinci's masterpiece, The *Last Supper*, was beautifully restored and protected for future generations to enjoy.

Like those artists who worked so long and hard to restore Leonardo's The *Last Supper*, God is a great artist who is also in the restoration business. As it so happens, His greatest restoration project involves His greatest artistic achievement—humankind. He created us in luminous splendor and beauty, but the corruption of the mold, smog, glue, and repaint that have polluted our lives has left all of us in dire need of restoration. No matter who we are, how well off we are, or how "*all together*" we believe ourselves to be, there is not a single one of us who does not stand in need of a touch from the "*Master Restorer*." We are quite helpless left in the hands of ourselves. In fact, we are often much like the ill-destined character in a nursery rhyme we all learned as children:

> *Humpty Dumpty sat on a wall,*
> *Humpty Dumpty had a great fall;*
> *All the king's horses and all the king's men*
> *Couldn't put Humpty together again.*

We live in a "Humpty Dumpty" world: a world of great brokenness that, for all our vast human intellect and medical, scientific, and technological advancements, we are unable to fix without the help of God. We advance all sorts of fancy theories and *brilliant* or innovative ideas for fixing what's wrong with the world—and with people—but nothing works. People still suffer. People still experience misfortune. People still endure tragedy. People are still in pain. People are still broken. And because the world remains a broken place, many are in need of restoration and healing. But unlike *Humpty Dumpty*, where all the king's horses and men couldn't restore him back to his original state, there is a King of kings who has the power to bring restoration and healing, and to make you whole again. God has not forgotten about you.

In the midst of our pain, sin, sorrow, suffering, and brokenness, there is good news. There is hope in the face of hopelessness. Yes, we *can* be restored! The Great Restorer is at work, and He is the prime expert. As Craig D. Lounsbrough said, "Jesus was and is the greatest restoration specialist of all time."

The team of experts that restored Leonardo's *The Last Supper* to its original beauty and glory succeeded in their efforts because of three essential factors: 1.) They knew exactly what needed to be done. 2.) They did exactly what needed to be done, and 3.) They took whatever time was required to do a thorough job. It is the same with Jesus—the *"greatest restoration specialist of all time"*—but to an even greater degree. Whether He is restoring a nation, a church, or an individual, Jesus knows exactly what is needed. Let's make it even more personal. If you need personal restoration in your life, if unexpected roadblocks, disillusioning setbacks, and disheartening deprivation have taken their toll on you and you are not sure how long you can keep going, and if your heart is crying out for restoration and renewal, then Jesus knows precisely what to do. He knows unerringly what you need and, if you let Him, He will do exactly what you need; He will take whatever time is needed to restore you and your situation completely. He will not do a slipshod job. When Jesus restores you, He will make you better than you were before; you will be better, in fact, than you have ever been.

Assuredly, if you are right now in the midst of pain, suffering, and trying circumstances, and if you wonder why God seems to be taking a long time to answer your prayers for relief, fix your situation, or change your circumstances, it may be that, in His timing, you are not *done* yet. His project of restoring you is well underway, but you need more time to *cure* and mature. We've already seen throughout this book how spiritual growth and maturity occur best when we learn to persevere through trials and hard times with faith and confidence. God knows exactly what it will take and how long it will take to bring you to the place He wants you to be, and He will not cut corners. He wants you to be a perfected son of God. First Peter 1:7 says, "These trials are only to test your faith, to see whether or not it is strong and pure. It is being tested as fire tests gold and purifies it—and your faith is far more precious to God than mere gold; so if your faith remains strong after being tried in the test tube of fiery trials, it will bring you much praise and glory and honor on the day of his return" (TLB).

If you are a child of God, then everything that happens in your life, whether you deem it to be good or bad, can and will be used by God to perfect you, restore you, and to deliver a harvest and your inheritance, and bring you to full maturity as one of His beloved sons. He does this for all of us who are His children. He allows and uses the most appalling things in life to work for our good and wellbeing because He is preparing us to reign with Him in this life and in the life to come. To the grace of Christ, and for the love of God!

Let us keep this glorious truth close in our minds as we progress through the rest of this chapter. Remember that no matter what you are going through now, God's restoration project for your life is already underway.

The Experience of Suffering Can Be Useful in the Restoration Process

One of the most critical keys to persevering through suffering, for a child of God, is to remember that all suffering is transitory and will eventually pass away, and then be replaced by victory. Suffering is not the end, nor is it the final, ultimate reality of life—restoration is. Full restoration is the ultimate and guaranteed destiny of every child of God; suffering is a means to that end. God allows and even actively utilizes pain and suffering in our lives in this current realm of existence to prepare us for the fullness of life as mature and fully restored *"God-images,"* in this world where possible, and in the eternal realm to come. With this in mind, let's consider carefully the following truths:

Suffering Used for the Purpose of a Greater Good

Our sufferings and misfortunes in life are often useful for the purpose of a greater good. One of the greatest lessons learned from suffering, when restoration takes place, is to recognize all the good things that emanate from our adversity and hardship. As the great apostle Paul reminds us in Romans:

And we know that in all things God works for the good of those who love him, who have been called according to his purpose. For those God foreknew he also predestined to be conformed to the image of his Son, that he might be the firstborn among many brothers and sisters. And those he predestined, he also called; those he called, he also justified; those he justified, he also glorified. (Rom. 8:28–30 NIV)

Nothing in the life of a believer happens by accident; God is never caught off-guard or by surprise. However, God allows both positive and negative circumstances into our lives to teach us, toughen us, mature us, and prepare us to minister to others, especially to those who are suffering, as well as to encourage them by our own example to have confidence that their suffering is temporary, and that they can make it through. At the same time, God is also preparing us to be co-rulers with and under Him in the new heaven and the new earth. Suffering often serves as an objective to help transform you into the spiritually mature man or woman He wants you to be. Because He has called you according to His purpose; He works all things for your good in order to restore you to the full likeness of His Son.

The Greek word for "*likeness*" is "*eikon*," from which we get our English word "*icon*." *Eikon* literally means "*statue*" or "*profile*," and figuratively, "*representation*," "*resemblance*," or "*image*." According to Scot McKnight, God's purpose in the atonement (Christ's death on the cross for our sins as our Substitute) is to restore those of us who are "*cracked*" by sin into unblemished *eikons* that beautifully display His glory: The atonement is designed by God to restore cracked eikons into glory-producing eikons by participation in the perfect eikon, Jesus Christ, who redeems the cosmos. To be an eikon, then, is to be charged with a theocentric *and* missional life. Prior to the fall, Adam and Eve did what they were supposed to do: they "eikoned." And cracked eikons are being restored so that they can eikon now, and so that they will eikon forever.

So, keep your suffering in perspective, because God has bigger plans for you. Your suffering is temporary; in due time, God will bring you relief and elevate you into greater usefulness in His purpose and, ultimately, into greater glory than you can ever imagine. The apostle Paul framed it this way: "The sufferings we have now are nothing compared to the great glory that will be shown to us. Everything God made is waiting with excitement for God to show his children's glory completely" (Rom. 8:18–19 NCV). Restoration often brings a greater glory and greater good out of the hardships you endure. The image of Christ will be seen in your restoration and elevation, because God wants to display you as a statue so that others may visualize His goodness. Yes, and amen!

Suffering Used for the Purpose of Increasing Spiritual Effectiveness

Sufferings we've experienced are often used to move us toward increasing our spiritual effectiveness. The primary principle of spiritual effectiveness is witnessed repeatedly in analogies like the crushing of grapes to produce wine to maturity, the pressing of olives to produce olive oil, and the squeezing of the flower pedal to produce the sweet-smelling aroma fragrance. All are examples of how the process of brokenness and recovery is often used to increase greater effectiveness. One of the basic principles of *horticulture* and successful gardening is the importance of pruning. On first thought, it may seem counter-productive to cut off branches or shoots of a plant that seem to be healthy, green, and thriving. If they are not producing fruit, however, they are detrimental to the long-term health of the plant. Such non-producing branches are called suckers, because they suck vital nutrients away from the branches that are producing fruit, and hinder the full growth of the fruit.

In an online devotional, writer and amateur gardener Candy Arrington described her initially frustrating experience trying to grow tomatoes one year. Although she carefully watered and fertilized the plants, they produced no ripe tomatoes even though the vines were green and lush. Remembering her father's advice from years before on the importance of pruning, she took a closer look. "Now, as I looked at my vines, I saw many non-producing shoots. I began pruning and soon discovered many more tomatoes than I realized hidden by the foliage. Although full and green, those branches were preventing the sun from reaching the tomatoes. And the nutrients in the vine were being used up by new growth rather than going toward enlarging and ripening the fruit."

The initial result of pruning is often ugly, even giving the appearance of doing more harm than good to the plant. But that is a false impression. Pruning actually makes the plant more fruitful. Ms. Arrington continues: "When I finished pruning, the vines were not as pleasing to the eye. In fact, they looked a little scraggly and sparse, but now, the sunlight was able to reach the tomatoes. Within days, we were enjoying delicious, ripe tomatoes."

Sometimes we have "*suckers*" in our lives that prevent the full life and light of God's Word and His Spirit from reaching us by sucking from us valuable time, energy, and attention that should be given to pursuing our godly purpose. Instead, we expend these things on distractions and on frivolous, unproductive, wasteful, unhealthy, or even sinful activities that hinder us from reaching our maximum potential. Indeed, part of Satan's central strategy is to use these things to suck the very life of God out of us, to the point where our godly influence and effectiveness, as well as our desire for spiritual things and the kingdom of God, become minuscule, even to the point of being nonexistent. Pruning, therefore, is vital for our spiritual effectiveness and steadfast devotion to the Lord. God often uses suffering to perform pruning in our lives. His pruning is often painful at first, but His purpose is to cut away anything that hinders our growth and threatens our fruitfulness. Quite often, it is out of the most desolate and devastating circumstances of life that our most abundant fruitfulness and faithfulness to God emerges.

Jesus said:

> I am the true vine, and my Father is the gardener. He cuts off every branch in me that bears no fruit, while every branch that does bear fruit he prunes so that it will be even more fruitful. . . . Remain in me, as I also remain in you. No branch can bear fruit by itself; it must remain in the vine. Neither can you bear fruit unless you remain in me. (Jn. 15:1–2, 4 NIV)

If you are a child of God—a *branch* of the *true vine*—the suffering in your life should drive you closer to God, not away from Him, because His goal is to grow you and increase you into a life of abundant fruitfulness and faithfulness to Him. And that is something you cannot do by yourself. None of us can. Suffering reminds us of our weakness and helplessness apart from God; it prompts us to cling closely to Him, trust Him in all things, rely on His Word, and depend on the indwelling of His Spirit to increase our spiritual effectiveness for Him as ambassadors of His kingdom. Whenever we start relying on ourselves—in our own strength, wisdom, and insight—our efficiency and effectiveness for God become stale and wither. In effect, we have cut ourselves off from the Vine that nourishes us with spiritual life, strength, wisdom, and power. It is only as we remain attached to Christ and His Word that we can be faithful and fruitful. Suffering helps us understand that we can't make it on our own, and that, apart from Christ, we can do nothing.

Suffering Used for the Purpose of Greater Dependency on God

Suffering is often used to get our attention to trust God and have greater dependency on Him and His Word. Sometimes we can be so stubborn in trying to go our own way, because we think we know what's best, that sometimes we have to reach rock bottom before we will look up. God has to get our attention before we will listen. Suffering is one of the means He uses to this end. Again, God is not endorsing or promoting evil, pain, or suffering, but rather sometimes allow it as a chisel to knock away some things that hinder growth, in order to bring a greater benefit to your life. He is a Master at what He does. In *The Problem of Pain*, his classic book on suffering, C. S. Lewis describes the attention-getting power of pain: "[W]e can ignore even pleasure. But pain insists upon being attended to. God whispers to us in our pleasures, speaks in our conscience, but shouts in our pain: it is His megaphone to rouse a deaf world." Because of our sinful, fallen nature, our perverse tendency, even as Bible-believing Christians, is to drift or turn away from God and His ways. We turn a deaf ear to His voice and soon become stubborn in our disobedience and resistant to change. Whenever this happens, God works to turn us back from the precipice of destruction to Himself again, usually gently at first. If we do not heed His words or the subtle promptings of His Spirit, then He will allow efforts to be escalated by employing stronger and more intense means to reach us, which sometimes involve allowing pain and suffering.

Psalm 119:67–68 reveals that suffering is sometimes the means to get us back on the right path when we have gotten off course: "Before I went through suffering, I went down the wrong path. But now I obey your word. You are good, and what you do is good. Teach me your orders" (NIRV). The psalmist suggested that suffering often produces a source of greater insight and a profitable reward. This favorable reward often comes to us only after we have endured suffering and hardships, allowing them to move us in the right direction by resetting our focus on the right priorities for our particular purpose and assignment. Suffering, pain, and hardship often furnish greater understanding and offer safeguards against making conscious decisions that are not in line with the path that God has set before us. Suffering not only helps us to get back on the right track, but it also helps us learn to stay there. Thus, the hard thing has turned into a good thing.

Consider, as a sobering example, the very tragic history of the Israelites in the Old Testament. Theirs is a story that is jam-packed with repeated instances of their unfaithfulness to God—followed by His calls for them to repent with warnings of judgment, and then by His delivering judgment of varying degrees of severity upon them when they continue to disobey. This cycle is especially apparent in the Old Testament Book of Judges. Time after time, the Israelites turn away from God to worship false gods; God permits pain, suffering, and oppression from external forces to fall upon them to get their attention; the Israelites turn away from their sin and back to God by praying to Him for relief, and then He raises up a deliverer: Jephtha, Deborah, Gideon, Samson, and others. The theme of the entire Book of Judges is summed up in its final verse: "In those days Israel had no king; all the people did whatever seemed right **in their own eyes**" (Judg. 21:25 NLT, emphasis added).

Anytime we, like the ancient Israelites, do whatever seems right in our own eyes rather than humbly submitting ourselves and doing what God has said to do, we get ourselves into trouble. We can also move unintentionally or innocently, but in all cases, our course must be changed if we are going to survive and thrive. God then disciplines us as a loving Father who delights in His children. Before He can get us moving back in the right direction, He must arouse us out of our deafness and stubbornness to get our attention. And He knows that one of the most effective ways to get our attention is to allow us to experience pain or suffering. Suffering always makes an indelible imprint on our conscience that we cannot ignore. He does not do this to punish us, but to teach us through it, and to draw us off the broad path of disobedience and self-interest that often leads to collateral damage or irreparable destruction, and back onto the *"straight and narrow"* path that leads to life, fruitfulness, and abundance. Restoration will often posture us for the right paths and reset us onto our proper priorities. King David understood this when he wrote: "He restores my soul [God revives life back into you]; He leads me in the paths of righteousness for His name's sake" (Ps. 23:3 NKJV).

Suffering Used for the Purpose of Encouragement and Empowerment

Suffering is often useful for the purpose of encouraging and empowering others who are suffering in similar situations. Within God's permissive will, our suffering is never accidental, and it is never about us alone. Pain or hardship tends to make us look inward and focus on our own discomfort—our own hurt and pain—to the point where we can miss the effect our pain and our response to it has on the people around us. Even worse, we can miss opportunities, not only to grow from our experiences, but also to see the pain of others who we could encourage and empower by the wisdom and strength we gain from persevering through our own times of suffering. For example, no one understands the effusive, emotional, and paralyzing trauma caused by a life-threatening illness better than someone who has gone through it. Many cancer survivors volunteer their time to encourage and support others who are currently undergoing their own cancer journeys. Alcoholics Anonymous groups consist of people who are attempting to recover from a common addiction, along with people who encourage and support each other from their firsthand knowledge of that addiction and its effects on their lives. Empowerment and encouragement are immensely important in helping to build up and save the lives of many who are going through devastating sufferings, misfortunes, and life tragedies.

Enduring suffering, if we allow God to teach us and impart wisdom to us through it, can make us more insightful and more capable of offering meaningful empowerment to others who are suffering, especially if their suffering is similar in nature or degree to ours. When people who are in the midst of pain and suffering see us after we have emerged in victory from our own suffering stronger than we were before, they will be encouraged to persevere through their challenges, because they know there is hope and, as a result, may seek to learn and grow through them. What God has done for you and through you will be evident when your restoration is completely revealed. He will do for others as He has done for you.

Paul the apostle reveals that encouraging, empowering, and comforting others is one of God's explicit purposes for allowing suffering in our lives:

> *Blessed [be] the God and Father of our Lord Jesus Christ, the Father of sympathy (pity and mercy) and the God [Who is the Source] of every comfort (consolation and encouragement), Who comforts (consoles and encourages) us in every trouble (calamity and affliction), so that we may also be able to comfort (console and encourage) those who are in any kind of trouble or distress, with the comfort (consolation and encouragement) with which we ourselves are comforted (consoled and encouraged) by God. For just as Christ's [own] sufferings fall to our lot [as they overflow upon His disciples, and we share and experience them] abundantly, so through Christ comfort (consolation and encouragement) is also [shared and experienced] abundantly by us. (2 Cor. 1:3–5 AMP)*

Restoration positions you to have the capacity to minister to others as they pass through the same or similar challenges in life.

Brandon was a precocious, smart, attractive, and athletic young man who appeared to be enjoying an idyllic life. But he also loved socializing and wild parties, where he often participated heavily in social drinking. One day, when he was 28, Brandon was inebriated while driving down a winding road with a friend who was sitting in the passenger seat. At one point, he misjudged a right turn, lost control of the car, and drove off the road down into a large embankment. His car flipped over and rolled multiple times, finally coming to rest some 30 yards off the main road. Brandon's friend died upon impact, but Brandon survived, though he sustained severe injuries, including a fractured back and head trauma as a result of hitting the windshield. In the days following the accident, Brandon found it increasingly difficult to cope with life after the death of his best friend, knowing that he was responsible for his death.

Brandon professed to be a Christian, but he did not walk in the light of God's Word; he was not heavily invested in the Christian life or spiritual things. His life displayed very little, if any, discernible spiritual fruit or consistent faithfulness to the Lord. Although Brandon loved life, he was not interested in righteous living and was undeniably headed in the wrong direction. In the long months of recovery and rehab following his accident, Brandon dealt with a dizzying array of devastating and potentially destructive emotions, such as guilt, fear, anger, depression, suicidal thoughts, and deeply unsettling doubts about his faith. He slowly began to recover and get back up on his feet, with some limitations. Most significantly, however, he recommitted his life to Christ, began attending church regularly, reading his Bible, and participating in prayer groups. He soon began to see drastic lifestyle changes in himself, especially in his moods and behavior. Brandon also joined a youth organization dedicated to helping and guiding youths to make solid decisions and to take the right paths in life. Eventually, Brandon became a counselor, and helped those who struggled with substance abuse and addictions. God's purpose and plans for his life began to come into focus.

Although he still lives with some pain and some limitations, Brandon has testified that the accident proved to be a pivotal turning point in his life that changed him forever. Whatever suffering you are presently experiencing, remember that it is temporary, and that it is not all about you. God wants to use you to empower and encourage others who have suffered and who are suffering. Restoration often brings with it the catalyst of empowerment and the impetus to also build up others' lives. Let Him turn your suffering into something meaningful, something glorious, and something of eternal significance in the lives of others.

Restoration and Victory Can Often be a Bittersweet Conquest!

Deliverance from hard times or suffering is always a welcome relief, but depending on your particular circumstances, in conjunction with your choices, God's will, and His purposes, your victory, in the end, may be bittersweet. You may agonize over particular losses you suffered that may or may not be restored. Certain relationships of yours may have changed in such a way that they can never return to their former state. There may be changes in your circumstances or overall situation that prove to be permanent. We can't always be assured of an ideal or favorable outcome for every situation that pertains to our suffering or misfortunes. One thing we can know with confidence, however, is that when we finally decide we want our lives repaired, God, if we allow Him, is able to restore us to a level of wholeness far beyond our present suffering.

Rest assured, child of God, that He will restore you in His time and season and in His own way. Restoration *will* come, but that doesn't necessarily mean that everything will return to the way it was. Sometimes you can't go back, at least not all the way—for various reasons. Experiencing restoration, even with permanently changed circumstances, is quite often a much better situation overall than what previously existed. This is particularly true when it is God who has done the restoring. Even so, your victory may, in some ways, be bittersweet. On the one hand, you are remarkably grateful for the progress, breakthroughs, and restoration that have finally come, but on the other hand, you feel a deep and cloying regret over certain things, people, and circumstances that you know will never be the same or be a part of your *"new normal"*—your new life going forward.

Comparatively speaking, this was Brandon's experience. Ever since his tragic driving experience several years ago, his life has not been the same. In fact, people who knew Brandon before the accident can hardly believe or recognize him as the same person. Brandon has been turned on to God, the Word, and spiritual things. Many people who know him can attest that he had a radical secular mindset before the incident, and would have never thought to be involved with *"Bible-thumping-stuff."* Even though it was a hard thing losing his friend, Brandon's life was saved and restored. His friendships were changed to new groups of people; he quickly realized that returning to past relationships was out of the question. Brandon's usefulness for God's purpose, however, is greater because of his suffering than perhaps it would have been had he never experienced the misfortune. God took a tragic event in his life and turned it into a blessing by bringing him into a lifetime of greater glory, faithfulness, fruitfulness, getting his priorities straight in life, and increasing his impact in advancing the kingdom of God.

King David, in the Old Testament, gives us another example of someone who dealt with an exorbitant amount of suffering, pain, loss (some of it of his own doing), and often felt as though he was drowning in a sea of difficulties. Through it all, however, he endured; by the grace and mercy of God, he lived to experience a full and thorough but bittersweet restoration.

The Bible describes David as a "man after God's own heart." This means that David loved God with all his heart. Throughout his life, his heart was in the right place—inclined toward God. David was a godly man and highly favored by God, but this does not mean he was perfect. Far from it—his life was an oxymoron. David's résumé of accomplishments and accolades, in addition to master shepherd, exceptional warrior, worshipper of Jehovah, and brave king, would also include conniving deceiver, lustful adulterer, premeditating murderer, and inattentive father. Although David was highly blessed by God throughout his life, he also, due to poor choices stemming from his flaws and human failings, experienced God's judgment, as well as had heartache, tragedy, and danger in his personal and family life, including a coup attempt by one of his sons. (For the full biblical background on what follows, see 2 Samuel chapters 13–18).

David fathered numerous children by several different wives, and the complex relationships that resulted created tension, rivalry, and jealousy, which eventually erupted into violence and revenge. Amnon, David's firstborn, was a half-brother to Absalom, David's third son, who had a different mother. Absalom also had a full sister named Tamar. In time, Amnon fell in love with his half-sister Tamar (or so he thought). In order to get her close to him, Amnon feigned sickness and asked his father, King David, to send Tamar to personally care for him. When Tamar entered Amnon's house and the two were alone together, Amnon forced himself upon her and sexually assaulted her. Afterwards, to make matters worse, Scripture says that Amnon "hated her more than he had loved her" (2 Sam. 13:15 NIV), and he cast her out. Tamar went away shamed, humiliated, sobbing, and stained with an undeserved stigma she would carry for the rest of her life, even though she was not to blame. Such were the social and cultural mores of that day, particularly with regard to women.

Amnon's lustful heart, exploitative behavior, and dismissive attitude toward Tamar were unspeakably despicable and abhorrent. Although Scripture says that David was *furious* over the notorious incident, it gives no indication that he ever directly confronted or rebuked Amnon for his actions. Absalom was also livid with rage over Tamar's disgrace and humiliation at Amnon's hands, but was unwilling to let it go at that. Although Absalom was unable to take immediate action, he bided his time while plotting an appropriate revenge. Two years later, when the time seemed right, Absalom lured his brother Amnon to his house on a ruse and murdered him. Absalom then fled the country, taking refuge in the homeland of his mother, who was of royal birth, where he lived for three years under the protection of his mother's royal family.

Unarguably, even as David mourned the death of his firstborn son, Amnon, Scripture says he also mourned the *loss,* through exile, of Absalom: "King David longed to go to Absalom, for he was consoled concerning Amnon's death" (2 Sam. 13:39 NIV). After three years, David was persuaded to deal graciously with Absalom by ending his forced exile, and the young man returned to his house in Jerusalem, with the stipulation that he could not be in his father's presence. David lifted this prohibition two years later, but by then it was too late. Even though Absalom went once again into his father's presence, and everything appeared normal on the outside, Absalom was secretly at work undermining, instigating, and subverting his father's authority, mounting a shrewd insurrection by cunningly winning over to himself the affection and popularity of the people. Then, once he sensed that the time was right, Absalom launched an outright open rebellion against his father, intending to take the throne for himself. David and the rest of his family, along with his greatest supporters and admirers, had to swiftly flee Jerusalem as fugitives, barely escaping from the city before Absalom and his numerically superior armed forces entered. Absalom's well-planned revolt was the greatest threat to the Davidic dynasty that David ever encountered as king.

One of David's counselors and advisors, a man named Ahithophel, switched his allegiance to Absalom, which prompted David to pray that God would "'turn Ahithophel's counsel into foolishness'" (2 Sam. 15:31 NIV). David also sent a trusted friend named Hushai back to Jerusalem to pose as Absalom's ally, in order to sabotage and discredit the counsel of Ahithophel, as well as to serve as David's eyes and ears in Absalom's inner circle. When Ahithophel suggested wisely that Absalom take a small army to pursue and viciously attack

David and his company by surprise at night while they were still weak and tired, kill only the king, and bring the rest of the people into Absalom's fold, Hushai countered with different counsel aimed to play to Absalom's bloated and twisted ego, vanity, anger, and vengeful spirit against his father. Hushai advised Absalom to take his full army in pursuit, with the intent to completely wipe out David and all who followed him. Absalom foolishly followed Hushai's counsel instead of Ahithophel's, because "the LORD had determined to frustrate the good advice of Ahithophel in order to bring disaster on Absalom" (2 Sam. 17:14 NIV). Hushai sent word to David regarding Absalom's plans so that the king could get ready.

As a result, Absalom and his army suffered a decisive defeat with enormous casualties. David sent out his army, which consisted of many mighty warriors to engage Absalom's men in battle. However, he specifically charged his commanders to "'be gentle with the young man Absalom for my sake'" (2 Sam. 18:5 NIV). Despite the bitter struggle and everything that happened, David still loved his son and wanted him alive and safe. In the end, however, Absalom's army was defeated in the epic battle, and Absalom, the prince himself, was killed by Joab, one of David's top commanders. The coup attempt was over. Absalom's revolt had failed. The king was safe, and the threat to his monarchy was removed. Yet, when David received news of the victory, his only concern was for Absalom's safety, and upon learning he was dead, the king was devastated. Instead of celebrating the stunning victory and the restoration of his reign, David retreated to his chambers, wept bitterly, and cried out: "O my son Absalom! My son, my son Absalom! If only I had died instead of you—O Absalom, my son, my son!" (2 Sam. 18:33 NIV).

In the greatest crisis of his life since the time when King Saul had pursued him with murder on his mind, David almost lost his kingdom to a rebellious son. God intervened, however, and restored David's rule, but not without cost: Amnon was dead, Tamar was disgraced and forever stigmatized, and Absalom was also dead. David was still king—his rule was restored—but in many ways, David was never again the same. His life and his rule after Absalom's rebellion and death were different than before those sad and tragic events. God gave David victory over his enemies and ended the war in his household, but that fresh victory left a bittersweet taste in David's mouth.

Reflections on Recovery and Restoration after Bitter Sufferings

A bittersweet victory is far better than living in a caustic environment of hopelessness and total defeat. If you are going through an intense crisis, a grievous hardship, or deep suffering, and if you are faithfully seeking God and praying to Him for help, He will restore you. Depending upon your particular circumstances, however, your restoration, like David's in the aftermath of Absalom's rebellion, may not bring everything back to the way it was before. You may have to adjust to permanent changes that may cause you periodically to wish that things could be the way they used to be. But let God use those changes to work a change in you, so that you can go forward restored in Him, wiser, stronger, and better than before. Overall, with this in mind, here are five practical principles you can embrace to help you become proactive in experiencing your full recovery and restoration.

1. **Focus your attention on being your very best—every day—rather than focusing on your weaknesses.** No one is perfect; everyone has potentially debilitating flaws, if you look hard enough. There are many people who can do many things very well, but no one can do everything well. All of us, without exception, have strengths as well as weaknesses. One of Satan's favorite tactics to trip us up in our walk with God is to trick us into bemoaning our weaknesses and failures instead of celebrating our strengths and victories. Stop letting yourself fall into that insidious trap by always insisting that you are just as human as anyone else. God has also made you uniquely you. No one else in the world is exactly like you. Proactivity pursues the promises of God, so focus your attention on doing your very best, getting better, and on what's going well. Believe in Christ's ability to help you make significant strides, and change things for the better. As much as possible, have a winsome perspective about life, and de-emphasize your hardships, struggles and sufferings. God has endowed you with special gifts, skills, talents, and strengths to equip and enable you to completely fulfill the plan He has had for your life since before the foundation of the world. Stop listening to Satan's trash talk about you. Change the channel, and turn the page. Learn to listen to—and embrace—what God's Word says about you. Know and believe that your full restoration is on its way, if it hasn't already begun to happen by now.

Adopt a new mentality and a positive mindset that says, from the moment you get up every morning, "Today, in the solid assurance of the Father's love and favor, and full of grace, I am going to do my very best, knowing that even in my weaknesses He is made strong. Weakness and failure won't stop me from reaching my fullest potential because His strength will prevail. Today, in His strength, I am going to make a difference!"

2. **Actively use and exercise your faith and hope muscles**. It takes faith to live in order to survive and overcome the difficulties and hardships of life. It's much easier to give in to hopelessness and despair. Our physical muscles will atrophy over time if they are not used. This is why astronauts who spend months at a time in the weightlessness of space on the International Space Station must spend an excessive number of hours every day on exercise machines to keep their muscles toned. Likewise, our spiritual *muscles* of faith, hope, and love will diminish, become depleted, and wither away if we do not exercise them continuously. Actively using and exercising your faith and hope muscles keeps your spirit person strong, healthy, and flexible. It doesn't make a difference how many faith failures you think you have had. Faith can increase and become stronger over time. Keep living by faith and keep believing God's Word. Faith-filled words and positive thoughts will eventually lead you out of defeat and into victory. Child of God, get your faith and hope muscles up. Get them up, and keep them up, despite what happens. The devil wants you to roll over and give in to his tactics. The devil is a liar; don't take his bait. Our faith as believers is not "*blind faith*," but it is "the confidence that what we hope for will actually happen; it gives us assurance about things we cannot see" (Heb. 11:1 NLT). And Christian hope is not merely wishful thinking, but it is "an anchor of the soul, both sure and steadfast" (Heb. 6:19 NKJV). In other words, the believer's faith and hope are not based on possibilities, but on *certainties,* which are based on the integrity and infallibility of the Word of God. We all live in this physical realm, and it is subject to failure and loss. But the God we serve is absent of any impossibilities. Thomas Edison said, "Many of life's failures are people who did not realize how close they were to success when they gave up." So, learn to approach each day with your life anchored on the "*sure and steadfast*" hope and confident faith in God's Word, that He loves you, and that He's "*got your back*."

When you learn to live each day with your faith and hope fixed on the unshakable certainty of God's love, grace, and favor, all the pain, suffering, and hardships you face in this life will diminish in comparison to God's ability and power. Real, biblical faith has a way of bringing things from the unseen realm into the realm where you can touch it, see it, and experience it. Live life faithfully and not hysterically—hopefully and not haphazardly.

3. **Learn to live and walk in the righteousness of Christ.** Knowing and living in the righteousness of Christ is a safeguard against Satan's daily accusations and assaults. Part of living by faith is walking daily in the confident knowledge that, in Christ, you are the righteousness of God. When you became a *"new creation"* in Christ, He took your sins from you and imputed to you His own righteousness; He made you a partaker of the righteousness that emanates from the Son of God. In Paul's words: "For He [God] made Him [Christ] who knew no sin to be sin for us, that we might become the righteousness of God in Him [Christ]" (2 Cor. 5:21 NKJV). So, let go of your past. Step boldly into each new day, confident in the eyes of your heavenly Father, safe and secure as one of His beloved children. As a child of God, you're not trying to make yourself righteous by some good deed or works. That will never work, but only lead to more vexation and frustration. This kind of righteousness only comes alive when you, as a believer in Christ, appropriate the knowledge of God's Word for your life. Satan wants to cheat you out of the best that God has for you. He wants to make you feel that you're good for nothing. Don't tip-toe around walking in the righteousness of Christ. Be bold about it! Learn to live, think, and walk as one adopted and beloved by God, not as an orphan; live as a son or a daughter of the king, not as a slave.

4. **Recognize your goals and balance your expectations in life**. Poet Robert Browning wrote, "Ah, but a man's reach should exceed his grasp, Or what's a heaven for?" Aspire to great things. Set goals with laser-like precision, but have specific, realistic and reasonable objectives, in order to achieve attainable goals for yourself. Even if you don't reach all of them, you will achieve more than if you had never set your sights or if you had lowered your standards. Have an energetic, positive, and contagious attitude when moving forward. Keep yourself motivated to succeed. Measuring the level

of your interest, time, and ability will always help you discover whether or not to pursue certain objectives. At the same time, recognize that you can't do everything. Develop the things you are able to do well and very well. Always remember that it is exceptionally rare for some things to always work out exactly the way you want them to. Keep yourself and your thinking flexible; be pragmatic about adapting to changes when necessary. Acknowledge that there may be some things in life you may not be able to achieve because of certain limitations. However, don't ever give up on your dreams and goals in life. You never know what might happen at some given point and time. Learn not to allow the fiascos and setbacks of life to become a monument to the death of your hopes and dreams, but use them as stepping-stones as you reach for the stars. Don't sweat it when things happen that are beyond your control, especially when you have done everything within your power to avoid it. Do not waste your days and years overindulging in unrealistic expectations exasperated by frustration that may push you to the brink of a meltdown. Life is too short. However, resist the temptation not to do anything at all. Dream big, but set your priorities wisely so that you focus your attention and efforts on the most important things. Les Brown said, "Shoot for the moon. Even if you miss it, you will still be among the stars." Never make valid excuses for an apathetic, complacent, and lethargic mindset; it will only rob you of your peace and potential future. Let God's eternal truths, His divine will, your purpose and assignment in the earth realm, and the certainty of God's eternal kingdom, guide and inspire your endeavors. As you embrace your recovery, learn to readjust your expectations, desires and demands. Maintain a healthy balance between your efforts, opportunity, progress, and reality, along with sensible living. Do all that you can do, do everything to the best of your ability, and don't worry about what you cannot do. Leave the rest to God and live your life to the fullest.

5. **Practice living your life without regret, fear, or pain from your past dragging you down.** Everyone has some kind of hardship, and we all encounter crises in life. In Christ, you are a new creation; the old has passed away, and Christ has made you and everything about you completely new—your spirit person (2 Cor. 5:17). He has not given you a new lease on life, but a whole new life! *Nothing* in your past matters anymore,

not even your failures, worst experiences, or deepest regrets. Christ has made all things new. He has taken away your sin and its shame along with it, and He has put it far from you, never to be remembered again. You have nothing to be ashamed of anymore. Satan will try to dredge up memories of your past sins and failures in order to condemn you, but when he does, just remember that the *you* he brings to mind is the old *you*—the *you* that passed away when Christ made you completely new in Him. You remind the devil of his future, so don't fall for his tricks. Let the old *you* stay dead; instead, walk in complete newness of life: free, fearless, and forever destined for glory as a favored child of God. So, stop trying to fix it! Don't worry about it or make yourself sick another day or another second. Waiting for others to give you affirmation, approval, recognition, and acceptance is a waste of your precious time and energy. Living in a perpetual victim state, clinically depressed and angry over how unfair life has been, is a sure recipe for disaster and failure. Make a quality, conscious decision to live vivaciously without regret or fear.

"The grass withers, the flower fades (life's brevity), but the Word of God endures forever!"

8

THE IMPACT OF OPEN DOORS

"As righteousness leads to life, so he who pursues evil pursues it to his own death."

— Proverbs 11:19 (NKJV)

"We are free to choose our paths, but we can't choose the consequences that come with them."

— Sean Covey

All Choices and Decisions Have Consequences

A POPULAR STORY WHICH WAS HEAVILY CIRCULATED REVEALED that one night in 1962, in a hotel in Seattle, Dr. Billy Graham woke from a sound sleep in the middle of the night, with what he later described as "a burden to intercede and pray for Marilyn Monroe," the popular Hollywood singer and movie star. When the feeling continued over the next several days, one of Graham's associates tried to reach the actress through one of her promoters and film agents. Dr. Graham wanted to present the gospel of Jesus Christ to Ms. Monroe, to afford her the opportunity to experience salvation by receiving Christ as Savior and Lord; he wanted to extend to her the chance to walk away from a life of sin to follow Him (Jesus), thus escaping hell and eternal damnation.

Once contacted, her agent offered Dr. Graham no hope for a meeting in the immediate future. "Not now," he said, "Ms. Monroe is too busy to meet with Dr. Graham. Perhaps two weeks from now." Two weeks later, however, Marilyn Monroe was found dead in a hotel room from an apparent suicide that shocked the world. Only two weeks—but it was too, too late. As far as anyone knows, Ms. Monroe died in sin, without ever finding salvation through faith in Christ.

All of our choices have consequences, even the choice concerning our eternal destiny. Suffering, pain, hardship, and trouble exist in the earth realm, and are impossible to completely escape. While we are able to avoid some things, it is impossible for us to live completely free of the rigorous contingencies of daily living. Some of our life experiences breed suffering because we live in the sphere where suffering, pain, and evil exist. In these situations, we should focus on limiting our pain and suffering as much as possible, and "*shut the back door*." This world is fallen and is presently under the dominion and control of evil humans, Satan, and his cohorts. Until it has been redeemed with the return of Christ on the earth, it will continually yield more and more conflict.

Many times, pain, suffering, misfortune, and crises appear to come without a cause, and often with little or no warning. Nevertheless, it is our Father's will that, as His children, we minimize the suffering in our lives and escape further damage, destruction, and calamity by living under His divine but limited umbrella of protection through the new covenant that He has provided. However, God never promised us a rose garden or sunshine all the days of our lives here on earth. Times of tribulation often force us to make decisions by putting us in circumstances where they can no longer be ignored or post-poned. Among life's biggest decisions are the clear paths we choose to take.

Essentially, the sovereign rule of God means that all things remain under His divine authority in the universe. Remember, nothing happens within the universe that is outside of His foreknowledge, allowance, and permission. Satan, demons, evil, wickedness, pain, suffering, and *all* human choices and actions are ultimately subject to God's sovereign rule. God has never endorsed evil, conceit, or the sinful practices and wicked actions of humanity. God has never condoned nor participated in evil. Because God is just and righteous alto-gether, He reserves the right and the authority to judge Satan and humankind for their sin, rebellion and evil works. When we make choices contrary to the will of God, His justice eventually falls upon us. Many often get by for a time or season, but no one ever escapes. God can never be fooled!

There is a vast difference between permitting evil and practicing it. However, both the demonic activity and the decisions of humans have a significant impact on humanity and the world. We humans cannot escape the latent consequences that are directly related to our choices and personal decisions. Some trouble and suffering are directly related to our actions while other circumstances are indirectly related, but all are a part of the **root causes** of our suffering. Consequently, much of our trouble and suffering is due to our leaving doors open through which we permit suffering, pain, hardship, and sometimes evil to walk into our lives. This is especially problematic for believers, because we have been given more power, ability, anointing, and knowledge than unbelievers have, in order to control (to some extent) the evil we allow into our lives. The Holy Spirit in us gives us the power to overcome all the wicked forces of evil, but we must learn to exercise it. Unbelievers lack the indwelling personal presence of the Holy Spirit; therefore, they do not have that kind of protection from the power of the Wicked One.

A door to evil, suffering, and pain often opens when a believer chooses to negate or disobey God in a certain area; the devil then has a legal right to attack. A decision not to choose is still a choice, and will ultimately lead to some paramount consequence of its own. God created humans with free choice, but with that freedom comes the responsibility for every choice we make and every action we take. All living things produce after their own kind. So it is with our personal choices. Wrong choices bring negative consequences, and often lead to needless suffering that affects our lives, and sometimes the lives of our families, and they even impacting society as a whole. This moral dimension of our free will leads many to think that the odds are always stacked against them, no matter what they choose, as if we all are pawns at the mercy of God's erratic impulses. But this is not the case. Why is it so important to choose the right thing? It is because Satan and evil spirits must have legal permission to enter into our bodies, minds, and lives; wrong choices give them that permission. Wrong choices unlock and open doors into our lives, which allow evil and painful things to enter. Paul, the apostle of Christ made this truth evidently clear when he wrote, "Leave no [such] room or foothold for the devil [give no opportunity to him]" (Eph. 4:27 AMP).

The Impact of Open Doors Can Bring Bad Things

It is extremely easy to indulge in a pity party—grieving, murmuring, fulminating, and complaining under your breath about why bad things have happened to you, especially when your world seems to have collapsed. Blaming God for your ills is not the answer. Take Christ's Word, and assert yourself in the heat of your trial. Ask yourself: What doors have I willfully left open, either out of a lack of wisdom, or out of my own disobedience and selfish volition? Some things we allow may seem small or innocent, but they are not. It is often the little foxes that trip us up. Praying to God to make your life easy and problem-free is a prayer He is unlikely to answer, at least in the way you want Him to.

As long as you are on this earth, you will never be completely free of problems or difficulties. However, you can minimize Satan's influence by shutting unsafe doors—and keeping them shut. No matter how much you may wish otherwise, there are no magical formulas, spiritual hocus-pocus rituals, or escape routes to make the dilemmas of life vanish forever. God has given you His Word and His Spirit. Know that He has overcome the world, and that if you have Him, you have His power and ability to overcome, just as He did. He has made you more than a conqueror, and the greater one (JESUS) lives within you. First John 4:4 reminds us, "You are of God, little children, and have overcome them [evil and wicked spirits], because He who is in you is greater than he who is in the world" (NKJV). Believers are able to have complete victory over Satan and this world's system if they accept and follow the leading of the "Greater One," because Christ won the victory for us at Calvary.

Also, rest assured that not everyone will understand you or be for you. Living the Christian life is not about other people's acceptance, but God's approval. No matter how nice or inoffensive you may try to be, not everyone will be on your side. Those who are of the world are blinded by the god of the world, which is Satan. Therefore, they will be against you because you, as a believer in Christ, are not living according to this world's pattern. Give thanks to God that your spiritual eyes have been opened to the workings of evil and to the devil's strategies. Jesus Christ was manifested that He might destroy the works of the devil (1 Jn. 3:8). Be fully aware that there are some bad things that do not have to happen, and they are within your power to stop by shutting the back door. You can bank on it!

I have devoted the rest of this chapter to examining 10 of the most common and perilous doors that Christians open, either inadvertently or intentionally, which allow Satan to legally attack them. These open doors allow him to steal your joy, destroy your effectiveness, and inject an exorbitant amount of deep suffering, trouble, pain, misfortune, and, in some cases, senseless tragedy, into your life.

Door One: Planting the Wrong Kinds of Seeds

The popular philosophy of our day sees no contradiction in believing one thing while practicing another. Many habitually rationalize their wrong by glossing over their questionable behavior with these short-sighted (and false) views: "*Nobody's really perfect, and God wants me to be happy in this,*" or "*Things will work out either way,*" or "*God will rectify my mess-ups,*" or "*Grace will make up the difference.*" Others insist that it doesn't matter, because God will casually overlook your indiscretions, flaws, and evil, fleshy nature, because He wants you to enjoy life. Well, it *does* matter; it matters a whole lot! Yes, God does understand our shortcomings, faults, and mistakes; He is very compassionate, forgiving, and full of mercy, and often the God of second chances. However, our constant foolhardy, thoughtless, and/or ill-considered, reckless actions can open the door to bad things happening to us. Proverbs 19:3 gives credence to this backwards, leisurely thinking which undercuts biblical virtues when it explains: "Some people ruin themselves by their own stupid actions and then blame the LORD" (TEV). In other words, our own actions can bring unimaginably negative outcomes into our lives. We can knowingly or unknowingly sow or speak something painful, evil, or destructive into our lives; when the crisis comes, our first response is often to make up valid excuses and/or to blame God for our predicaments. Our life is a seed, and our actions are seed. What we speak out of our mouths and hearts becomes seed. What we practice becomes seed. When we plant the wrong kind of seed, we will reap the harvest of what we have planted, whether good or bad. Seedtime and harvest is a universal law that transcends time and dispensations (Gen. 8:22). God makes this significantly clear in Galatians 6:7–8, "Don't delude yourselves: no one makes a fool of God! A person reaps what he sows. Those who keep sowing in the field of their old nature, in order to meet its demands, will eventually reap ruin; but those who *keep sowing* in the field of the Spirit will reap from the Spirit everlasting life" (CJB; emphasis added). Many of today's so-called "*Christian belief systems*" teach that the law of sowing and reaping has neither lasting consequences nor repercussions for those who are forgiven and live under the grace covenant. This is simply nonsense! It is more "*new age*" thinking than biblical truth. Nothing could be more hazardous!

Moscow officials made a huge error that sparked a major scandal when, in one part of the city, on city-owned property near a metro train construction site, they accidently planted marijuana seeds where they had intended to plant regular grass seeds. Over time, some 230–plus cannabis plants grew, and eventually had to be removed at considerable time and expense. What should have been a simple grass-growing project turned out to be a horrendous embarrassment to the city and its officials. Every seed that is planted can only produce after its kind. You cannot plant apple seeds and reap orange trees. No matter what your intentions are, or what your plight is, or how sorry you may be after the damage is done, if you plant the wrong seeds, then you will still reap a ubiquitous harvest of *exactly* what you have planted. Sowing things in your life that are contrary to God's Word will ultimately bring increased sorrow, destruction, disaster, and misfortune, regardless of how good you feel at the time. Things may be ever so wonderful today, but the bill will come due! I promise you!

Be very mindful of what you are planting presently; it is a surety that you will reap *precisely* what you have sown. If you expect to live peacefully and harmoniously, and to make it through life without creating unnecessary drama, crises or extra hardship, and without bad things happening to you, then be cognizant of the fact that you need to plant seeds that are conducive to righteousness rather than planting the wrong kinds of seed, which will produce a harvest after its kind. God's design is for you to plant the right kinds of seeds so that you can experience a quality life. Randy Alcorn said, "Sow a thought, reap an action. Sow an action, reap a habit. Sow a habit, reap a character. Sow a character, reap a destiny."

Door Two: Poor Judgment

Again, life is about the choices we make, and not merely the chances we take. God never created us as robots and then sealed our fate. Our personal judgment in life choices is more than just a fun merry-go-round. God has given us a free right to make unwise moral decisions. Because we all have free will, however, God is not responsible for our impaired judgment—nor for its consequences. We are created in God's image, which includes the free will to choose between good or evil and right or wrong. Our spirits have already been preprogramed to know right from wrong and light from darkness. God built this into our conscience. Our decisions determine the sum total of who we are and who we have become. Our impaired judgment and poor lifestyle choices are often a direct result of a sequence of wrong thinking. Our paradigm for decision-making gives a strong indication of where we are headed in life (see Ps. 119:30).

Incontrovertibly, we (believers) sometimes exercise our free will in ways that lead us away from God's perfect will and into our own selfish desires—continually doing dumb stuff. God always informs and instructs us regarding what to choose, and why to choose a certain path. We have the power to bring God's hand of blessing or cursing into our lives and into the lives of others, simply by the decisions we make. Although we face many complexities and troubles in this world that are not of our making, it is our own judgment in the circumstances of life, more than external forces, that affect our lives for better or worse. Joshua laid it out straight for the Israelites as they prepared to cross the Jordan river into the promised land to experience God's best, and his advice is apropos for us as well when he says, "'Serve the LORD alone. But if you refuse to serve the LORD, then choose today whom you will serve'" (Josh. 24:14–15 NLT).

All too often, many of us make poor choices because we don't want to consult God about our lives. And many others mistakenly believe there are no serious consequences for their poor judgment, because they view their salvation as a bullet-proof protection plan from their poor decisions. They never take time to consider what is before them, and what will be the end result. The Christian life is more than repeating a prayer at a church altar with chills running up and down your spine—thinking that's the end of it. If the truth could be told, this warped, common, mystical concept of authentic Christianity is utterly ludicrous, dangerously deceptive, and corrosive. The genuine Christian life is about the transformation that touches our lifestyle, our thinking, and our actions, which translates into changes in our character and behavior for the better. God does not control the decisions we make; however, He does empower us through His Word and His Spirit to overcome our deficiencies, in order for us to make better choices, although this is not effortless. It is our responsibility to discern and to learn how to recognize the differences between right and wrong, good and evil, and wise and foolish. God often prompts us to do the right thing, but the decision of response is ours and ours alone.

Conclusively, we cannot allow destructive forces into our lives without being influenced and affected by them. God has made protection available to us under His Word and through the witness of His Spirit, but we can't blame Him for what happens if we disregard His safeguards and don't strategically take the necessary precautions. The person who smokes three packs of cigarettes a day for 30 years and develops lung cancer has no grounds for asking why it happened. Likewise, the person who is undisciplined in their diet for years and then develops clogged arteries or other health complications has no basis to complain that God has cut their life short because of heart disease and stroke. We can bring curses into our lives by desensitizing our moral compasses, and by our own poor judgment and actions. We cannot violate God's natural and/or moral laws (adultery, sexual promiscuity, perversion, pride, worshipping money, power, success, addiction, or unwholesome pleasure, etc.) or abuse our physical bodies and the environment (excessively drinking alcohol, habitually smoking, abusing drugs, overeating, chronic worrying, fear, stress, etc.) without expecting any consequences from these actions. Participation in actions and decisions that are outside of the bounds of their intended purpose or outside of God's will is always detrimental, and will eventually bring harm.

Human beings have a moral compass that gives us the freedom to choose, and to direct our actions as we will. More often than not, our poor judgment is rooted in our free will, which results in our suffering, deprivations, and in other bad things happening to us. Poor and/or sinful choices are not the only reason for, and do not answer all the questions of why bad things happen to good people. They are, however, one good, solid reason why some believers suffer loss, pain, tragedy, and, sometimes, even premature death. Thomas Aquinas said, "A small error in the beginning becomes a great one in the end." Start immediately by making better decisions and implementing sound judgment. You'll be amazed at the positive results it will bring.

Door Three: Fear

Fear is another door we open unintentionally anytime we stop walking by faith and trusting God's Word, and instead start walking in the flesh, following our own logical reasoning, our own direction, our own wisdom, and our own abilities. Satan sees it as an open invitation to set up shop and to operate in our lives. That's why fear is one of his chief weapons against us. Fear is a paralyzing force, just as faith is an empowering force. More than that, fear is the opposite of faith; it is a demonic counterfeit. The spirit of fear usually begins to manifest itself in the areas of fearing people, things, failure, diseases, rejection, the unknown, betrayal, or in some kind of lack or insufficiency, or some physical limitation. The Bible clearly instructs us not to fear people (Prov. 29:25). Fear operates in the negative, just as faith operates in the positive. We have to overcome fear by using the power of the Word of God and the Holy Spirit, which God gave us to trample over all the forces of evil. I have heard many believers speak of things that they feared, and, before they knew it, the very fear they spoke of came to pass right before their eyes. Job experienced this reality for himself when he said, "'What I fear most overtakes me. What I dread happens to me. I have no peace! I have no quiet! I have no rest! And trouble keeps coming!'" (Job 3:25–26 GWT).

Part of the reason why trouble, evil, crisis, and even disaster fell upon Job was because he opened a door to fear in his life. Fear is a negative, supernatural force that brings not only the presence of evil and suffering, but also a great deal of other demonic activity along with it. If it's a warning from God, then we have to take the necessary precautions, so that we are in a position of faith and not weakness. We can allow fear and paranoia to become so powerful that they produce a reality that manifests a stockpile of evidence in the physical realm. It's the devil who orchestrates events to captivate us by secretly building fear and other negative, insidious forces into our minds and consciousnesses. As believers, we must stand our ground and push back in the Spirit against the kingdom of darkness. We must understand and know how to claim and utilize our rights in Christ to rebuke Satan and live in the Holy Spirit's power. Yes, and amen!

Definitively, it is not the will of the Lord for us to live and operate our daily lives in fear. Second Timothy 1:7 concludes, "For God has not given us a spirit of fear, but of power and of love and of a sound mind" (NKJV). One of the main keys to overcoming fear and safeguarding your mind is operating your life through God's power. The reason God instructs us not to fear is because He knows that when we place our trust completely in Him, and not in any person or worldly thing, fear cannot enter in. If our hearts are filled with love and faith in God's Word, then there is no room for fear and shame. God's endorsement is victory for us, because the Holy Spirit has given us guaranteed power, love, and a sound mind—as long as we continue to walk in the Spirit and not in the flesh—to walk by faith and not by sight. To display fear is to displace faith, which shows that we lack confidence in God. This displeases God because it shows Him that we do not trust Him neither His Word for our security. If we are not careful with our spoken phobias, then fear is a subtle door that often opens up the spirit world, creating a reality. Don't let the devil have a single opportunity to open a door to bring suffering and misery into your life through fear. The battle has already been won.

Door Four: Sin – Wrong Behavior

God has already judged our sins and laid our iniquities upon Jesus at Calvary. The eternal punishment for our sins has been paid once and for all by Christ Jesus! However, when we begin practicing sin habitually as Christians, it puts us on shaky-ground—Satan's territory. We cannot persist in wrong living and sin, and then expect God to wink at us and turn His head even as we reject His Word by our actions. Sin is always extremely destructive, dangerous, and poisonous. We must understand that we open ourselves up to consequential ramifications whenever we become insensitive to our proclivity to sin by willfully and continually disobeying God's Word. Yes, God is full of grace and mercy; however, there are always ripple effects to our actions, whether they are good or bad. God cannot and will not bless us, nor override our self-destructive behavior—especially our irresponsible insistence on minimizing our sin, rebellion, disobedience, and wrongdoing.

Whether you are missing the mark of God, involved in illegal practices, slipping back into impulsive-neurotic behavior and sinful conduct, continuing in daily willful disobedience, or committing any other kind of systematic and habitual transgression, you must absolutely come to a place of humble, heartfelt repentance. With honesty and sincerity, confess your own sinful wrongdoing, and turn away from it. One of the doorways that brings bad things into the lives of believers is living in unrepentant, willful sin and continual wrongdoing. When you continually live this way, God's grace is always available to help you change, but sometimes it is impossible to avert a bad harvest from coming to you. You cannot keep walking in the wrong direction, and still expect to reach the right destination. As Proverbs 11:19 cautions us, "As righteousness leads to life, so he who pursues evil pursues it to his own death" (NKJV).

We must remember that pursuing life or death is our personal choice. God allows you to make your own decisions. That's why it is called *free will*. God does not force anything on you that you choose to do or not do. If you are sincerely struggling to overcome certain sinful desires, the Spirit of God is right there to strengthen, encourage, and aid you until you have total victory in your life. It is especially self-deceptive to hide behind a religious façade, thinking you will never be held accountable for your actions. If your proclivity is bent toward the wrong thing, then you must learn to practice disciplining your flesh. This is not always easy, but it can be done through the power of the Holy Spirit. Hebrews 12:1 explains, "Let us lay aside every weight, and the sin which so easily ensnares us, and let us run with endurance the race that is set before us" (NKJV).

Each one of us must make the personal decision to walk in harmony with God's Word, or to walk contrary to it. Walking with God must become a daily decision; it must become a habitual practice that we follow every day, whether we are high or low, happy or sad, and whether we feel like it or not. We must not let our God-walk be governed by our frazzled emotions and volatile feelings. To walk with God is a deliberate, cognitive choice we make with the full engagement of our spirit, soul, and body.

Far too often, many believers make the mistake of interpreting the grace of God as a license to excuse wrongful behavior. Yes! We are to lean totally on Christ for deliverance, courage, and strength; however, we must still repent and turn from our wrongdoing. Many contemporary Christian thinkers don't believe in practicing contrition and penitence anymore. They say that repentance is no longer necessary for Christians, that "*it doesn't take all that anymore.*" They often take passages from God's Word out of context, and misinterpret other Scriptures to support their lop-sided belief system. To be perfectly blunt: The devil is really crazy! It takes whatever God says it takes—nothing less. Repentance is not just for those who are professing Christ and seeking salvation, but it is also for those who possess Christ (2 Cor. 12:21; Rev. 3:19). Let no one deceive you! The Word of God says, "If we say that we have no sin, we deceive ourselves, and there is no truth in us. But if we confess our sins to God, he will keep his promise and do what is right: he will forgive us our sins and purify us from all our wrongdoing" (1 Jn. 1:8–9 TEV).

God wants us to rest in what Christ did on the cross—in that He paid the debt of our sins by His Son's blood sacrifice. However, many of us reason within our own minds that, since God is a merciful and a forgiving God, even if we continue in our sin, He'll forgive us and we won't suffer any aftereffects or consequences for our actions. God is very concerned about His children not harboring or hiding sin away in their lives. Remember, child of God, that there are always consequences to what you do, even though you are forgiven. You cannot hoodwink God so that He will bypass the consequences of your negative choices; you cannot plead the grace of God to avoid any repercussions from your actions. It simply doesn't work like that—not one bit! Unfortunately, it is a rarity anymore to hear instruction on God's righteous judgment against sin. The fear of God (reverence) has become almost a lost virtue among many believers, including many Christian leaders—I'm sorry to say. Sin runs rampant in our churches, and preachers are afraid to touch the subject for fear of suffering some kind of retribution in their ministry. Anyone who speaks out on the subject of sin is considered *"out of touch"* with modern culture, and into fanaticism, behavior modification, works-oriented religion, sin management, or reactionary legalism. Contrary to popular thinking, God's grace should never be abused or mocked. God's grace is not greasy grace or cheap grace. He sent Jesus, His Son, to die for us so that we could be transformed into the image of His Son—not what we think we should be or what we want to do, but what God has purposed us to be. Our thinking has to change first if our behavior is going to change for the better. The modern-day teaching is totally fickle and backward—God please help us!

We understand this concept even in our workplaces. Most employers allot their employees a certain number of *sick leave* days per year, to be used for sickness, medical care, or other similar areas as needed. But if you take advantage of those days, and start calling in sick for trivial things, clearly abusing your sick leave, you are likely to be fired. We are not to abuse the spirit in which something is given by abusing it according to the letter. Abuse of sick leave is a major problem in the corporate world. A similar problem exists among believers, regarding the abuse of spiritual things. Many believers are quick to point out all the evil, suffering, pain, misfortune, and injustice in their lives and in the world. They abhor all the evil, and the things they don't like that are happening to them. They tend to blame others and God or point their finger at Him for not responding or not intervening quickly to relieve their inward misery and suffering. At the same time, they rarely turn inwardly to see the sin, rebellion, corruption, disobedience, or moral evil that they commit against God—things they do that they know God disapproves of and has clearly told them not to do. Somehow, they want or even expect God to overlook their persistent sin, disobedience and stubbornness without any penalty. Even when we miss it, we should always be proactively pursuing the right things, and making sure we are doing the right things.

The *"X-factor"* in all things is that, as believers, we should discern and judge whether and how we are using what God has freely given through the cross— the riches of Christ—to enjoy, but not to abuse them. God gives His grace, mercy, and forgiveness to us freely, but we are not to take advantage of Him, nor cheapen the gifts He's given to us by continuing in our disobedience and rebellion, or by lowering our standards. Our heavenly Father is patient and slow to anger, but if we persist in abusing His grace and forgiveness, eventually He will judge us and bring forth the chastisement that is fitting for our sin and wrongdoing. If we don't judge ourselves—if we do not guard our own steps—God will judge us, and He will do so with great precision. So, let us all take warning. Remember that God will judge His children more quickly for spiritual sins or sins of the heart (pride, arrogance, evil, unforgiveness, etc.) than for physical sins. It is extremely important that we keep our hearts right before the Lord. The apostle Paul said, "But if we would examine ourselves, we would not be judged by God in this way. Yet when we are judged by the Lord, we are being disciplined so that we will not be condemned along with the world" (1 Cor. 11:31–32 NLT).

Door Five: Wrong Associations

Many good-hearted Christians are disillusioned and don't believe that associations have a great impact on their lives and on the lives of others, especially when those associations are not in their best interest, or in agreement with positive behavior and good conduct. Even with the rise of social media, such as Facebook, Twitter, Instagram, and blogs, we all must be explicitly cognizant of cyberspace, which brings a plethora of chatter, clamor, and clutter that tries to infiltrate our relationships with turmoil as we build our lives. Essentially, many of the social media networks are designed to impose their own preferences, which shape our mindset and thinking by oversaturating us with worldly ideas, secular, humanistic beliefs, and a degraded system of values. Satan uses deliberately crafted influences of associations to gain access into our lives and to turn our thinking away from God's Word. Amos 3:3 reminds us, "Can two people walk together without agreeing on the direction?" (NLT). You can't walk closely with someone or next to something for a long period of time and not have it affect your life, thinking, attitude, and behavior. We always need to be aware of others' compulsory motives, influences, and intentions. The Word of God also says, "Do not be misled: 'Bad company corrupts good character'" (1 Cor. 15:33 NIV). Wrong associations can often have lasting and even fatal consequences.

A 19-year-old Texas man was sentenced to 25 years in prison for being an accessory to murder; he assisted in the commission of a crime, but he did not actually participate in the crime as a joint principal. He didn't commit the murder himself; he simply went along with the one who did. Sometimes we can't just go along to get along; we must make a conscious decision not to participate in someone else's wrongdoings or bad choices. Every association in our life matters. Whenever we (as believers) associate with morally-compromised individuals who display wrong thinking and wrong behavior, whether actively or passively in sympathy with them, we become partakers of evil, even if we were never the chief initiator. Wrong associations lead to an advancement in evil that's destined to knock you off course, which only gets worse with time. The opposite, however, is also true. Proverbs 13:20 simply states, "He who walks with the wise grows wise, but a companion of fools suffers harm" (NIV).

The wrong associations can lead us down the wrong path, where we are lacking the supernatural wisdom of God to keep the appropriate doors shut, that will otherwise rob us of our greatest potential and cause us to miss once-in-a-lifetime opportunities. We can be fooled and swiftly led astray by becoming involved with dubious people, questionable activities, or by running after so-called popular cliques, fueled by our own carelessness, stubbornness, and failure to listen to the Spirit in order to make good associations and from positive relationships. As a wise but anonymous quote reveals, "Show me your acquaintances and friends and I'll show you your future." It is always good practical wisdom to move every individual out of your inner circle that does not fit or belong. Keep your eyes open, listen, and stay attentive!

Door Six: A Negative Disposition

Suffering, trouble, trauma, and other bad things often enter in through the door of a negative disposition. A negative disposition is the inclination to view most of life and its experiences through a negative lens. This skewed perspective usually comes through in a sour attitude, a fixed and inflexible mindset, and venomous speech, all of which eventually saturates one's mood, behavior, decision making, and personality, ultimately poisoning one's quality of life and outlook on the future.

One of the most hurtful, notorious, and damaging aspects of a negative disposition is the nasty habit of spewing hateful and derogatory words into the atmosphere with no thought or care as to where they might land. When I was a little boy, we had a popular saying when someone spoke hurtful things: "Sticks and stones may break my bones, but words will never hurt me." Well, that is absolutely false. Words are amazingly powerful. They can be used for good or evil purposes. God spoke this universe and everything in all creation into existence by speaking words. Many people today are living and dying by words spoken over them from individuals who are not alive any longer. Our predisposition toward life, and the words that we constantly speak and hear have a permanent impact that is not always easily broken or diverted, especially negative words.

Many believers misunderstand or grossly underestimate the power of a negative bent toward life that is resistant to change. Your life is greatly affected by your attitude, mindset, and spoken words, whether negative or positive. Many things, both positive and negative, will come to life because you speak them and believe them in your heart. Allowing those thoughts to pulsate through your thinking eventually causes you to roll the words off your tongue with great ease, thus speaking those things into existence. If your life and world are filled with constant anguish, clutter, envy, bitterness, and strife, then most likely it has a lot to do with the negative force of your perspective on life, and with the words spoken around and through you. Inexorably, negative words habitually spoken will bring much dark drama, pain, sorrow, and conflict into every facet of your life, blocking the flow of God's greater blessings. Would you ever deliberately produce negative circumstances for yourself or others? Yet, it is done inadvertently because so many do not adequately understand the power of their words to cause either good or evil to manifest around them when they speak. Proverbs 18:21 explains, "What you say can preserve life or destroy it; so, you must accept the consequences of your words" (TEV).

We must learn to tenaciously guard our attitude, filter our thought life, and take great care about what we speak over our lives and the lives of others around us. We carry the very destiny of our own lives through our WORDS. Your words are containers; they create LIFE or activate DEATH. Your words are more powerful than you think; even little word curses and silly phrases on others can produce a boomerang effect in your own life. You think that you are settling a score with someone, but in essence you are really cursing yourself. Again, remember, God spoke the universe into existence, and so it was established by His Word. In fact, He Himself is called "The Word." God's creation models Himself, displaying the *power* of spoken WORDS. Allow your words to be used constructively. Stop frivolously using your vocabulary to speak vulgar and stupid-stuff by allowing anything and everything to flow out of your high-strung, snappy mouth. Your words will either make or break you.

We, likewise, use words to get things done, to pray, to worship, to encourage, to lead others to Christ, and to fellowship with our brothers and sisters. When our attitudes and speech are negative, they release toxic energy and power into the atmosphere, which allows an open door for the negative to attach itself to our lives. Watch what you say. The very thing you speak could be an open door to your reality. I am not suggesting that if you don't believe something in your heart or have spoken incorrectly out of context, that those things will come to pass. Nonsense, don't even go there! I am speaking of the things you believe wholeheartedly, speak out regularly, and practice on a consistent basis, that give power to the spirit world to create them and make them a reality. Don't let a negative disposition destroy your hopes and dreams of your potential future. Learn to speak words that are filled with love, peace, faith, confidence, and expectancy by maximizing positive thinking and speaking. God's Word has the power to turn any tragedy into triumph, if we believe it. Death and life are in your MOUTH!

Door Seven: The Absence of Knowledge

A few years ago, a 37-year-old father and his 15-year-old son went cave diving at an underwater cave system in Florida. The two were eager to test the new scuba diving equipment they had received as Christmas gifts. The underwater cave system was notoriously dangerous. Even though the father was an experienced ocean-certified diver, he was not certified for cave diving, and had little experience with it. His son had far less experience, and had no certifications at all. Despite a posted sign warning of the dangers of the location and advising that only advanced divers engage in the activity, the father and the son proceeded with their diving excursion anyway. They were reported missing that evening. Later that night, search crews found their bodies in one of the deep- water caves where they had apparently become trapped, ran out of air, and drowned.

Later, a friend of the father said that even though he could tell that the father had very carefully prepared the equipment used in the dive, it was still not adequate for cave diving, especially in that particular location. According to him, their lack of experience and understanding of how to use the proper gear in such a dangerous place proved fatal. An aquatics specialist had warned the father several times, but the father didn't think it was a big deal and dismissed it. "They were pretty much doomed from the start because they had no knowledge of what they were doing in such deep-water caves," said the emergency worker. Often, we think we have enough experience and knowledge to proceed, but in many situations, we are working with inadequate information or a limited scope.

What you don't know and can't see *can* hurt you. Knowledge is power. In many cases, it becomes the catalyst that brings us out of much of our suffering and pain, causes us to thrive and excel in life, and often prevents us from accidentally creating future catastrophes. It is not enough to think that we know, or to think that we are good, well-rounded people. We are bound to hit a brick wall eventually, if we don't keep our minds and hearts open to the continuing challenge of being lifelong learners, especially when it concerns things that affect our lives. There are too many blind spots in life; it is impossible to always know what's up the road, even when you think you have great intuition. The best of the best doesn't know everything. We must continue to seek God's guidance, and ask Him to impart to us His knowledge and wisdom. God wants to guide us by His wisdom, so we can make better decisions and affirm past solid choices rather than continuing to repeat the same mistakes and duplicate cycles of failure. The Word of God gives us insight into the mind of God when He says, "'My people are destroyed for lack of knowledge because you have rejected knowledge . . . [and] because you have forgotten the law of your God'" (Hos. 4:6 NKJV).

When people lack the proper knowledge, they often make decisions without any forethought, which are frequently based on wrong teaching, selfishness, ignorance, or faulty information. Ignorance and wrong information can often mean the difference between life and death, success and failure, health and sickness, and also, the satisfied, balanced life that God intended for it to be. In fact, God is explicitly frank in telling us the cause of our destruction and calamity when He says, "'My people are destroyed for lack of knowledge.'" Maybe you think that sounds quite harsh, or maybe you think that "spiritual stuff" doesn't really matter much, but it's the naked truth. Without God's knowledge, we often suffer an incredible amount of additional suffering, pain, misfortune, unpredictability, messiness, rejection, evil, unfairness—and the list goes on and on. Sad but true!

God also warns us that we can acquire proper knowledge and then reject it. Christians who have the knowledge of the Word, but reject its instruction, will pay a high price for their rebellion, stupidity, and folly. What a sad tragedy it is for an all-knowing God to be Lord over a people who stubbornly resist receiving His wisdom and instruction. It just doesn't make any sense, does it? Here is the all-powerful God who wants the best for His children, and yet they are defiant and deficient in their level of blessing and protection, because they refuse to act upon the knowledge of His Word, and suffer because of it—not because it is His will. He doesn't want us to suffer needlessly when His truth has been made available to us. Some of the negative, hideous, and painful things that happen to us could simply be averted or avoided by knowing and following God's proper instructions, and the wisdom found in His Word. Decide today to begin developing and investing your time and energy in gaining God's wisdom.

Door Eight: A Lack of Discipline

Another reason why many believers are afflicted with pain, suffering, and other bad things is because of the lack of discipline they exhibit in their personal lives. More and more, many Christians are prone to blame God for their mistakes and misfortunes, often making logical excuses and mixing creative reasoning with it that seems valid as to why they are unable to discipline themselves. Well-meaning Christians often complain that life is unfair because they have not had the right "breaks" in life, when their real problem is that they fail or refuse to order their lives according to the standards, principles, and commands that God has given in His Word.

This general lack of discipline is at epidemic proportions in today's society and is quickly leading to enormously tragic and appalling consequences. These include widespread deviation from biblical values and principles which, sadly, has led many believers to embrace the decay of values and the moral filth that abounds in our culture. This is partly the result of false teaching by many modern-day preachers who have espoused to the New Age mysticism and other secular belief systems, while leading astray many biblically astute Christians. Parents and guardians who do not train and discipline their children from an early age are also part of the problem. Consequently, the "hip-contemporary" church has produced a generation of ignorant, immature, and self-centered believers who have brazenly imbibed and assimilated such basic attitudes and behaviors as: "*I deserve to be happy,*" "Do what's works, *for you,*" "*Live to do you-boo,*" and "*Nobody can tell you how to live your life.*" In the minds of these selfish believers, the "*nobody*" in that last statement includes God. Immature, underdeveloped, undisciplined, and untrained believers insist on living their lives according to their own wishes and selfish desires, by trusting in their own faulty wisdom and intuition, and then wonder why so much pain, trouble, and hardship enters into their lives. They wonder why they are never happy and why nothing ever seems to work out for them. There is a reason for everything!

Such New Age-style thinking is both foolish and destructive. Christians who may have the best of intentions, yet who are naïve or careless, can easily fall into the trap of this false, deceptive mindset and prevailing philosophy, ultimately suffering great spiritual harm and ending up confused, conflicted, unable to hear the voice of God, and thus incapable of having a successful, Christ-centered relationship with Him. A solid, well-integrated Christian life is not rooted in false teachings, defective theology, or a bunch of popular, feel-good clichés, but in a consecrated life that is devoted to the Lord Jesus Christ and His Word. As we have already stated, the Bible says that we reap whatever we sow. Let me say to you straightforwardly: Whenever we sow undisciplined behavior, we will reap a harvest of precisely the same kind in great measure. No amount of wishing for something different to happen will keep you from reaping a bitter harvest, from repeating foolish behavior, or from an undisciplined lifestyle. It's just the naked truth, plain and simple.

Believers who refuse to walk in the ways of the Lord, or to discipline their flesh, thinking, and lifestyle, often find themselves on the receiving end of God's discipline. He allows certain negative circumstances and events to enter into their lives to grab their attention, wake them up, rebuke their stubborn, hard–hearted rebellion and destructive behavior, and to call them to repent and return to Him. Yes, repent! The Bible says that God disciplines the children He loves. God's spiritual discipline often results from our failure to implement discipline and set boundaries in our personal lives and behavior. Assuredly, we must understand that God's spiritual discipline is not punishment for our sins and wrongdoings. God does not hold our sins against us. Jesus Christ paid the price for our sins at Calvary. Rather than pursuing punishment, God uses spiritual discipline to help us navigate our lives to produce righteousness, holiness, and peace. God's motive for spiritual discipline is His love for us and His desire to bring us to a place of maturity. Just as parents love their children by disciplining them in order to bring the best out of them and to help them become mature and well-adjusted individuals, our loving, heavenly Father does the same. We as believers could avoid many of the sufferings, tragedies, hardships, and other bad things that happen to us simply by learning to live a disciplined life, characterized by obedience to the will, ways, and Word of God.

Remember, God allows spiritual discipline because of our own rebellion, sins, and poor choices. The Bible says that God chastens those He loves; it is the love of God that drives Him to chasten us. Proverbs 3:11–12 reveals, "My child, don't reject the LORD'S discipline, and don't be upset when he corrects you. For the LORD corrects those he loves, just as a father corrects a child in whom he delights" (NLT). You can avoid a lot of bad things from entering your life by simply listening and following.

A 28-year-old man was serving a 15-year prison sentence for crack cocaine distribution and conspiracy to sell illegal drugs. His sentence was eventually reduced, and he was released from prison after only four years. After leaving prison, the man testified that going to prison had saved his life. He said that the first two years of his sentence were especially difficult, because he felt that the world owed him something. However, the mentorship of an older inmate made him realize that he needed to swallow his pride, take responsibility for his actions, and focus on changing his behavior for the future. He finally concluded that the destruction and suffering that took place in his past life was due to a lack of discipline. He decided to use the chastisement of prison to rebuild his life. Once he began to focus on the gifts and positive qualities that were buried underneath all the toughness he had tried to portray on the outside, his life drastically changed for the better. Acknowledging that he was ultimately responsible for the precarious position he had put himself in, he eventually earned his GED and a college education, lectured across the country, wrote a book about his life experiences, and became a positive influence in his local church and in the community.

The words *"chasten," "chastening,"* and *"chastisement,"* all relate to the idea of correction, discipline, teaching, training, and instruction. It speaks of an intimate bond of mentorship between two persons with the intentions of the "greater" one checking the "lesser" one for restraint. It is a type of correction that results in the "lesser" one receiving education and training. When the Lord chastens us, He does so with the intention of bringing us to a better end result. However, we still have to submit to God and choose to receive His discipline. Life can be propelled by carelessness, distractions, haphazardness, inattentiveness, sporadic behavior, and dysfunctional emotions, which often bring additional trouble, misfortune, suffering, and pain upon us when we refuse to obey God and His Word. God will allow short-term discipline in our lives to bring about long-term spiritual fruit. His desire is for His children to be fully committed to Him and completely available to Him with no strings attached. A disciplined life always yields results, no matter what you're facing. Using your own free will to choose the wrong thing can bring about God's spiritual discipline in your life. Author Timothy Keller writes in his book *Walking with God through Pain and Suffering*:

> Some suffering is given in order to chastise and correct a person for wrongful patterns of life (as in the case of Jonah imperiled by the storm), some suffering is given not to correct past wrongs but to prevent future ones (as in the case of Joseph sold into slavery), and some suffering has no purpose other than to lead a person to love God more ardently for himself alone and so discover the ultimate peace and freedom.

Door Nine: Violating Spiritual Laws

One of the most dangerous doors that we can open and allow bad things to come upon us is when we violate spiritual laws that God has already set into motion. There are natural laws as well as spiritual laws. One example of a natural law is the law of gravity: whatever goes up must come down. Because gravity is a natural law, it is impossible to defy it; the most that we can do is to compensate for it in certain ways or cooperate with it. An airplane, for example, does not defy gravity. Its wing surfaces shape airflow in such a way as to produce positive lift that, combined with the velocity produced by the engine, temporarily overrides the pull of gravity. Likewise, a spacecraft or a satellite orbiting the earth has not defied gravity and is not truly *weightless*. In reality, gravity is always pulling the spacecraft, and it is continually falling toward the earth, but the surface of the earth curves away from the spacecraft at the same rate of speed, so that the spacecraft is literally *falling* around the earth. God has already established fixed, natural laws in the universe. Natural laws, like gravity, were put in place by God, and they cannot be put aside.

Like natural laws, spiritual laws are always in force and always operate with either a negative or positive impact on our lives, depending on the manner in which we encounter them. Violating spiritual laws often opens doors of suffering that expose us to fierce, inescapable, negative circumstances. As we have previously discussed, one example of a spiritual law (which has a parallel in the natural) is the law of sowing and reaping. We reap what we sow, whether we are talking about natural seeds that we plant in a garden or spiritual seed (either good or bad) of thoughts or behaviors that we plant in our minds or in our lives. The reaping may not come immediately; it may seem very slow in arriving, but it will eventually show up. Yes, sir!

Most people, including many believers, break spiritual laws every day, because they are often unaware that spiritual laws are at work. Every time we make contact a spiritual law, it automatically works, whether we realize it or not. While many people don't understand or even have any concept of spiritual laws or how they work, others may be aware and yet not understand how or when they come into contact with them—much less violate—spiritual laws. Many nonbelievers are essentially oblivious to the reality of the more powerful spiritual world that exists beyond this dimensional, physical world, and to the fact that it was God who created them both. Spiritual laws exist; it is our responsibility to know what they are, and to make sure that we are on the right side of them.

In Ephesians 6:1–3, the apostle Paul not only quotes a commandment of promise, but also a spiritual law, when he points out concretely, "Children, obey your parents in the Lord, for this is right. 'Honor your father and mother,' which is the first commandment with promise: 'that it may be well with you and you may live long on the earth'" (NKJV).

Many children in our society today have become defiant, indifferent, unthankful, and disrespectful. Sometimes they come from good families and have the best of parents. One of the greatest problems in modern society, which affects the thinking of so many, is diversionary influence, that is perpetually echoed by the politically correct culture that runs counteractive to Judeo-Christian values and beliefs. When children come of age, they are responsible for their own actions and the consequences that come with them. Children who constantly disobey, dishonor, disrespect, and ignore their parents' commands and instructions eventually cut their lives short in some way. Sometimes they suffer a poor quality of life and find themselves with limited opportunities or options for change. Far too often, they suffer needlessly from the great pain and nerve-racking heartache they have brought into their lives because of their rebellious and disobedient behavior. Little can be done to prevent a spiritual law from operating once it has been set into motion. Again, this is not just a New Testament promise, but a spiritual law. We cannot violate spiritual laws and not expect to suffer the unavoidable negative repercussions of our wrong actions.

Door Ten: No "Apparent" Reason

When I say *"no apparent"* reason, I mean that the reason for our current situation is not presently known to us, and sometimes we're victims of circumstances that are beyond our control. Some believe that things like chance, chaos, natural selection, and accidents simply reflect the random nature of the universe. This is foolery! There is always a reason for everything that happens, whether we know it or not. Nothing just *happens*! God is the Lord of all things, and nothing happens in the universe without His divine knowledge or permission. In Matthew 5:45, Jesus said, "'He [the Father] causes the sun to rise on good people and on evil people, and he sends rain to those who do right and to those who do wrong'" (NCV). For some reason God allows it to happen. Notice that, when it rains, it hits everybody. The rain does not discriminate because of circumstance, age, ethnicity, sex, origin, or the presence or absence of faith. God chooses to allow both good and evil to shine on the righteous and the unrighteous alike. God is neither participating in, nor endorsing, evil, but He allows it to come to pass.

Time after time, when the rains of life come pouring in, we don't always immediately know why. However, it could be that we unwittingly may have opened a spiritual door somewhere or have precipitated the problem in some other way we are unaware of. God does not always stop bad things from happening to righteous people. We don't always hear Him when He's telling us to close the front door or the back door of our lives. Many times, we are simply too busy because we never trained ourselves to listen to our born-again, recreated spirit. So, we simply don't get it when He tries to tell us to stop this or to do that. Thank God that He will intervene on our behalf if we trust Him to deliver us! Whether we have opened a spiritual door through innocent ignorance or through defiance of God's will, trouble, like the rain, comes upon us anyway, and it comes whether we are ready for it or not. God has placed some things in our hands as believers that we can do something about. He has given us the authority to overcome life's difficulties.

In 1 Corinthians 13:12, Paul states, "Now we see things imperfectly, like puzzling reflections in a [as in a cloudy] mirror, but then we will see everything with perfect clarity. All that I know now is partial and incomplete, but then I will know everything completely, just as God now knows me completely" (NLT). God eventually makes His will known to those who believe in Him—to those who have His Spirit. However, this doesn't always happen immediately or instantaneously, nor are all the answers revealed when we think we should have them. To the believer, the Holy Spirit reveals and explains the mysteries of God. God wants us to know and to understand what is going on, and His rationale behind things that relate to our lives. Although He doesn't always give us every single detail, He will give us a basic understanding of what His will is for our lives if we will simply ask. To live as if we never know what's going on or why some things happen the way they happen, is basic frivolity. He is a God of definitive purpose, order, and communication. God speaks, He reveals, He writes, and He gives unction; He goes out of His way to share and to make sure we understand Him. Humanity is without an excuse. We should not waste time blaming God for the bad things that happen in life that we don't have an answer for yet. Hold on—one day it will come. Life in Christ is one of surety, purpose, and calculated moves which yield expected, measurable results. Thank God for what we do know!

Some things God purposely decides not to reveal in this life. Some things are the *"secrets of time."* It may not always be possible to know every answer in this life of why good people suffer bad things or even why some good things happen to bad people. Of course, we do know that God is a merciful God. The *"secret things"* or the *"secrets of time"* are bound by the limits of God choosing to release them in time or in eternity. In Deuteronomy 29:29, Moses said, "There are some things the LORD our God has kept secret, but there are some things he has let us know. These things belong to us and our children forever so that we will do everything in these teachings" (NCV).

For whatever reason, God sometimes chooses to remain silent on certain questions and answers. He doesn't offer details to every answer of evil, misfortune, deprivation, tragedy, or suffering that takes place in the world. No one, I don't care how spiritually deep they are in the things of God, knows every complete revealed plan, purpose, and pursuit of God—not even about their own life. God's foresight is not meant to grant humanity total knowledge and wisdom of the universe and all its mysteries, but it is to provide enough information to guide us through life. However, God has granted us to know the things that are revealed, and these things belong to humanity as a whole. God's ultimate quest is for His creation to follow His Word and the path He has set before them. One thing is always certain—His Word!

Reflections on the Consequences of Open Doors

Our present-day pop culture has rejected the Word of God as the final source of God's authority. It denies even the possibility of any absolute standard of truth and morality that should guide human life and conduct. Although its politically correct language and values dazzle us with the appearance of wisdom and brilliance, it is in reality morally wicked, destructive, deceptive, and thoroughly debased. Too many Christians and non-Christians alike, refusing to believe that there are **root causes** to their litany of problems and challenges, endeavor vainly to find easy escape routes in life by maneuvering, finagling, vacillating, and masquerading through their poor lifestyle choices. Rejecting the idea of moral absolutes, today's jaded postmodernists embrace, instead, the *"new rules"* of a superficial tolerance, relativism, and a nonjudgmental ideology that calls for no submission, sacrifice, or surrender. Truth and morality are whatever you choose them to be for you. This new agenda has widely opened the door to rampant pluralism, secularism, and narcissism, as well as every other diabolical position and every kind of moral filth, degradation, and depravity. This pressing agenda says to do whatever you want, regardless of how destructive and immoral it may be or how much it runs contrary to biblical principles. Many believe you won't suffer any repercussions or be held responsible for your decisions and actions—even many Bible-believing Christians.

Humans are not robots; God has given us moral freedom of choice. He has placed options before us. On the one hand, God has set life, goodness, prosperity, abundance, empowerment, wellness, favor, peace, and joy if we love, obey, and cleave to Him, and to what He has spoken in His Word. This will bring the good side of life to fruition. Failure to love and obey God, on the other hand, will lead to a plethora of evil, wickedness, sin, suffering, pain, destruction, and oftentimes, premature death, and, in some cases, suicide. God never wishes anyone suffering, pain, tragedy, or misfortune; He is simply telling us how to avoid additional, unnecessary suffering as much as possible and the misery that exists in this fallen world. Making critical calculus of sound decisions and implementing good judgment involves more than just a simple agreement with what God has spoken; it has to become in us a new way of thinking and behaving, and a living reality.

God doesn't automatically eradicate some things from our lives after we make Him Lord and Master; however, God never chooses to remove our free-will, which guides our actions, and determines the consequences of those actions. More often than not, we have to permanently live with some of the deficiencies resulting from past poor choices. God has already promised us in His Word that we will reap whatever we have sown with respect to good and bad lifestyle choices. Much of the suffering, pain, tragedy, and misfortune we face in life is a direct result of actions and choices that were within our control. The consequences of our conscious decisions and actions are never canceled out simply because God is a loving God, because He understands our personal preferences and feelings, or because we have experienced the grace of God, without any conditions for our lifestyle.

Regardless of the way many have been informed, any pattern of moral decay or bad choices must change before the cycle of suffering, pain, and misfortune can be halted or broken. God's truths and standards are not based upon our personal feelings or assumptions. Many even in the Christian community of believers are confused, doodling, and diddling over God's grace and the consequences of their wrong choices in life. The grace of God, and His forgiveness of our sins, does not wipe out all the past, present, or future consequences of our mistakes and failures in this life, even after we come into union with Christ. Some of today's religious leaders are now questioning and struggling, calling any New Testament instruction for living, abiding by the law or a works-orientated salvation. Let me be perfectly clear: To accept and to fully believe this is to be blatantly misguided and ignorant of any solid, biblical truth, forgiveness, real grace or reality! Nowhere in the entire Bible is there even the tiniest shred of evidence to support this belief system. I don't care who's teaching it!

The grace of God is not God turning His head so that we can continue to repeat our well-ingrained sins, pursue our failing choices, persist in subverting and dodging His written Word, or live rebelliously in a lifestyle that is totally contrary to biblical virtues. Our choices and actions will always lead to either good or bad results. It is impossible to make any choices without having consequences. God's design is that we overcome, rule, and reign in life by Christ Jesus, if we stay focused on His way. If you decide to make habitual good choices, then you can expect perpetual results that will be good and lasting. But if you decide to make bad, foolish, unwise choices and to take haphazard chances, then evil consequences will automatically attach themselves to you. Many ask: "*Why me, w*hen bad things happen?" "*Why is God allowing* *this to happen?"* "*I don't deserve this?"* If you have asked these questions or if you are asking them now, keep in mind that what you are experiencing may be directly related to your actions, or lack thereof. This is not always the case, but quite often it is at least a main factor in the equation. God often allows us to experience the consequences of our own choices in order to get our attention and help us to learn from our checkered past behavior.

Sometimes grievous suffering can serve as God's megaphone, to turn us to make the necessary changes. Even as a Christian, if you continue to abuse your body, your physical health, and wellbeing, then you will eventually deteriorate and fail, sooner rather than later. If you do not follow the Word of God on how to be a good steward and manage your money sufficiently, then you will more than likely experience financial mishaps that could dog your steps and drag you down for years to come. If you abuse or misuse your relationships, then you will surely lose the trust and confidence of those individuals. If you fail to feed, and nurture your faith, and neglect your spiritual walk with God, then you will open yourself to much unnecessary sorrow, trouble and suffering. Devastating consequences from perpetual wrong choices and decisions are simply inescapable!

There is also a positive side to our consequences that we must not forget. When we tap into the positive, it will always bring success and new levels of achievement and advancement into our lives. This should be the motivating factor when we make decisions that are set before us on a daily basis. When we make wise, sound decisions and choose to follow God's laws, we will eventually triumph as champions. God will ensure that our sound decisions bring us great reward, results, favor, and blessing. After all, your choices will affect your whole life on the earth as well as your life throughout eternity.

"He's the Alpha and the Omega, the Beginning and the End, the First and the Last—His kingdom has no end!"

9

RESPONSIBILITIES OF THE CHRISTIAN LIFE

"'Getting *wisdom is the wisest thing you can do! And whatever else you do, develop good judgment. If you prize wisdom, she will make you great.'*"

— **Proverbs 4:7–8 (NLT)**

"Trouble springs from idleness, and grievous toil from needless ease."

— **Benjamin Franklin**

Understanding the Essentials of Christian Responsibilities

IT IS OBVIOUS THAT SATAN HAS LIMITS TO WHAT HE CAN AND cannot do. What he would like to do is destroy the entire world, along with the human race, so that he can laugh at God. However, he cannot. In the case of Job, God placed a hedge of divine protection around him, so that his life would not be utterly destroyed. We can make decisions and choices freely that are obviously wrong, and yet convince ourselves they are not. That always gets us into trouble. Aside from that, God sometimes does allow the devil to attack us, but only within limitations. Even when there is death, Satan is not permitted to kill just anybody willy-nilly. Satan does not have carte blanche to attack us anyway he pleases and anytime he pleases. This is especially true for believers, particularly when we are focused on listening to God. If we are accessible to God's voice, God's will, and God's Word, some things can be averted, while some other things can be reversed or changed. By no means am I suggesting that every tragedy, crisis, or misfortune will be thwarted. Not one bit! However, the All-powerful God desires to establish good in the earth where He is believed and trusted.

In order for calamity and chaos to be dismantled, and for righteous individuals to live peaceably and fulfill their lives in the earth realm, the human spirit must be regenerated and developed to the point of being in sync with the mind and Spirit of God. Many Christians' spirits have been regenerated, but their thinking has not been renewed with God's Word. Their minds are well-educated, but their spirits lack wisdom and spiritual sensitivity to the mind, will, and purpose of God. Many Christ-professing believers are behind schedule in their spiritual development, knowledge, and empowerment in the abundant life.

When I say abundant life, I am speaking of the life (God-kind) that God intended for every believer to have while living on the earth. Abundance doesn't mean that you will never have any trouble; abundance comes from the source who not only provides, heals, and delivers, but also sustains us. More often than not, many believers set their spirituality on a shelf and only use it when there is some kind of crisis. In addition, too many Christians have a discernibly weak spiritual immune system. In this day and age, the politically correct culture adheres to the reinforcement of superficial spirituality through acquiring lots of material things and entitlements, the avoidance of personal responsibility, passing of the buck to others for their own failures and apprehensions, and much more. These addictive, self-destructive behaviors only accentuate and perpetuate the intensity of the suffering, pain, and sorrow that occur in their lives while upon the earth.

Winston Churchill said, "Responsibility is the key to success." Responsibilities of the Christian life are relative to our personal and behavioral choices. Oftentimes, the wrong choices we make are a major source of the *root causes* of unnecessary sufferings, failures, tragedies, crises, and misfortunes. Some bad things do not have to invade our lives. All we have to do is simply follow God's instruction.

In times of adversity, we tend to seek God and His Word for spiritual strength and guidance. In the immediate aftermath of the deadly terrorist attacks on the twin towers of the World Trade Center in New York on September 11, 2001, many Americans, trying desperately to sort out the tragic event, turned to God for spiritual insight, comfort, and answers. For the next few months, many hearts were turned toward God, and churches all across America were filled, but that spiritual focus soon dissipated as the initial shock and fear from the attack diminished.

When things are going well, people easily delude themselves into believing they don't need God. During good times, even many believers with good intentions find it more difficult to stay focused in their Christian journey, fulfill their responsibilities, and build their personal relationship with the Lord. Prosperity and success often prove to be a much tougher test in life than times of adversity in drawing shallow believers away from practicing a balanced Christianity. Prosperity is never wrong in itself, so the question is: Can you be trusted with more? As believers, we need to learn to focus more intently on God when things are going well in life, so that abundant prosperity doesn't cause us to lose the vibrancy of our faith and relationship with the Lord! Shallow Christianity is a threat to our survival and spiritual development. Satan always stays busy trying to trip us up. Yes, sir, and Amen!

The New Testament clearly warns us of the evils in the world, and gives instruction on how to limit the damage that comes from living in this present evil environment, in a way that minimizes our chances of falling victim to the devil's schemes, influence, and dominance. We certainly can't stop every crisis and dilemma from arising. However, it is not the will of God that we should be destroyed in the midst of solving and conquering life's issues. We need to always be aware of Satan's devices, plots, and schemes. While trusting ultimately in God's enabling ability, each of us has the responsibility to do everything in our power to protect ourselves against the evils that try to overtake our lives.

Pop culture doesn't make it any easier, as it constantly validates irresponsibility, arrogance, stubbornness, and gross immorality that undermines the authority of God, His Word, and biblical principles. This backward, perverse, and pervasive culture seduces many Christians into abdicating their personal Christian responsibility for their own lives and actions, even to the point of blaming and calling God cruel or hard-hearted for inflicting suffering, deprivations, and/or misfortune, which they have actually brought upon themselves. The Bible and, most specifically, the New Testament, provide direct instruction that brings clarity to the Christian walk, and an understanding of the basic fundamentals of Christian responsibilities. God is ready and willing to give you wisdom so that you can make better decisions in life. Your living and walking in victory, as well as overcoming defeat, has more to do with your actions than with God's reactions to your circumstances.

Responsibilities of the Christian Life

The remainder of this chapter is devoted to elucidating 10 of the most important fundamental truths regarding the spiritual aspects of personal Christian responsibility, in which each person must take the initiative in order to experience more favorable results in their spiritual journey. Please be aware that this list of Christian responsibilities is not all-inclusive; I have intentionally downsized it to provide glimpses into some of the most pertinent and basic spiritual disciplines, with the definite purpose of helping you to prevent many of the unnecessary bad things that might otherwise happen in your life.

1. **Regularly nurture and develop your relationship with Christ.**

It is almost inconceivable that so many Christians seem to think that it is perfectly okay to become a born-again follower of Jesus Christ, and yet not bother to nurture and develop their relationship with Him on a consistent basis. Nothing could be further from the truth. Everything in the earth realm must be developed, nurtured, and maintained for stability and longevity purposes. Every Christian is responsible for being proactive in maintaining his or her relationship with Christ. God wants us to do this, but He will not force us. This is absolutely pivotal for spiritual growth and maturity—not to mention for avoiding unnecessary trouble and suffering. Many modern-day believers don't think in terms of nurturing and maintaining their faith in Christ, and seldom practice any Christian disciplines. They mistakenly assume that developing a mature relationship with Christ is automatic, with no effort on their part. Well, it isn't! You have to devote time and energy to serve the Lord.

The secret to a successful and purposeful Christian life is a well-watered, well-balanced, and well-maintained relationship with the Lord. You cannot finagle your way through life, hoping and praying that things will automatically turn out for the best if you pay only casual attention to God's Word and your spiritual life. For your faith to remain strong and stand the test of time, you must learn to practice basic spiritual disciplines regularly. There is simply no substitute for spiritual discipline when it comes to obtaining wisdom for building and maintaining a stronger anointing, as well as growing a vibrant and reciprocal relationship with Christ. Our relationship with God is the most important relationship in our lives. It greatly affects everything we do, how we interact with the lives of others, and how we understand and carry out our assignment while on the earth.

Your quest for a successful and meaningful relationship with the heavenly Father is ultimately is your responsibility. He will be quick and eager to assist you in your quest, but you must take the initiative. Having a real, personal relationship with the Lord is more than learning spiritual jargon or wearing a customary piece of jewelry around your neck. It's a lot more than that! It is a lifetime of application in the Spirit of the Word of God to grow you into the fullness of the stature and character of Christ. Good character far outweighs fame, fortune, short-term happiness, prestige, or any other thing we might deem important. None of us will ever graduate from the school of the Spirit or reach spiritual perfection in this earthly life. However, every one of us can develop into a mature spiritual person. Every believer should be in regular fellowship with a local church. There are no activities, ministry endeavors, or spiritual quests that can substitute for one's commitment and responsibility to a local church. This is God's set design and purpose for all Christians. Anything outside of God's original plan only breeds more confusion, abuse, instability, and chaos. We are not free to make our own rules, but we are bound to follow His. Chip Ingram said, "God's dream is that Christians would actually live like Christians."

2. **Consistently listen to and obey the voice of the Holy Spirit as He speaks to you through God's Word.**

Nothing in life works properly unless we are consistent with it. Listening to the voice of the Holy Spirit is one of the key disciplines for deepening and strengthening our walk with Christ. The Holy Spirit leads and guides us into all truth, tells us of things to come, and brings back to our remembrance the things that God has said to us (John 16:13). It is critical that we learn to be sensitive to the voice of the Holy Spirit, in order to receive exact instruction on how to live out our everyday lives, especially in the midst of crisis, suffering, and hardship. If we are open to the voice and leading of the Holy Spirit, then He will lead us out of difficulty, suffering, and hard circumstances. Deliverance may not come right away, but it *will* come. Many Christians suffer needlessly because they are disjointed, disconnected, and are not in regular communion with God's voice and His Word. God is strong and powerful enough to deliver anyone from every affliction in life—but are you humble enough to listen!

Likewise, it is important as believers that we become well-acquainted with the voice of the Holy Spirit before a crisis strikes, so that we may properly discern between the voice of the Holy Spirit's leading and the voice of mendacious deception, destruction, and death. One of the main reasons why God gives us His Spirit at the time of our rebirth is so that He may guide us by illuminating our hearts and minds through His Spirit and His Word. It is God's will that we have the ability to discern clear direction. Through the leading of the Holy Spirit's proddings, we have spiritual discernment, and we receive guidance through a knowing on the inside, inner promptings, spiritual intuition (*gut sense*), and/or the voice of God. God has made His voice available to every born-again believer. Romans 8:14, 26 explains, "For as many as are led by the Spirit of God, these are sons of God. . . . Likewise the Spirit also helps in our weaknesses. For we do not know what we should pray for as we ought, but the Spirit Himself makes intercession for us with groanings which cannot be uttered" (NKJV).

Notice in these verses that, first, God leads His children by His Spirit—not by sense, knowledge, or feelings. Second, the Holy Spirit helps us in areas of fragility, debilitation, and ignorance, where we lack knowledge and instruction. Third, He helps us in bringing the will of God and the best for our lives into focus.

An NFL football player shared the personal leading of the Holy Spirit in his life, regarding the financial wealth he built during his career. In particular, he explained how he was able to preserve his fortune, and to make big plans for living after the NFL. Despite the millions of dollars he made during his NFL career, he was led from the beginning by an inward inclination not to touch one dime of the signing bonus or salary from his actual NFL contract. Most NFL players live extravagant, high-profile lifestyles during their careers—some of which are very short—only to find themselves broke within a few years after their large paychecks have ended. They never learned how to manage their wealth assets wisely—often indulging in many frivolities. This one NFL football player, however, took a different approach. After making over $3 million during his first two years in the NFL, he signed a 6-year, $100 million extension in his third year. As a matter of strict priority, he refused to touch any of the $80 million that he had made over the next eight years of his career. Instead, he lived off the money he made from his endorsements and marketing. He did not blow any money on extravagant purchases, such as expensive cars, jewelry, multi-million-dollar mansions, or other such items. When he retired, he was able to accomplish his dreams and live out his life enjoying the wealth which he had made during his football career, all because he obeyed the voice of the Holy Spirit, instructing him on how to manage his money strictly and wisely.

Essentially, learning to obey God's Word is in harmony with listening to God's voice, because they are basically the same. The Holy Spirit will never contradict God or His Word. The Holy Spirit is the Spirit of God. He is a perfect gentleman, and He doesn't force His way into our affairs. It is one thing to hear God's voice, but quite another to act upon what He says. Moreover, the discipline of obeying God's voice must be learned and practiced. Isaiah 1:19–20 reveals that if we are willing and obedient, then we will eat the best from the land. That doesn't mean we won't have any troubles or crises in life. Rather, it means that God ensures that good will come into our lives through obedience. But, all too often, Christians are disobedient and do not practice listening and obeying the Word of God consistently, and then wonder why so many bad things storm into their lives. Verse 20 states, "'But if you refuse and rebel, you shall be devoured by the sword'" (NKJV).

Disobedience, rebellion, and stubbornness often open a door that allows bad things to enter into our lives—not because God wishes them to or delivers bad things to us, but because of our unwillingness to obey His Word. Bad things come as a natural consequence of our disobedience. When we disobey God's Word, we are unable to discern correctly. This makes us a direct target for Satan. Yes, you can be a *good* person and still rebel against God, but there is a price to pay for disobedience—a steep price. Don't be a hardhead! I promise you, disobeying God will cost you a great deal—much more than you can imagine or afford.

Diligent attention to hearing the Word is not the complex part. That comes with learning to esteem what God says and placing obedience to His Word above our own thoughts, agendas, and philosophies. This requires us to discipline our flesh, which usually doesn't feel good. Many of us are masters at self-deception. It does not make a difference how many times you rest in the finished work of Christ (and you always should)—you must still learn to practice God's Word if you want to avoid needless suffering and minimize its effects and havoc from invading your world and life. Listen to the wise counsel of the apostle James:

> Do what God's word says. Don't merely listen to it, or you will fool your-selves. If someone listens to God's word but doesn't do what it says, he is like a person who looks at his face in a mirror, studies his features, goes away, and immediately forgets what he looks like. However, the person who continues to study God's perfect teachings that make people free and who remains committed to them will be blessed. People like that don't merely listen and forget; they actually do what God's teachings say. (Jas. 1:22–25 GWT)

Many believers have learned to trust their feelings; they are skeptical, and reluctant to act upon what God says. But when we learn that God is trust-worthy and infallible, our confidence in Him grows to the point where we automatically turn to Him for counsel rather than relying on our own faulty thinking. Within our hearts, we must judge or conclude that God is faithful, and we must trust Him and obey His Word for our own good.

3. **Carefully watch all the associations and influences in your life.**

Your associations are those things, people, places, ideas, etc. that you are linked to and influenced by. There are countless people whose lives have been affected and, in some cases, damaged or destroyed by wrong or ill-conceived associations. It's not as important to hobnob with the in-crowd as it is to protect yourself from potential threats. Who could count the number of people who have taken stock of their messed-up lives and wondered how they got there? Some eventually realize they have self-destructed with the wrong things or the wrong crowd, and are left feeling tremendous grief and regret over the irreparable, negative consequences of their unwise associations. Associations can be good and fruitful or evil and destructive. It is vital, therefore, to keep a close eye on them, because they can ultimately help secure either your promotion or your downfall. Consider these words from Psalm 1:1–2: "Happy are those who reject the advice of evil people, who do not follow the example of sinners or join those who have no use for God. Instead, they find joy in obeying the Law of the LORD, and they study it day and night" (GNT).

Our associations have a profound impact on our lives, and on those that are nearest and dearest to us. We can never underestimate the power of outside influences. Associations are so strong that they often define who we are, how we think, and what we believe. When we hear a person's name, usually we think of all the people and things they are associated with. When we hear the name Michael Jordan, we think Chicago Bulls, basketball genius, and billionaire entrepreneur. When we hear Charles Manson, we think killer, monster, and lunatic. When we hear Richard Nixon, we think Watergate scandal, crook, and corrupt politician.

The associations we are solidly linked to, once embedded in our minds and spirits, are oftentimes virtually impossible to undo. It's exceptionally difficult to make great progress or to avoid dangerous situations in life when we are linked to the wrong things and the wrong people. Al and Laura Ries said in their book, *22 Immutable Laws of Branding*, that the most powerful thing a business can own is a word in the minds of consumers. They give the example that the most successful brands in the world are those that, when people hear the brand name, are automatically synonymous with every product in that category. So much so, in fact, that people may attribute a particular brand's name to a product that is also made by others. For instance, people may refer to all cola drinks as Coke, and all cotton swabs as Q-Tips, or may ask someone to Xerox a document for them. Coke, Q-Tips, and Xerox are all brand names that have become so thoroughly identified with their specific products that they now serve as generic designators for every product in that category. When an association is strong, a name becomes one with the actual person, action, or entity. Of course, the lesson from branding is that associations can be very positive when they are integral, but bring great repercussions when they are not. Socrates said, "The unexamined life is not worth living." Beyond mental soul-ties and associations, we must also keep a close watch on and examine our actual relationships with other people. Those who we surround ourselves with, confide in, and call friends, must be in sync with God's plan and will for our lives. Otherwise, the wrong influences and unhealthy relationships will ultimately contribute to our downfall and destruction.

4.   **Habitually return your tithes and offerings to your local church and give purposely to the kingdom of God.**

When it comes to the Christian responsibility of tithing, giving, and sowing seed under the New Covenant, there is a wide range of controversial teachings, information, feelings, opinions, and a whole lot of personal nit-picking concerning what and how Christians should and should not give. Although there are many additional examples of giving across the whole spectrum in the entire Bible, tithing remains the basic Scriptural standard-bearer for Christian giving. Tithing is referenced in the New Testament in Matthew 23:23; Luke 18:12; and Hebrews 7:1–10. God warns of the repercussions and adverse effects of not returning your tithes (God-robbers) back to God in Malachi 3:8–10. Tithing is a part of your personal responsibility for biblical stewardship in the kingdom of God, and is a foundational pillar in a well-watered and fruitful spiritual life. Tithing goes beyond just a religious routine and exchange of money from one hand to the next; it encompasses and affects your total life prosperity in God's economy for the Christian's provision and long-term financial stability.

Jesus, in the New Testament, explains and illustrates through many parables the beneficial truths of being a faithful steward over what God has placed into our hands as believers. At the same time, He also gives clear warning about the cost and detrimental dangers of becoming an unfaithful steward. The New Testament Greek word for "*steward*" is "*oikonomos*," which is defined as a "*manager*," "*supervisor*," or "*administrator*"; "*a person of authority entrusted to manage the business affairs of the master's household*." The Lord's affairs would include our ability to manage the finances He has set into our hands, as well as the ability to return our tithe to God on a consistent basis. As the old anonymous saying goes, "Money is a bad master, but a good servant." God's design is that we master the stewardship of handling our money, so that it doesn't master or eventually destroy us. You can't be a poor steward and expect things to work out well for you in life. Make up your mind that, no matter what comes against you financially, you will remain a faithful steward over what God has placed into your hands; God is sure to prepare you for promotion, and bring you increase.

The biblical concept of stewardship implies, first, that God is the owner of everything in the universe, and He appoints us to be wise and faithful managers or administrators, exercising supervision over His affairs. God not only created everything in the material world, but also sustains all of life (Ps. 24:1). Since God is the owner and sustainer of all life, humankind becomes a steward or manager over the life that God has placed into its hands. Tithing is more than just fulfilling a religious requirement; it is about our relationship with God and His Word. When we understand this concept, transformation begins in our thinking, and it becomes much easier for us to manage our responsibility in returning our tithes and offerings to God—instead of being selfish and greedy.

Beyond tithing, being a good steward also includes living sensibly within our means, setting aside finances for emergencies, paying our bills on time, planning for retirement, making wise investments to expand our wealth, etc. None of this was ours in the first place; we are just managers. A manager is always accountable to the owner. Christians should not shrewdly shrug off their responsibility and say that it doesn't matter. God doesn't overlook our unwise dishonesty, greed, selfishness, rebellion, rationalization, or inconsistencies to reward our personal greed or dog-gone laziness. "Whatsoever a man soweth, that shall he also reap" (Gal. 6:7 KJV). God expects you to be a responsible steward with the provisions He has given to you. The Christian doesn't decide whether or not to participate in the stewardship of his life; his entire life (what he has and what he does) is the stewardship—good or bad.

Good stewardship hinges on the awareness that everything we have ultimately belongs to God. A little girl was given two dollars by her father. He told her that she could do anything she wanted with one, and that the other was to be given to God on Sunday at church. The girl nodded in agreement, and asked if she could go to the candy store. With visions of all that she could buy with her dollar, she happily skipped toward the store, holding tightly to the two dollars in her hand. As she was skipping along, she tripped and fell; the wind blew one of the dollars into a storm drain at the curb. Picking herself up, the little girl looked at the dollar still in her hand, then looked at the storm drain and said, "Well, Lord, there goes your dollar." Sadly, many Christians have the same selfish attitude toward giving: "*First me, then God—maybe.*" Tithing is all about making God the first priority in your finances and in your life, and not about giving Him leftovers or tipping Him with driblets.

God always looks at the intent of our hearts in all things, including our financial matters. Faithful stewardship is one aspect of a genuine expression of our faith. Like the little girl in the story, our actions always reveal what's inside our hearts. Our thinking and values must line-up with God's if we are to receive His best. We must view things in line with God's Word rather than our feelings, opinions, or personal desires. Most Christians trust their money more than they trust God. For some, their cupidity for material things and money has become a god; they are more concerned with their pocketbooks than with having the attitude of their hearts right before God. The money test often reveals the reality of Christ's Lordship in our lives. For many Christians, tithing—returning 10 percent to God—seems too great a sacrifice to make, yet they still want God's greatest blessings, and for Him to work miracles in their finances. Of course, many scandalous God-robbers never witness the fulfillment of God's greater blessing in their lives. Learn to trust God with your tithes and offerings; indeed, trust Him with every area of your life, and don't become dishonorable in your giving. Hang in there when the going gets tough. Demonstrate your trust by faithfully returning to God your tithes and offerings. Watch God's covenant work for you!

5. **Develop your born-again human spirit, which is a safe guide to follow.**

The spiritual part of you can easily become the most neglected part of your life with Christ if you're not careful in your spiritual quest. The only person who has a consistently safe instinct is a born–again believer, because the nature and life of God reside there. Most believers don't spend much time educating and training their "*spirit person*." Your spirit person is the real you. Oh, Yes! Many gladly devote much time and money to educate their minds and become intellectually smart, yet remain spiritually stupid. Don't misunderstand me; I wholeheartedly believe in and promote education. However, I don't believe in educating your mind at the expense of educating your spirit person with God's Word. Feeding, meditating and training yourself spiritually and learning intellectually are two totally separate things.

Many modern believers are simply very shallow, empty, and tragically devoid of spiritual discernment, and even of basic knowledge regarding many spiritual truths. Too many Christians today are led more by their flesh, dominated by their unrenewed minds, frivolous emotions, carnal senses, or external circumstances, than they are led by the Word of God. Day in and day out, people starve themselves spiritually, and never take the time to train their spirit person, because they are under the illusion that the visible, tangible things of this sophisticated world are more real, thus more important and more worthy of their time and attention, than the invisible things of the Spirit. Proverbs 20:27 concludes, "The spirit of a man is the lamp of the LORD, searching all the inner depths of his heart" (NKJV).

In the sum total of things, a person's spirit becomes the Lord's flashlight for exposing human thoughts, dangers, and inclinations in the unseen world, and brings God's illumination and understanding into even the darkest recesses of a person's life. People who fail to develop their human spirit beyond the external world may be functional in many aspects of life, but will be spiritually ineffective. A person with a well-developed spirit, however, possesses the capacity to successfully navigate through all the troubles of life that are spiritual (invisible) in origin. Depression, anger, anxiety, uncertainty, death, divorce, addictions, and the like can all dominate a person who is spiritually underdeveloped or stagnant. One of the reasons why bad things sometimes happen to good Christians is because their spirit person is underdeveloped, so they cannot discern and recognize the unseen forces and hear the voice of God. The developed, born–again human spirit is a safe guide because it is sensitive to the light of life within it—Jesus Christ. As Paul explained to the Corinthians:

But God has given us the revelation of these things through his Spirit, for the Spirit makes search into all things, even the deep things of God. For who has knowledge of the things of a man but the spirit of the man which is in him? In the same way, no one has knowledge of the things of God but the Spirit of God." (1 Cor. 2:10–11 BBE)

As believers, we must be built up in our faith in order to be stretched, enlarged, and renewed in our spirits day by day. We must be transformed in our mentality and well-equipped with truth in order to dominate the challenges and crises that confront us, by going beyond the veil of our physical senses, emotions, and intellect. If the physical body requires detailed, daily attention in its many complexities, then the human spirit requires even more, because it is even more real than the things we can sense in the physical world.

What a tragedy it is for a physically mature Christian to function throughout life as a spiritual infant. Babyhood should never be the permanent state in the spiritual life of a Christian, any more than remaining a baby in the physical life. Both are tragic because they reveal a serious dysfunction. Babies are supposed to grow by design. Absence of growth is a sign of impending death. Genuine spiritual development requires daily care, attention, and the application of God's Word. We must learn to develop, discern, and follow the "*still, small voice*" on the inside, and learn to be more conscious of the spirit world, where many of the things in our lives rise and fall first, before they touch the physical world.

6.   Constantly guard and control your thought and speech life.

Christians cannot say anything with their mouths and not be affected by it. Not just Christians, but anybody. The thoughts and the words that you speak will either free you or trap you; they will bring success to you or rob you of the best in life. You are the sum total of your thought life, what has already been spoken over you, and your actions. Speaking activates the realm of the spirit world. The spirit world is more real than this physical, material world we live in. In the spirit world, verbal words often work like a written contract in the earth realm. Your words often carry weight and power, which activate spiritual laws and set them into motion over your life. Proverbs 6:2 warns us, "You are trapped by the words of your mouth; you are ensnared with the words of your mouth" (WEB).

Unwittingly, you often inflict negative consequences on yourself by the rash of thoughtless words you speak. The words that come from your mouth cannot be separated from the intent of your heart, which is the bedrock of what you believe. In fact, the things that you speak reveal the essence of who you really are: your pattern, your design, and your expectations. Your words reveal your thoughts, express your likes and dislikes, and declare what you promote and reject; in short, your thoughts are all the things that form the core of your spirit.

An old but true adage states, "What's in you will eventually come out of you." Words do not suddenly and inexplicably appear upon your lips and then just roll off the tongue without thought or origin. Even *spontaneous* words give expression (often unintended) to whatever lies in the recesses of your inner being. Your words only carry as much weight as your conduct under-writes, but eventually what you continue to speak flows into your actions and becomes reality. In truth, your words drive your behavior. When you speak words, the way they are received and how far they go depend largely upon the painted canvas of your heart that has already been predisposed to your beliefs, thinking, and inward speech. Most contracts and agreements are built entirely upon the integrity of words. Words are responsible for underwriting, executing, and enforcing written contracts and agreements that require the mutual confidence of all parties. The moment our words don't deliver on what has been specified in the contract, they immediately lose credibility, value, and authenticity. God's Word is a divine contract; it is a covenant with His children that He will neither alter nor break.

Likewise, we must be careful to monitor what we speak by choosing our words deliberately and thoughtfully. We must be aware of what we should speak and what we should withdraw from our thinking and hearts. We must consult with God to find out what His Word says about a matter, and then align our speech to coincide with His thoughts. If we do not know God's Word, then we cannot know His will. God's Word *is* His will. We must also be careful not to continu-ously release negative, destructive speech into our lives and into the lives of others, thus giving power to evil things and calamity to gain entry into our lives. Let go of your old way of negative thinking and speaking; take hold of what God's Word says and learn what to think and speak. Whatever you say in the midst of sufferings and hardship will have a direct result on your outcome.

Your words can either be toxic and spread poison that eviscerates the potential for positive outcomes, or they can be curative and release blessings. Learn to keep a lid on destructive speech, cancel and renounce every word spoken in unbelief, fear, and ignorance. Start speaking faith-filled, hopeful, and life-changing words, even in the middle of adverse circumstances (Heb. 4:12). Your words always count!

7. Take the time to pray firsthand about everything.

Most modernized believers don't take enough time to pray and seek God concerning the major decisions and activities they embark upon in life. Seldom do many Christians seek God's counsel as to whether or not they should participate in a particular issue, a relationship or make a choice that will affect them long term. Rather than seeking His direction in life's matters, many brazenly make decisions out of their own egoistical and selfish desires, or out of ignorance, and then ask God to bless their choices. It takes time to pray, and, more importantly, to wait on God for a clear answer. Most people in our modern society are programed for a quick, fast-paced, microwave solution to every decision, and are too impatient to wait. This method of thinking doesn't work well in most cases. Prayer is foundational and essential to a successful Christian life. Martin Luther said, "To be a Christian without prayer is no more possible than to be alive without breathing."

Unwillingness to wait on the Lord and to seek His direction often leads to failure, disappointment, disillusionment, and other unpleasant or even disastrous outcomes. Trying to use God like a *genie* or a *magic wand* simply will not work. Too often, when we want something material or some other need fulfilled, we try to *rub* God the right way, hoping He will grant our wish. This is a very sad commentary, but it is the thinking of many shallow, modern Christians. They act as though they know what they need better than God knows, or think that He simply doesn't understand their situation. God cannot be manipulated. He already knows and sees what we don't know and cannot discern.

I am not suggesting that every believer should become a super saint or a prayer warrior who spends 12 hours a day facedown before God. Absolutely not! For many, this would not be practical, expedient, or beneficial. However, it is clear that many believers have gotten themselves into jams and messy situations simply because they did not acknowledge God first and seek His wisdom before making critical decisions. We must pay careful heed to Paul's counsel: "Never worry about anything. But in every situation let God know what you need in prayers and requests while giving thanks. Then God's peace, which goes beyond anything we can imagine, will guard your thoughts and emotions through Christ Jesus" (Phil. 4:6–7 GWT).

Life in this complicated, mixed-up world will give you more than enough reasons for worry, anxiety, hostility, and pressure in crisis situations without you making things worse by failing to seek God's direction on a regular basis. Don't allow yourself to worry or despair over things you can't change. Learn to pray firsthand, no matter what you are facing in life, and then trust God's providential care to act on your behalf. Allow time for His intervention before you make a move. Refuse to allow the problems and circumstances of life to destroy your faith in God. Satan is a master at working through your thought life to sabotage your faith in God and His Word. Stop allowing your thought life to run wild, zapping your reservoir of strength, energy, and courage. Take the time to seek God first in every circumstance of life.

As a child of God, you are to present your needs to God and tell Him about the things you want to see come to pass in your life without fear, anxiety, or fretting over the unknown. A thankful heart is the attitude you should have every time you ask God to act on your behalf or on the behalf of others, and always remember the goodness of God for what He has already done and for what He will do. God's peace, which is completely beyond all power and human comprehension, is able to guard your heart and mind.

8. **Avoid practicing generational curses and repeating cycles of failure.**

As Christians, we must embrace responsible behavior and the right-kind of thinking that has been set before us in God's Word. All too often, curses and cycles of failure work in our lives because we lack discipline, and have fallen into patterns of self-destructive behavior. A curse works like a spiritual law and is often set into motion through ignorance, fear, undisciplined behavior, or hurtful and habitual practices. Curses give demonic spirits legal entry into our lives, relationships, and families, usually through our bloodline. A curse can be defined as a vilification, a reviling, a reproach, and a maligning of an individual and/or a family. It comes in the form of a possessive spirit, and it is almost like a dark cloud or shadow that constantly hovers over someone. It is the opposite of "*the blessing*."

Curses are often repetitive and cyclical, where the same or a similar sequence of negative circumstances repeats itself over time. In many cases this cycle of negativity appears to be unbreakable. Someone's sins, and the sins of their predecessors, give the devil and his demons the legal right to implement and perpetuate suffering, pain, misfortune, destruction, wickedness, havoc, and even premature death in their lives. This pattern of curses returns periodically and frequently to terrorize the individual to whom it is attached. Curses feed and grow strong on negative emotions, and states of mind such as constant self-pity, the desire to quit, laziness, chronic depression, uncontrollable anger; personality, psychotic and bizarre behavior, psychological disfunction, and all other mental disorders; addictive behaviors, stubbornness, living in denial, unbelief, doubt; fear, a pessimistic, gossip spirit, constant complaining, financial instability, codependence, obstinacy, hostility, resistance, guilt, irrationality, insecurity, neuroses, narcissism, obsessions, and just plain lunacy.

Redemption is a part of the new covenant that gives born-again Christians the legal right to break curses and cycles. However, this does not happen automatically. It is the responsibility of all believers to forsake and renounce sin, implement discipline into their lives, take authority over the curses and cycles that have operated through their bloodline or through other open doors, seek deliverance, and continually walk in God's Word.

Two female prison inmates hold the dubious honor of being part of three generations of the same family in prison. A 39-year-old mother, her 21-year-old daughter, and her daughter's 8-month-old baby all resided at a state correctional center for women. The 39-year-old mother's mother had also served time in prison in the past, but was now deceased. She was serving a 15-year sentence for robbery, while her daughter joined her some time later in the same prison on an assault charge. Soon after entering prison, the daughter learned that she was pregnant. Subsequently, as part of a special program, she was allowed to keep her baby with her while in prison. This family's sad story is a clear example of how negative cycles and generational curses can affect an entire family's bloodline.

Proverbs 26:2 provides pertinent counsel here: "Curses will not harm someone who is innocent; they are like sparrows or swallows that fly around and never land" (NCV). This proverb provides insight into the effects of curses and cycles. Curses cannot injure or attach themselves to innocent individuals if there is no foothold of negative or evil forces operating in their lives. A curse which has no root is ineffective; it simply will not work. It can circle aimlessly and without purpose, just like sparrows and swallows that fly around but never land or rest. On the flip side, a curse that has a cause has a right to attach itself to someone who has opened the door or given it a foothold through negative and hurtful words or through wrongful, habitual behavior. It enters with a vengeance, wreaks havoc with negative consequences in abundance, and leaves in its wake a life full of regret.

The devil is well aware of spiritual laws. What may seem like merely a foolish, spontaneous decision here or there may grow into a succession of life-altering errors that cause permanent damage to our lives and to the lives of others. Even worse, that damage can be to innocent family members, thus setting them up to fail even before they get started. Cycles of bondage start with a string of instances of bad decisions that are repeated until they eventually become a way of life. You must avoid generational curses and cycles of failure at all costs. Begin to live your life every day in a way that reflects what is good and positive, reshaping your future, and beating the odds of the inevitable.

9. **Always allow love to be your guiding compass in life—not hate or revenge.**

Christians are responsible to walk in love toward others. Our lives as Christians will not work very well when we don't learn to love others as Christ has loved us. Satan will exploit every opportunity to stir up offences, resentment, anger, and an unforgiving spirit in our hearts. We can't allow seething bitterness, fumes of irrational hatred, or deep grudges to build inside of us against others and still expect the blessings of the Lord to be in abundance in our lives. They certainly will not! Simmering resentment, smoldering anger, steeping bitterness, or the savoring of vengeful thoughts in your heart against others will only open the doors to much trouble, pain, affliction, sickness, and disease. Do not allow anger or hurtful feelings toward anyone who has wronged you cause you to speak curses or retaliate against them; this will only release toxic fumes within your own spirit. Always remember the law of reciprocity is built into the earth's systems. Instead, you must learn to release these things, pray for your fellow man, and let God take care of the rest.

Romans 13:10 brings clarity, "Love does no wrong to others, so love fulfills the requirements of God's law" (NLT). To have great fellowship with God, and for things to work out in your behalf, you have to learn to practice and walk in love (Jn. 13:35). God is love—that is His very nature. If you have been born-again by the Spirit of God, then God's nature of love is resident inside you. But you have to allow that love nature to shine through you. You can't choose to allow your flesh and your feelings to always dominate your life and insist on being right and having your way all the time, because you will always pay a price for that—a great and painful price. If you will always allow love to be your guiding compass, then you will never fail at life. For believers in Christ, love is the best way—the *only* way—to live!

A single mother who worked as a preschool teacher was on her way to work one morning when a drunk driver swerved into her lane and crashed head-on into her vehicle. Her injuries were so severe that her spleen, her appendix, 2/3 of her colon, and the upper intestine had to be removed. She also lost her right foot, her right arm was broken, and her left heel was shattered. Convinced that she might die, she even penned a letter to her 13-old son expressing how proud she was of him, and how she was saddened to have to leave him. The injured, single mother didn't find out until weeks after the crash (during her recovery) that the woman who'd slammed into her was intoxicated well over the legal limit. That is when anger and resentment set in.

To make unexplainable matters worse, the drunk driver only had minimal auto insurance, thus leaving the single mother with heavy medical bills after the accident. The next devastating blow came when the single mother was let go from her job, and was given an eviction notice from her landlord the day before Thanksgiving. This series of horrible events thrust her into a deep depression. She became very resentful and bitter against the woman who had literally wrecked her life. She began seeing a professional therapist and taking antidepressants. It was during the trial of the woman who had hit her that the injured woman experienced something quite profound. During the sentencing of the 63-year-old homemaker who had hit her, the unemployed preschool teacher took note of how scared the woman looked. After the woman was sentenced to 16 to 28 months in jail, the injured woman went up to the public defender, without any rancor, and said, "Please let your client know that I forgive her." She said that she had chosen to forgive rather than to hold animosity and harbor hate in her heart for the rest of her life. She also said that forgiving the woman who hit her and literally destroyed her well-being gave her a huge sense of relief. Forgiveness enabled her to experience healing and to move on with her life.

Martin Luther King Jr. said, "Darkness cannot drive out darkness; only light can do that. Hate cannot drive out hate; only love can do that." Dr. King was in agreement with the law of love, that whoever loves his fellow man will never do him wrong. He will not harbor grudges in his heart or take revenge in retaliation for a hurt inflicted by another. He will not try to get even with the person or desire, that something bad will happen to him in return. Love doesn't curse others' lives. By loving our neighbor, we obey and fulfill the whole Law. The Christian life is a life guided by love, not hate, even when suffering wrongs at the hands of others. Never get stuck in the rut of having unforgiveness in your heart. Hebrews 12:15 instructs us, "Make sure that everyone has kindness from God so that bitterness doesn't take root and grow up to cause trouble that corrupts many of you" (GWT). Refuse to harbor bitter, hateful, and malicious thoughts in your heart. Always be the first to say that you are sorry. Be quick to repent, forgive, and reach out in love to create a win-win situation. You'll always be ahead by surrendering to the law of love. Love never fails!

10. Purposely submit to sound biblical, spiritual leadership.

One significant responsibility every Christian has is to submit to the established spiritual authority that God has set over him or her. One reason why so many bad things happen to so many Christians is that they don't possess a biblical perspective or understanding of the purpose of spiritual leadership as God has established it in the church (Eph. 4:11; Heb. 13:17; 1 Tim. 5:17). Failure or refusal to follow, abide by, and live under a spiritual covering is why so many believers run into so much adversity and are so easily defeated in life. Integral spiritual leadership is a gift from God, just as natural, godly parents are a great gift and blessing to their children.

Every believer needs a pastor, church, and a spiritual covering in his or her life at every stage of spiritual development. Every believer also needs to purposely submit to spiritual covering. You never outgrow the ministry gift of a pastor in your life; it doesn't matter where you feel you are spiritually, where you think you are going, how spiritually equipped you are, or how deep you think you are. Every instruction the Lord gives us must match up with His Word. Period! God is not the author of confusion (1 Cor. 14:33) concerning His church or anything else.

Unarguably, many Christians would have been much better off if they had simply listened to the instructions from the Word of God that their pastor had given to them. Our consumer-driven society has drawn many Christians into becoming active consumers (shoppers and hoppers) of church, often by looking for a more relaxed, attractive, and subjective Christian experience, without any strings attached. Much of the shopping and hopping eventually leads to dropping church altogether. Many run in and out of different churches and ministries as though churches are like fast-food restaurant chains; some people regard God's leaders as disposable products. Some have personal, deviant agendas and motivations looking for platforms for spiritual stardom and popularity. Most, however, are unable to identify exactly what they are looking for. Even if they think they know, and even if it hits them right between the eyes, most are still not able to identify it, because they believe everything they hear—and nothing—all at the same time, while only obtaining bits and pieces. Paul the apostle, instructing young pastor Timothy, warned, "A time will come when people will not listen to accurate teachings. Instead, they will follow their own desires and surround themselves with teachers who tell them what they want to hear" (2 Tim. 4:3 GWT).

A transit spirit of monolithic proportions has overtaken the body of Christ in recent years. If you don't like something in a church or if you get tired of the spiritual leadership, though it may be sound and morally good, then you criticize it, condemn it, and simply pick up your belongings and head down the street to the next church, where you repeat this vicious cycle of rebellion and destruction—and on and on it goes. Many have fallen into this tragic trap and have become spiritual vagabonds with no anchor, no spiritual roots, no real anointing, no identity, and no church home. Sadly, many never recover from this chaotic pattern.

Many modern-day believers are spiritually dysfunctional and biblically illiterate. Never having enrolled in *"Basic Christianity 101,"* they don't possess a strong or solid foundation in the Word of God. Our culture and our world are greatly affected by biblical and spiritual ignorance. Consequently, they are also absent of any established spiritual-structure, the need to have a church family, and void of any spiritual lineage, protocol, and etiquette; living their spiritual lives aimlessly or haphazardly hitting and missing—with many mostly missing. Some believers are trapped in backward thinking; they are going nowhere and accomplishing nothing—a human *train wreck,* destined eventually to crash and burn somewhere if they don't turn around. Some have ended up on a *"spiritual junk-heap"* (unfit for any good spiritual purpose) because no one is able do anything with them. Sad, but true!

This is a great travesty, because most have placed themselves under their own spiritual authority, and have endangered themselves and others by their stubborn refusal to submit to the real spiritual authority that God has placed in His church. To their own great detriment, they are temperamentally unable to discipline their flesh, sit down, be still, and listen. They are notoriously negligent with their spiritual walk. This short-sighted and foolhardy behavior often leads to extensive, far-reaching, and long-term spiritual damage. Nothing good ever results from one's biblical illiteracy, obstinate will, and reckless approach to faith—nothing at all. There can never be any lasting spiritual change, progression, or growth until we learn to surrender to the spiritual authority that God has placed over us. The purpose of spiritual authority is to guide us in our spiritual development in the Word of God, to help us to reach spiritual maturity, to lead us into service work in ministry, to unify the body, to set biblical standards, and to settle, encourage, and strengthen us in our life of faith (Eph. 4:12). In order for these things to take place, we must be submitted under the established spiritual-authority of the local church, not in isolation. Far too often, many weak and feeble believers remain immature and undeveloped or underdeveloped spiritually because they simply won't listen, submit, and follow instructions. When you are truly submitted to the Lord, then you will be submitted to His Word; when you are submitted to His Word, you will be submitted under the spiritual authority that He has set before you. It's not spiritual rocket science!

In the final analysis, the remedy for this unguarded and irrational behavior toward defying spiritual authority is for believers to return to their responsibility of respecting biblical structure and order, to submit to their spiritual parents with a heart of genuine humility to receive the Word of the Lord, and to have patience and faith in anticipation and expectation that change and growth will happen in their lives. Change will not happen overnight, but spiritual growth will happen when Christians get into their rightful place and stay put.

The path that God has laid out in the Scriptures is for all believers to be conscientious in submitting to all kinds of authority. Submission to legitimate authority is essential to a quality of life that is peaceable, attainable, and successful, whether it is the authority of the nuclear family, the authority in a marriage relationship, the authority that exists in societal governments, or any other authority in the kingdom of God. The path of submission to spiritual authority may not always be easy for our flesh, but it is God's way of bringing great dividends and benefits to those who will adhere to it, which will far outweigh the destructive forces that will certainly come for those who vigorously oppose it. The payback for godly submission and obedience will most certainly be tremendous!

Reflections on Taking Personal Responsibility Seriously

All of us begin life with absolutely no responsibility for our personal well-being and lifestyle choices. In the early stages of life, everything is done for us, and nearly all decisions are made by those who are responsible for us. Normally, as we grow toward adolescence and into adulthood, we are gradually allowed (and expected) to assume more responsibility and to make more of our own decisions. Eventually, through the modeling of parents, grandparents, or guardians, and by much trial and error in frequently falling down and picking ourselves up, we learn (hopefully) to take responsibility for ourselves even in the most minuscule areas of life. We learn through things like taking on small tasks, doing schoolwork, holding down small or odd jobs, and obeying higher authority. From an early age, our decisions often bring with them an understanding of the good and bad consequences which result from either accepting or shirking our personal responsibilities.

One of the main evidences of maturity is the ability and willingness to take responsibility for one's actions in all areas of life. This includes making wise, solid, and sensible decisions on a consistent basis, and understanding the gravity of the harsh consequences of failing to do so. Mature persons are those who reach adulthood with a familiar acquaintance with both the rewards of being a responsible person and the hardships and pitfalls that result from irresponsibility. Once positive mindsets of responsible thought and behavior become embedded in our brain, it is highly unlikely that we will fall into irresponsible habits, such as castigating others for our own mistakes, and cloying through life, evading our personal accountability.

The word responsibility is a compound word of two different words: "*respond and ability.*" It is one's ability to respond to any given situation or circumstance. One of the main reasons why so many Christians don't comprehend why bad things happen to them unnecessary is because they take very little personal, reasonable initiative in their Christian faith and lifestyle choices. Yes, child of God, bad things *will* happen in this life. This world is a fallen place that is decayed by sin, suffering, evil, violence, and perversion. It is vitally important to know that when things in life go wrong (and they will), you don't go wrong with them. There is not a single person who walks through life unscathed. Some things in life we have no control over, but many other things are within our grasp—even how we respond to our circumstances and what we allow— and those are the things we are responsible for. More often than not, if we experience a plethora of bad things in our lives, then it is probably because we refuse to accept personal responsibility for our actions and decisions.

This modernized age and culture strongly promotes in people a spirit of entitlement, and encourages a mindset that the world somehow owes them something (or even anything and everything they want). They perpetually blame others for their wrong choices, mistakes, and failures. This is the backward spirit that pervades this age. Personal responsibility is an individual independence and freedom to think, exert choices, seize control, and react positively or negatively to any given circumstance. Each one of us is completely responsible for all his or her life's choices. I know that is a hard pill for some people to swallow. However, one thing is clear: your personal choices and decisions will follow you until you have breathed your last breath in this life. Taking responsibility and making wise choices will always pay off in the long run.

Christians, above all others, should reflect good character and mature accountability for their personal lives, because the Bible teaches clearly and precisely, with many vivid examples throughout, of the *root causes* and effects of personal responsibility and the dangerous consequences of irresponsibility (Isa. 3:10–11; Ezek. 18:20; Lk. 16:10-13; Gal. 6:7–8; Eph. 4:25-31).

Here are three essential life principles that will help you to develop, mature, and maintain responsible behavior:

Avoid blame-shifting, making excuses, and complaining about things not going your way. Sometimes things in life will go wrong without warning; other times, life will go so well that it feels like nirvana. Life can be tough at times! When things go wrong, don't go wrong with them. Acknowledge your mistakes and failures, even if there were other contributing external forces in the mix. You can never control the actions of others, but you can always control your own actions and reactions. Stay out of the habit of always passing the buck or pointing the finger when things are perfectly within your degree of control. Get rid of the kind of speech that says: *"I never asked to be born," "It's not my fault I act like this," "My parents are the reason I'm so jacked up," "There is no hope for me," "I can't change, I'll never get ahead in life," "What's the point in life?," "We are all just pawns in God's hands," "I wish the world would stop so that I could get off, and Life is so unfair."*

Well, who said that life was meant to be fair or would be fair some day? At times, life isn't fair; it can throw you a raw deal. This earthly life is not designed to make a perfect world for you to live in. The sooner you learn and except that, the better off you will be. Always feeling sorry for yourself and wallowing in a pity party is not the answer either. All of these are negative, hostile, and pessimistic mindsets that only breed more anger and hostility inside an unguarded heart and mind. They will never change things for the better or help you to achieve your basic duty and crucial responsibilities as a human being and as a Christian. You will only produce more failure, which will make you feel worse.

Instead, wake up each day, and begin to posture your attitude and confess these positive statements: *"With Christ all things are possible," "Greater is He who is in me than he who is in the world," "I am an overcomer, and I am more than a conqueror through Christ."* You can do all things through Christ Jesus who gives strength! Change your thinking, and your life will change. Make a conscientious effort to speak positive things rather than always accentuating the negative. Take sole responsibility for your choices and actions. Don't allow distractions to cause you to expend your time and drain your energy always harping on the negative. Do whatever it takes to courageously seek and obtain the wisdom of God. God always rewards faithfulness, even in the midst of hardships and sufferings. God will always show Himself strong on behalf of those whose hearts are devoted to Him (2 Chron. 16:9).

Take your personal relationship with God wholeheartedly. Again, a big part of your personal responsibility in the Christian life begins with taking your personal relationship with the Lord seriously. You can't have a successful and purposeful Christian life without pursuing and developing your relationship with Christ. It is impossible! You can't squish God into a convenient, dusty corner of your life and expect Him to help you solve your most difficult problems. Either He is Lord of all or He is not Lord at all. God's timetable has to take precedence over your personal ambitions and scheduled agendas. God is looking for the hearts of people who are loyal to Him and to His Word. Tear down all the rationale and the defense mechanisms that keep you from total dependency upon God and His Word, His structure, His way, and His order. Take the time and be devoted to serving God. Yes, you are solely responsible for all your spiritual choices, your natural choices, and your actions in life. However, God is able to help you make better decisions and develop good judgment. Nurturing and maintaining your relationship with the Lord will bring direction, purpose, strength, growth, and emotional well-being to your spiritual, relational, emotional, physical, and financial life.

Learn to live by faith and practice patience. Our Christian faith is impossible to operate and execute accurately when we try to evade personal responsibility. Faith is a way of life. The Bible instructs every believer to live by faith (Rom. 1:17). In a nutshell, we should live our lives responsibly with hope and expectancy. As Christians, we must learn not only to live by faith, but also to release and build our faith when times are easy so that when the rough times of life come—and they surely will come—we are not blown away or destroyed. We must learn to practice believing God, standing on His promises, and confessing what He said belongs to us.

Even when it seems like your faith isn't working, or when you have experienced faith failures, keep trying! Sometimes results can be very slow in coming, which can make you prone to give up. Using your faith is like learning anything new for the first time. You have to keep at it until you master it. One of the most powerful things that builds unshakable faith, and allows it to remain resilient and strong, is patience. Building the good fruit of patience inside you has cumulative value in helping you to shoulder your crucial responsibilities in the Christian life. Patience is what undergirds, bolsters, and sustains your faith until you are able to see the results manifested in your life (Heb. 6:11–12). Patience will often add an extra dimension of strength, power, and perseverance when using your faith. Without patience, your spiritual walk will constantly be frustrating, which will keep you on edge, annoyed, agitated, and constantly upset. You have to practice being patient; it doesn't come easily.

Patience is your ability in the Lord's power and might to remain consistently constant after your faith has been released in His Word. Hebrews 10:35–36 concludes, "Therefore do not cast away your confidence, which has great reward. For you have need of endurance, so that after you have done the will of God, you may receive the promise" (NKJV). You must stop thinking that patience is designed to make your life miserable and increase your suffering. Patience that waits in faith and hope (Rom. 8:23–25) puts you on a course to victory; begin expecting the unexpected while you wait. Patience is the power to remain consistently constant when all hell breaks loose, and it seems the situation is hopeless. Patience is the thing that takes over when bad things continue to happen to you, and it helps you to continue to trust that God's Word cannot and will not fail; it will ultimately lead you to success. Faith and patience work together to bring the promises of God to fulfillment in your life. Faith in God's Word allows the promises of God to flow to you; patience keeps that flow (window) open until the promise of God has arrived.

10

OVERCOMING LIFE'S CHALLENGES

"For I know the thoughts and plans that I have for you, says the Lord, thoughts and plans for welfare and peace and not for evil, to give you hope in your final outcome."

— Jeremiah 29:11 (AMP)

"Our attitude towards what has happened to us in life is the important thing to recognize . . . The last of human freedoms, to choose one's attitude in any given set of circumstances, is to choose one's own way."

— Viktor Frankl

Grappling with Life's Disappointments and Moving toward Recovery and Wholeness

EARLY ON IN LIFE, LOUIS ZAMPERINI SEEMED DESTINED FOR greatness. His life growing up was characterized by discipline, confidence, a commitment to excellence, bull-dog determination, and an irrepressible spirit that never lost hope. Little did he know in those years how essential those qualities would be to his survival in the ordeal that was soon to come.

By the time he competed in the 1936 Summer Olympic Games in Berlin, Germany, Louis Zamperini was one of the fastest distance runners in the world. A mere five years later, however, he was a young lieutenant in the U.S. Army Air Corps (later the U.S. Air Force), serving in the Pacific Theater of Operations as a bombardier aboard a B-24 Liberator bomber. It was a dangerous life, not only because of the peril of air combat and performing bombing runs over enemy territory, but also for witnessing the frequent accidents and other mishaps during the course of the war that caused the deaths of thousands of American airmen, due to noncombat related incidents. One such incident engulfed Louis Zamperini and changed his life forever.

While on a search and rescue mission to find a downed bomber one day, Zamperini's own airplane experienced mechanical problems and crashed into the sea. He and a fellow crew member survived 47 days adrift in a life raft; they sustained themselves by drinking water and catching fish. One of the reasons they survived is that they never lost hope. They were able to maintain their morale by keeping a positive spirit, despite the privations and uncertainty of their situation. However, their ordeal was only beginning.

Eventually, they were picked up by the Japanese and taken to a prison camp as prisoners of war. The camp was brutal in its environment, and in the treatment the prisoners received from the guards, but Louis Zamperini suffered the most. Ironically, his fame as a runner and a competitor in the 1936 Olympics made him well-known to his unsympathetic captors. One Japanese guard, in particular, singled out Zamperini for especially brutal treatment. At the hands of this guard, known by the prisoners as *"the Bird,"* Zamperini was subjected to unpredictable and repeated beatings, terrible deprivation, the unrelenting threat of starvation, physical and psychological torture, and unimaginably brutal and dehumanizing conditions that would have thoroughly broken most people. In fact, that is just what *the Bird* was determined to do: break the body and spirit of this famous American, who was at the mercy and whim of his cruel captors.

Louis Zamperini refused to break. He tenaciously endured, even under the worst punishments, and the cruelest, hardhearted abuse that *the Bird* could dish out, but his spirit never broke. The discipline, confidence, and hope that had always sustained him in life also carried him through the greatest challenge and the worst ordeal he had ever faced.

His horrific experiences in that prison camp did not leave him unaffected, however. Two years after his capture, he was liberated when the war ended. He returned home to the United States as a man with tortured memories, extreme hatred, and bitterness toward his captors and tormentors—*the Bird* in particular. Night after night, he woke up screaming from nightmares of his time in the camp. He married soon after returning to the states, but the emotional trauma of his experiences (what today would be diagnosed as post-traumatic stress disorder) was so intermittently disruptive that it, along with his abuse of alcohol, began to threaten his young marriage.

One night, reluctantly, but at his wife's urging, he attended a Billy Graham Crusade with her, and his life was transformed when he embraced the gospel message of forgiveness and life in Christ. His newly found faith truly made him a new man; in the strength of that faith, he was able to overcome a tidal wave of mental and emotional aftereffects of his ordeal in the war. This transformation was so great, in fact, that in 1950, after having vowed earlier that he would never return to Japan, he did indeed return, visiting in prison some of his guards from the camp who were serving time for war crimes. He expressed to each of them his heartfelt forgiveness of them for the way they had abused and mistreated him. The resurfacing of the horrendous memories brought feelings of déjà vu all over again. He even sought to meet personally with *the Bird* for the same reason, but the man refused. Undaunted, Zamperini wrote the man a letter, expressing his feelings in completely honest and transparent terms, but also explaining that he had completely forgiven *the Bird* for all of his mistreatment.

Freed from the terrors of his past, Louis Zamperini went on to live a full, fruitful, and enjoyable life, during which he saw success as an inspirational speaker, started a camp for troubled youth, and even carried the Olympic flame in the Olympic Torch relay for the 1998 Winter Olympics in Nagano, Japan.

Louis Zamperini overcame tremendous challenges and obstacles through a combination of four significant factors:

- **Faith**. His conversion to Christ gave him the spiritual fortitude, empowerment, and resources to triumph over the terrible emotional and psychological trauma from his wartime experiences, which would otherwise have crippled his postwar life, and eventually destroyed him. Through the development of his Christian faith, he was able to overcome the weaknesses and inadequacies that had threatened to plague and cripple him even after his captivity had ended.

- **Forgiveness.** Zamperini's visit to Japan to forgive his captors and tormentors was an expression of his faith that did as much good for him, as it did for them, if not more. Forgiveness is the key to releasing the past, thereby not permitting the power of the past to destroy your present or rob you of your potential future. It allows you to stop rehearsing things that should be forgiven and forgotten, even if they are your own mistakes. Unforgiveness is a poison and a cancer that eats away at a person. Forgiving those who have wronged you not only removes hindrances in your fellowship with God, but it also reduces paralyzing anxiety and depression, and it leads to better overall physical health and a prosperous spiritual life.

- **Hope.** Even when circumstances seemed hopeless during the 47 days on that raft and 2 years of brutal captivity, Zamperini's hope never died, and that is one of the main reasons he survived. Hope displaced his fear and inspired him to continually work for his survival. The power of hope and his audacious faith enabled him to persevere and look confidently to the future beyond his present circumstances. Hope is the virtue that empowers us to overcome every debilitating circumstance that we encounter, whether it is indifference, deprivation, despair, discontentment, discouragement, doubt, unbelief, or fear.

- **Letting go.** Another main reason Louis Zamperini's life after the war was fulfilled, happy, phenomenally successful, and productive is that he learned to let go of the fear and pain of his past. Even though his body was free when he returned home after the war, his mind was not free until he learned to release the trauma and the painfully bitter memories. In all of these things, his faith and his relationship with Christ were the decisive factors for overcoming the greatest challenges of his life.

How to Overcome the Challenges and Misfortunes of Life

Everyone faces challenges in life, but not everyone knows how to deal with those challenges effectively, positively, or productively. Many people fumble their way through life, never finding their path to wholeness and soundness. While there are many different ways to approach the issue of dealing with the challenges of life, I want to focus the bulk of this chapter on four wisdom principles for overcoming obstacles and achieving success in life. These principles are particularly timeless, powerful, and relevant.

Turn the Disappointments of Life into Opportunities

Learn to turn the lemons of life into lemonade. Most of us are familiar with that little bit of folk wisdom that says, "When life gives you lemons, make lemonade." That is a lighthearted way of saying that we should work to make the most of whatever circumstance we are in; to make the best of a terrible situation. While the wartime experiences of Louis Zamperini certainly were much more dire and grim than can be compared with getting *lemons* from life, they certainly illustrate the principle of making the best of a bad situation and triumphing over horrendous conditions that would have broken most people. Under the most brutal and inhumane treatment imaginable, Zamperini refused to bow, refused to break, and refused to surrender to all depredations, even when singled out for particularly abusive treatment by one particular guard. The lessons that he learned in life prior to the war had prepared him mentally, emotionally, and physically for the ordeal to come. And after the war, his encounter with Christ equipped him with the spiritual strength not only to overcome the trauma of his precarious experiences, but also to forgive his tormentors, including that one particular guard that made his life hell.

While few of us will ever go through privations or depredations to the magnitude of what Louis Zamperini lived through, all of us, at times, must deal with challenges in life of varying degrees of intensity, including some that are so serious that they could destroy us or knock us down for the count, unless we are prepared to deal with them before they arise. When life gives you lemons, learn to make lemonade. The key to turning the lemons of life into lemonade is to alter your skewed perspective. Learn how to see opportunity where

221

others see only oppression, and possibilities where others see only a litany of problems. Many of the challenges and hardships in life are often disguised as opportunities to advance to something greater. So, the key to overcoming the challenges in every facet of life is to learn how to look beyond the guise of the dilemma to see the treasure beneath.

As a young businessman in his early 30s, Sir James Dyson became increasingly frustrated with his Hoover vacuum cleaner, because of its loss of suction. He suspected that the unit's disposable bag design might be part of the problem. As far as he was concerned, the vacuum cleaner was a lemon. This sparked an idea in his mind to innovate a new approach that would solve the loss of suction problem, and do away with the need for disposable bags. After much trial and error, Dyson succeeded in creating a vacuum system that used the concept of cyclonic separation, which removes particulates from an air, gas, or liquid stream without using filters through vortex separation. This was a totally new concept for the vacuum cleaner, and it took him 5,126 failed attempts before he made his idea work properly on the 5,127[th].

Dyson's idea met with resistance in his native UK, as no distributor was willing to take on his product. He was 36 at the time, and the disposable bag vacuum market was a $130 million-plus per year industry. Dyson moved forward with his idea in the Japanese market in 1983; the hot pink version of his vacuum won an industrial award. By 1986, he'd won a U.S. patent for his invention, although he was still unable to get manufacturers to take on his product. In the face of repeated rejection, he formed his own company and, by age 46 in 1993, he began marketing the product himself. His idea was eventually met with acceptance, with millions of satisfied customers around the world. Dyson's estimated net worth, as of 2016, was nearly $5 billion. Dyson achieved great success because he saw a lemon and turned it into a lemonade product that, ultimately, many people were thirsty to drink—and did!

There are many things you can do to make the best of the negative circumstances that life can often bring. The important things are to know your options and to formulate a winning strategy. For instance, when you are enduring negative situations, first look for the lessons contained in it, instead of complaining and whining about them or being condescending, cynical, callous, or critical. What can you learn from your experience that will help you grow? What can you take from it that will make you stronger and more resilient in the future? Train yourself to see your negative circumstances as teachable moments and opportunities.

Invariably, a second crucial part of your strategy would be to take control of the things that you have the power to control. You can't always control the negative situations that come your way, but there are many things, within the context of those situations, that you can control. Louis Zamperini could not control the unimaginably miserable conditions of his imprisonment in a Japanese prison camp or his brutal treatment by the guards. What he could control—and did—was his response to those dismal conditions. He made a conscious, deliberate decision that he would not be broken—that he would prevail in the end.

Third, make the most of social support networks. For some reason, many of us have a counterproductive tendency to back away from social contact when challenges or hardships come, and try to deal with them alone. Don't fall into that tragic trap. Reach out to friends, family, your local church, and other support groups. It is highly likely that someone within or near your circle of acquaintances has probably gone through the same thing or similar situation what you're experiencing, and, if so, try to reach out to that person. Let that person share the wisdom that was gained from that experience, and apply that same wisdom to your situation.

A report published by the American Psychological Association described the results of a 12-year study of the effects of stress on the lives of the retained employees in the wake of a massive downsizing in their company. In 1981, the Illinois Bell Telephone company reduced its workforce by almost 50 percent over a period of 1-year—from 26,000 to a little more than 13,000. The study revealed that 2/3 of the remaining employees suffered severe anemic performance and health declines due to the challenges and stress associated with change. However, the other 1/3 actually thrived during the same period even though subjected to the same tensions and stress. What made the difference? The employees who thrived displayed three key winning attitudes that helped them turn adversity into an advantage:

- *They had an attitude of commitment that led them to strive to be involved in ongoing events rather than feeling isolated.*
- *They had an attitude of control that led them to try to influence outcomes rather than lapse into passivity and powerlessness.*
- *They had an attitude of challenge that led them to view stress changes, whether positive or negative, as opportunities for new learning.*

The second fundamental key, then, to turning life's lemons into lemonade is, in a word, *attitude*. Another word for attitude is mindset. A consistent positive attitude and mindset frees you from fickle mood swings, sudden and destructive mental collapses, and unsteady decision-making even in the midst of chronic and unfair treatment, bitter hardships, undeserved sufferings, horrific losses, fleeting dreams, unexplainable misfortunes, and unexpected failures. You will find yourself overcoming all the obstacles and challenges of life once you set your mind to succeed and develop an attitude of endurance.

Eliminate the Power of the Past, Going Backwards, or Stagnating

Eliminate the power of the past from your present and future. The challenges you grapple with in life will either make you or break you; the choice is yours. You can't always choose your challenges, but you can always consciously choose how you will respond to those challenges. The power of the past is one challenge we all share in common. All of us have been manipulated or dominated by memories from our past that we would rather forget: memories of excruciating pain, abuse, betrayal, ridicule, rejection, humiliation, derision, vilification, or condemnation. Other memories could be of colossal failures, sharp contrast, disappointing others, or hurting someone dear to you. Regret or guilt over your past has the potential to prevent you from moving forward and getting on with your life. Someone said it best, "Never let the pain from your past punish your present and paralyze your future." Only you can keep that from happening.

Too many people impoverish their present and imperil their future because they are immobilized by their past. Don't let yourself become one of them. Don't allow previous disappointments, disasters, or detours on your journey of life trap you in the quicksand of regret, self-pity, bitterness, discouragement, despair, or chaos. They will prevent you from getting past your past. Don't fall prey to the mindset that you'll never be able to get out or to get ahead.

Time is unalterable. None of us can truly live in the past, no matter how much we might think we want to, or how hard we try. The present keeps impinging on us relentlessly, and it will not be denied. Life, with all of its ups and downs, will continue to happen whether we like it or not. If we are not prepared to face it because we insist on living in the past, then we will only become incredibly absorbed and agitated from piling up more failure, self-pity, disappointment, and regret about the inevitable.

So how do you get free from the *"paralysis of the past?"* Most of the answer involves your perspective. First of all, make a deliberate and conscious decision to break with your past. Nothing will improve for you until you let go of that which you cannot change anyway. Determine within yourself that you will stop analyzing, rehashing, and rehearsing the mistakes or the dreadful experiences of your past, which only predispose you toward weakness. Only then will you gain mastery over them.

Deciding to break with your past means accepting your past as it is, and not trying to shape it into what you wish that it could have been. No prodigious amount of wishing, *"if onlys,"* or *"what ifs"* will change your past. Without neglecting preparations for the future, concentrate on the present moment, which is the only thing you can influence at this point. Your past is your past, and it cannot be changed. Accept it, and let it go. It's over and done!

Dealing with your past can stir up strong emotions that wage war back and forth inside you, even years after the fact. The frazzled and haunted emotions that are often associated with horrifying memories can rise up screaming from the back of your mind so loudly that they may be difficult to resist and overcome at first. So be patient with yourself. Even though your emotions and feelings are vital to your true experience, they can also become very volatile when you are trying to overcome challenges. Continually resist them, and fight back negative feelings of animosity. Emotional healing over past experiences seldom happens quickly. Feelings you thought you had conquered long ago can unexpectedly pop up and trigger certain sentiments from the past. When they do, don't berate yourself. Accept the feelings as they come, deal with them the moment they arise, and rejoice over every victory. Eventually the pain will go away. You'll still remember how you felt, but those inferiority feelings will no longer control you. It is particularly important to not only release every negative mental picture frame of the past, but also not to bring those areas up in current conversation.

Another strategy for breaking from your past is to examine it from a different perspective. Your past, for good or bad, for better or worse, has helped to make you the person you are today. Instead of brooding disconsolately over how your deplorable experiences and grievous hardships have hurt you, harried you, and hindered you, start thinking about how they have strengthened you—how they forced you to rely on abilities and resources you might never have known you possessed otherwise. Steel is tempered in fire, and tempered steel is the strongest.

You cannot change your past, so don't waste your time trying. Don't expend your energy cogitating over missed opportunities or lamenting over past misjudgments. The best thing you can do about your past is to learn from it—your mistakes and failures as well as your successes. Your past cannot control you, nor control your present or future unless you allow it. When you became a Christian, you became a *"new creation"* (2 Cor. 5:17). In Christ, all things are new, including you, so don't let the faults or the mindset of the *old* thwart the growth of the new you. Don't allow your old past that is dead and gone to hamstring you, while chipping away at your future potential. There is absolutely nothing in the present or the future that you can ever do which will change or alter your past. The only profit from the past is the lessons we learn, that help us live positively and productively in the present and prepare us for an immensely prosperous future. When you are able to eliminate the power of the past, you become less distracted by your past hurts and wounds; it becomes easier to focus and concentrate on securing a positive and successful future. In Isaiah, the Lord said, "'Do not cling to events of the past or dwell on what happened long ago. Watch for the new thing I am going to do. It is happening already—you can see it now! I will make a road through the wilderness and give you streams of water there'" (Isa. 43:18–19 TEV). Break the power of the past, and repeating cycles of stagnation and failure, by resisting to dwell on past negative events and realities that you are more than likely not able to change. Put your energy into and focus your efforts on the new horizons, new opportunities, and new possibilities that will advance future prospects.

Focus on the Present and Make Efforts to Move Ahead in Life

Determine to focus on what's ahead of you, not what's behind you. It's dangerous to look behind you when you are supposed to be moving forward. In the Bible, Lot's wife, fleeing with her husband and their two daughters from the destruction of Sodom and Gomorrah, looked back and became a pillar of salt (Gen. 19:26). Whether from irresistible curiosity or irrepressible longing, her failure to let go of the past destroyed her. This story is a warning and a reminder to all of us of the potential danger of continually *"looking back."* Affection, focus, and curiosity all can cause you to build fortresses of the past in your mind. Then you ferociously attack those fortresses while allowing your time and energy to be consumed in the frivolous and futile attempts to change the unchangeable past. Many good-hearted Christians, driven impetuously by their mental propensity for contemplation, and fascination with wishing for something to have been different, eventually cause harm to themselves by ignoring the lessons of wisdom to leave the past where it is. Paul the apostle made this same analogy of concentrating on what's ahead of you instead of what's behind you when he wrote, "Don't you realize that in a race everyone runs, but only one person gets the prize? So, run to win!" (1 Cor. 9:24 NLT). Ask yourself: *"What is my purpose in living?"* *"What direction am I going in life?"* *"What do I want my future to look like?"* Nobody's life just stands still; you are either advancing or you are digressing. You can bank on it!

Time is linear, and so is life. There is no profit in looking at the past except to learn from it, and then to use those lessons to grow toward greater success in the future. Success lies in the future. Advancement lies in the future. Maturity lies in the future. Fruitfulness lies in the future. Destiny lies in the future. Overcoming the obstacles of today prepares you for a more successful future. While all these things can be enjoyed to some degree in the present, they do not lie in the past, and that is the point. You never succeed in the game of tennis until you learn to keep your eye on the ball, or in golf unless you keep your eye on the green. You can't hit your mark if you keep taking your eyes off the target. You can't reach your destination if you lose track of how to get where you want to go.

Draft horses are often fitted with *blinders* on the outside of each eye to keep them from being distracted by what's around them, so they will stay focused on what's ahead. Runners preparing for competition are taught to keep their eyes fixed on one thing—the finish line—and to ignore everything else. They know, during the race, not to look to either side to see where the other runners are, and never, ever to look behind them. Olympic gold medals have been lost to runners who would have won, except that they glanced aside at the last instant. Consider this: You must first realize where you are presently before you are able to move forward. Start now by assessing how and what needs to change for you to experience a successful end result.

Vigorously, be firm in your determination to let the past be the past, and stay right where it is. Once you have gleaned from your past experiences and circumstances all the useful wisdom and knowledge they have to offer, release the past from your life and let it recede into the background. Whatever you did not appropriate to help you grow you no longer need. Don't stop and build a monument after you have forgotten and released your past. Use the wisdom and knowledge from your past to help you set positive and progressive goals for reshaping your future. Then, concentrate and focus your eyes on those goals, taking incremental steps, if necessary, but never losing sight of them. Don't regret or replay the past. Don't get distracted by peripherals in the present. Zero in on pressing ahead.

The apostle Paul learned to let go of the futile activities of his past that he had once prized so highly in his efforts to be right with God, in favor of embracing the much greater, more glorious, and eternal riches available to him in Christ by the grace of God. Like Paul, learn to consider your past as "*worthless because of what Christ has done*" and "**press on**" to reach the end of the race and receive the heavenly prize for which God, through Christ Jesus, is calling us" (Phil. 3:7, 14 NLT).

The Greek word "*dioko,*" "*press toward,*" used here in Philippians literally means "*to pursue, to chase, to strive for purpose, to bear down hard and go after.*" This word gives indication of a hostile pursuit in a good sense; it means to press or to pursue with an inexorable persistence, hounding, desire, diligence, and earnestness in order that one might obtain the prize. In a race, all who aspire to finish press to the end and become winners. Paul also uses another Greek word with a similar, but slightly different meaning in the same passage: "*epektenino*," "*reaching forth*." This Greek word means "*extending oneself*" or "*reaching forward by strong straining*" or "*forward progress and advancement*." The Christian race is not effortless, painless, smooth-sailing, cheap, or chintzy, but ultimately it is supremely rewarding. Success depends on keeping your eyes on the prize or goal. And that means always looking ahead optimistically. You will always find successful people and super-achievers refusing to fret over missed opportunities because they are goal-oriented pursuers, pressing, reaching, progressing, and focusing all their attention and energy on what's ahead of them, and not on the disparities of the past.

Be Guided by Gratitude, Thankfulness, and Appreciation about Life

Begin cultivating in your heart and mind genuine gratitude, thankfulness, and appreciation about life. There is enough negativity and chaos in the world already; don't be responsible for adding more to that poisonous mixture, even in your own personal life. Move away from demanding that life should always be a certain way. Stop viewing everything in life as broken or adversarial; it isn't true! You will come up defeated when you purposely ignore or refuse to be grateful, thankful, and appreciative about the ordinary good things, the everyday joys of life, and about what's going well. Don't allow yourself to slip into a mindset characterized by constantly ridiculing everything, and by damaging words that blow things way out of proportion about your circumstances in life. Negativity breeds discontentment, dissatisfaction, displeasure, and more negativity in speech, thought, behavior, and life. Proverbs 16:24 emphatically states, "Pleasant words are like a honeycomb, making people happy and healthy" (NCV). Pause for a moment, and think about how fortunate you really are!

It is true that genuinely grateful, thankful, and positive people generally live longer, experience fewer health problems, especially chronic ones, and are more robust, satisfied, and content in life than people without such a positive, amicable disposition. Carefully controlled scientific studies have revealed that positive people have lower heart rates, lower levels of the stress hormone cortisol, and lower concentrations of the plasma associated with heart disease. Companies on average spend 25 percent less on health-related costs for employees who are positive, happy, and healthy than on employees who are not. An analysis of no less than 30 separate studies, shows that positive people are less likely to get sick. People who are positive because their lives have meaning and purpose experience healthy changes at the cellular level; people who consider themselves happy, but who are negative by nature and whose lives lack meaning, follow a general pattern of being chronically distressed, which often leads to caustic criticism and adamant resistance to change. This only exacerbates their problems, which lead to even more negativity in life and more debilitating disappointments.

Not only is there a direct corollary between happiness and health vs. negativism and deterioration, but there is also a link between gratitude and happiness vs. ungratefulness and unhappiness. Research shows that consistently grateful people are happier, more energetic, more hopeful, more helpful, more empathic, more spiritual, more giving and forgiving, quicker to have faith, and less materialistic. They're also less likely to be depressed, anxious, lonely, envious, neurotic, or sick.

Gratitude pervasively always boosts one's happiness. According to Dr. Sonya Lyubomirsky, gratitude:

1. *Promotes savoring of positive life experiences.*

2. *Bolsters self-worth and self-esteem.*

3. *Helps people cope with stress and trauma.*

4. *Encourages caring acts and moral behavior.*

5. *Helps build social bonds, strengthen existing relationships, and nurture new relationships (and we know lonely people have twice the rate of heart disease as those with strong social connections).*

6. *Inhibits harmful comparisons.*

7. *Diminishes or deters negative feelings such as anger, bitterness, and greed.*

8. *Thwarts hedonistic adaptation (the ability to adjust our set point to positive new circumstances so that we don't appreciate the new circumstance and it has little effect on our overall health or happiness).*

What we speak over our lives is what tends to manifest in our lives. Trouble will not last forever, so strive to learn how to outlive the adversity and suffering in your life. If you want to be more satisfied and feel better about life, then make a conscious effort to be more positive and cheerful, freely expressing gratitude and appreciation, and nurture a thankful spirit instead of panicking and losing control, being nervous, agitated, frustrated, and negative. Yes, and amen!

"Unyielding Faith" for Overcoming the Fiery Challenges of Life

Many people liken a great challenge in life to going through a fire. Concerning the story of three young Hebrew men in the third chapter of the Book of Daniel, this was the literal truth. King Nebuchadnezzar rose to prominence when he built one of the most majestic, architectural cities ever constructed in the ancient world. He was the most powerful man on the earth of his time. Not only did the height of his monarchy bring him great power, prestige, and self-glorification, but his pride and arrogance also rose to an unbearable level as well—to the extent that he effusively viewed himself as a great god.

In a classic case of the age-old conflict between one's devout faith and the idolatrous state, Shadrach, Meshach, and Abednego, who were among the thousands of Hebrews taken into exile in Babylonia where they also rose to prominence in loyal, competent service to the oppressive King Nebuchadnezzar, steadfastly refused to bow in idolatrous worship to an idol set up by the king. In defiance of his arrogant decree, the three Hebrew men made no attempt to rationalize, temporize, and compromise with worldly philosophy. They refused to look for loopholes or make concessions with idol worship when they knew and were loyal to the one and only true God Jehovah, the Most High. The mandatory worship of the king's monstrous golden image was to bring solidarity to and acknowledgement of his sovereignty and his imperial power throughout all of Babylon. However, these three young men were courageously convicted, and determined to remain absolutely and exclusively faithful to God, regardless of personal cost. Their unyielding faith to remained steady was the key, with their minds made-up to radically fixed their eyes on God, even if it meant death.

They openly defied King Nebuchadnezzar. His arrogant and ill-conceived decree to manipulate them with fear, intimidation, and to compulsively coerce them into submission in acts of allegiance to worship a false god, had back-fired. Their defiance resulted in being condemned to execution. In a furious fit of headstrong rage, the king ordered them to be thrown into a furnace burning with fire and sulfur that had been heated to seven times its normal intensity. A moment after the three men were thrown into the fiery furnace and engulfed in flames, Nebuchadnezzar rose up in absolute shock. Although he had thrown three men into the fire, he saw four men in the heart of the fiery blaze, walking around completely unburned, unharmed and unscathed; he described the fourth man as looking like "'*a god*'" (Dan. 3:25 NLT). It was a physical impossibility for anyone to remain conscious, let alone unharmed, in the midst of such a raging inferno. God stepped into the fire and intervened with miraculous protection to prove His faithfulness to the three Hebrew men, and to honor their faithfulness to Him. The king, humbled and awed by this undeniable demonstration of divine protection and power, hastily called Shadrach, Meshach, and Abednego out of the furnace where they were walking around in the fire, praising and worshipping the Almighty God. Then, he made a public proclamation of praise to the God of the Hebrews and elevated the three men to even higher positions of leadership in his kingdom.

While it is unlikely that many of us will experience such visible and tangible proof of God's presence as in this story, we can all take from it the truth that God is always with us in life's challenges. He is walking with us through grievous suffer-ings, whether we see Him visibly or not. If we trust Him in and through all things, then He will bring us eventually to a place of victory and triumph. On rare occa-sions, someone is blessed with a visible, angelic manifestation of God, but for the vast majority, it is through the eyes of faith which is how we see Him, where we are also able to experience and witness His delivering power. God has provided all the evidence we need to *see* Him by faith with what He has given to us in His Word.

There are many principles of "**Unyielding Faith**" that we can learn from the three Hebrew men's real-life experience. Here are a few:

- *Unyielding faith testifies (points towards) to what the power of God can and will do.*
- *Unyielding faith always has a good report when faced with severe opposition and hardship.*
- *Unyielding faith has confidence in God's grace for deliverance.*
- *Unyielding faith refuses to back down in the face of real threats and seemingly utter defeat.*
- *Unyielding faith rests in the promises of God and not in human effort or self-righteousness.*
- *Unyielding faith holds fast to its confession of faith.*
- *Unyielding faith is unwavering and never compromises.*

Concretely, this encouraging story of the three young Hebrew men crystallizes for us the truth that God will never abandon His people. He will always be present to strengthen and sustain us as long as we look to Him, trust in Him alone rather than in our own resources, and remain true to His Word. Satan often brings dreadful trials into our lives to trip us up and cause us to back off of our faith. Many are tempted to give up too quickly when Satan pours on the pressure. This story also shows us that God won't necessarily keep us out of the fires of life. Satan often uses the fiery trials of life to take his best shot to destroy us. However, God, in turn, allows the pressures and sufferings of the furnace of affliction to come into our lives in order to develop our faith in His Word, eventually bringing promotion, deliverance, and victory. God permitted the three Hebrew men's faith to be tested and tried in a place of extreme suffering and evil so that His glory and power could be seen and manifested before all.

Sometimes we have to go through the furnace of affliction, but when we do, we can take courage in His Word, that He has promised to sustain and protect us through it all and to bring us out victoriously on the other side. God knows that the fires of life can often temper us, test us, and purify us, and also make us ready to take our places when elevated and promoted. God's rewards to us for our faithfulness are not always readily material, tangible, visibly understood, or immediate in this present world; they are nevertheless real, much greater than we can possibly imagine, and awaiting us also in the next world. That is why Paul said that the temporary sufferings of this world are nothing in comparison to the glories that await us (Rom. 8:18). What looks like defeat, turns out to be victory. What looks like a death sentence, turns out to be life and peace. What looks like total failure, turns out to be a total success. Your faith in God's Word has the power to overcome and defeat every opposing obstacle you face in life. When you refuse to give up or give in to the pressure of the devils' tactics, they soon dissipate. So, hang in there! Your current troubles and challenges will soon pass. Your greatest days are still to come! Payday is on its way!

Overcoming all Obstacles, Recovering, and Finishing Well

American baseball legend Yogi Berra famously said, "It ain't over till it's over." He may have been talking about baseball, but the same is true with life. A cheerful heart and a thankful spirit will carry you far in life, even all the way to the end, and it can help you immensely to finish well. In gymnastics competitions, how one finishes can be just as important, or more important how one performs. Whether on the vault, the horse, the rings, the parallel bars, the uneven bars, or performing than the floor routine, an otherwise flawless performance can still lose if the gymnast fails to "*stick the landing.*" A stumble, an extra step, or a fall at the end can undo much or most of what went before, no matter how good it was.

Finishing your life well—*sticking the landing*—is just as important, and perhaps more so, as living your life well. Some people simply stop when the going gets too tough. Bad breaks in life end up breaking them so that they never recover their stride. One of the challenges of life that we all encounter is the strength and the will to keep going even when things go against us. What we need is a standard to pursue, or a *hero* to follow. In Hebrews we read:

> *Therefore, since we are surrounded by such a huge crowd of witnesses to the life of faith, let us strip off every weight that slows us down, especially the sin that so easily trips us up. And let us run with endurance the race God has set before us. We do this by keeping our eyes on Jesus, the champion who initiates and perfects our faith. Because of the joy awaiting him, he endured the cross, disregarding its shame. Now he*

is seated in the place of honor beside God's throne. Think of all the hostility he endured from sinful people; then you won't become weary and give up. (Heb. 12:1–3 NLT)

Comparatively, the Academy Award-winning movie *Chariots of Fire* contains a dramatic scene that illustrates how doggedness in the race can lead to victory, even against setbacks. In the scene, Scottish Christian and champion sprinter Eric Liddell is knocked down accidentally by another runner during a race. While most runners would call it quits at that point, assuming they were now too far behind to have a chance, Liddell responded differently. He got back up, looked at his competitors so far ahead of him, and with a fierce look of determination on his face, he set off after them. Exerting what appeared to be an almost superhuman effort, he poured on an additional burst of speed, closed up the lost distance, and actually won the race. As a committed Christian, running was more than just an athletic activity to Eric Liddell. Believing that God had made him fast, he used his running—and his winning—as a way of bringing glory to God and affording him opportunities to bear witness to Christ. Winning a gold medal in the Men's 400-meter sprint in the 1924 Paris Olympics, Eric Liddell went on to a fruitful ministry as a missionary in China until his death in 1945 while confined in a Japanese internment camp. All who knew him spoke of his integrity, character, and unfailing self-sacrificial faith in Christ. But he was a man who knew how to finish well.

Sometimes the best cure for discouragement and defeat in the challenges of life is to look to someone who has succeeded in those same challenges, and even in greater ones. Looking to Jesus and others who have gone before us and seeing how they faced and overcame greater challenges than any of us will ever face can encourage us to persevere, to lay aside the pressing weights of our past sufferings, pain, failures, unhealthy proclivities, and mistakes, and keep on running the race of life all the way to the end. Don't let past disappointments or current challenges of life prevent you from recovering, pressing on, and finishing well.

Finishing well means taking into account the end from where you are now. Keep in mind what you want your end to be as you press through every obstacle in life. Finishing well means that you will have to learn, and sometimes relearn as you go, forgetting those things you need to forget, and relearning new things, always adding depth and dimension to your experience with winsome perspective. Finishing well means that you don't allow discouragement to get the best of you when the going gets tough and when things work against you without cause. Finishing well means you have a bulldog determination, persistence, and stick-to-itiveness in the midst of adversity, suffering, and hardship. Finishing well means putting forth your best effort. It means never quitting, never counting yourself out, never giving-up, never underestimating yourself, never throwing in the towel, and always believing you can overcome every one of life's challenges.

Reflections on Conquering the Challenges of Life

In conclusion, I have provided five action points to focus on that will help you to deal successfully with the unavoidable challenges that life often brings. Because we are all subject to the same or similar hardships in life, it is our mindset and focus which ultimately determine our outcomes and end results. Many of the severe and extreme challenges in life often fall beyond our control to exterminate quickly. Overcoming challenges is usually a process that we must walk through with steadfast faith in Christ. Even in the worst kinds of circumstances of life, we don't have to lose control and "*quit life*." So, with this in mind, let's consider these five action principles to help us stay in focus:

1. **Keep in mind one certain truth about trouble and hardship: "Everything passes."** Let's face facts. Nothing in this world lasts forever. Good or bad, pain or pleasure, it makes no difference; whatever is of this fallen, trouble-ridden, physical, material world will come to an end and be replaced by something else eventually. Life is never here to stay; it's always passing. Everything we experience in this world has a limited shelf life and will soon expire. When you realize this truth, you will not waste valuable time philosophizing and scrutinizing over temporal things. Life has seasons, and every season of life eventually is replaced by a different season. Do your best to make every season count, because you only have one shot at life. It is of paramount importance to know with a surety that when going through the challenges of life: **Everything passes**.

So, don't treat your troubles as though they are here to stay. They are not. No matter what you may be going through right now and no matter how grievously difficult, repulsive, or hopeless things may seem at any given moment, rarely are they as bad as they appear. God's design is that life should be much easier than most make it out to be. Most of us have a natural tendency to exaggerate the seriousness of our negative or painful circumstances, especially when we are in the midst of them. Yet, as Paul reminds us, our current "light affliction" is momentary and insignificant when compared to the "eternal weight of glory" that awaits us as children of God (2 Cor. 4:17). However dreadful, painful, or oppressive your situation may seem, it will not last forever, even if it feels otherwise. It is sorely temporary and will pass eventually. The key is to trust in God for the faith and strength to persevere longer than your problems do. "This too will pass."

2.   **Don't engage in every battle in life. Choose your battles wisely going forward.** General Douglas MacArthur, who helped orchestrate the U.S. victory in the South Pacific during World War II, famously said, "In war there is no substitute for victory." One of the surest paths to defeat is to treat every predicament or hardship as a life-and-death conflict. You will face many battles in life, but some will be more intense and important than others. Be extremely careful of how you keep score in life, pursuing personal vendettas and jumping to what seems to be obvious conclusions. Don't wear yourself out or expend your resources engaging in trivial battles and fruitless conflicts you don't need to fight, trying to put out unnecessary fires. You don't have to lash out at every falsehood, and provocation, or respond spontaneously to every attack. Not all challenges have equal weight; calibrate the relevancy of every demand. Evaluate with objective measure, because some challenges exist as byproducts of other, weightier challenges; deal with the bigger challenge, and the lesser challenge often will fade as well. One of your greatest regrets, in hindsight, will be that you allowed yourself to be pulled into dilemmas that wasted your valuable time, siphoning off your ingenuity and energy that wasn't worth the effort. Some challenges or difficulties, as annoying or problematic as they may seem, simply aren't worth your time, because they won't affect the ultimate outcome of your life and eventually will be resolved simply

by subsequent developments. Learn to work your due diligence; decipher and discern exclusively which battles are more important—which challenges will affect your life the most depending on how they resolve—and focus on those.

During wartime, generals don't commit troops and resources to every possible skirmish or *hot spot* on a battlefield; that is a recipe for defeat and disaster. Instead, they analyze the overall situation—the big picture—and devise a strategy to win the war by identifying the most important battles and engagements, in which victory will bring the greatest strategic gain. It's all about wise and proper—or *economic* allocation of limited resources; approach life the same way. Don't let yourself be incited into fights that distract you from the overall objective by drawing your focus to side issues. At the end of the day, learn to fight the primary and principal battles that will guarantee your success, and in doing so, you will have foresight to take care of the little ones as well.

3. **Focus on the scope and magnitude of your purpose and assignment in life, and not side issues.** Before tackling the challenges in your life, make sure you understand your purpose and assignment in life as given to you by God. Then, armed with that knowledge, examine carefully the various demands you encounter or expect to face in order to determine how they relate to your God-given call and assignment. In this way, you can decide which disputes to address and which ones to ignore or place on a back burner. Only then should you proceed; otherwise, you may end up trying to play catch-up over time-consuming distractions, wasting your potential, and expending resources on things that matter little to fulfilling your purpose.

In other words, make sure that you understand your mission. Soldiers in battle, in order to achieve victory, must first understand their mission. Only when they understand their mission can they devise and execute a strategy to achieve it. This involves considering many possible options, and rejecting any that are irrelevant to the mission at hand in favor of those that directly relate to it. Some options may have easily achievable goals, but if they do not advance the mission, then they need to be rejected, or else they would require the commitment of resources that could be used better and more wisely elsewhere.

The upshot of this is: *set your priorities*. Not everything in your life will advance your purpose or help you fulfill your assignment—even every *good* thing. Some things in your life that are good may not help you advance toward your goal; they may, in fact, hinder you by pointing you in a different direction. Many well-meaning Christians live everyday life as if there is no tomorrow. Your choices today are what bring into focus your purpose in the future. Making solid choices today is what ensures that you will have a prosperous tomorrow. You must decide what things are vitally important and most strategic for accomplishing your mission, and then focus on them. Don't worry about the rest, and put it on the shelf.

4. **Move away from the false perception that life has to be a certain way.** You have your own ideas of how life should be, but how do you know if those ideas are true, realistic, or practical? Things happen in life—sometimes redeemably and sometimes irreparably. It's perfectly fine to plan and dream about the life you wish to live; just be ready to change your plans or adapt your dreams, because reality seldom matches your original ideal-picture plans. Success in dealing with life's quagmires, as well as in dealing with life as a whole, depends on flexibility and adaptability—not in your core values and principles, but in the ups and downs of day-to-day living. Our self-created image of a *glossy-finish* life does not always stack up against reality. You may have great dreams and plans for your life, only to become disgruntled and disillusioned when reality comes along to thwart, delay, alter, sidetrack, or even destroy them. When that happens, just remember that God's ideas for you are greater, higher, and more glorious than you can possibly imagine or create. Don't let rigidity in your off-kilter thinking reduce you to zero, or your perceptions about life keep you from trusting God to shape your life and destiny according to what He knows is best and in line with His plan for you. You owe it to yourself not to live with the false hopes that replace sound judgment, or with the irrational and unrealistic expectations of yourself and others.

5. **Know the latitude of your limitations as well as the parameters of your potential.** Don't be afraid of some honest self-analysis. Success in facing life's predicaments requires that you recognize your weaknesses as well as your strengths; your inabilities as well as your unique capabilities; your ignorance as well as your knowledge. Self-awareness of your limitations is crucial and critical to your success in meeting demands, because it will show you where you need help. And whenever you need direction, don't be afraid to ask for it.

Be confident in facing your challenges, but make sure your confidence rests in God, who can do all things, rather than in yourself, who cannot. Paul said that God's grace is sufficient for our every need (2 Cor. 12:9 NLT), and this includes our grievances and overcoming every difficulty in life. He also said that God's strength *works best* in our weakness. When God's power works in and through our weakness, we become stronger in Him (v. 10).

So be wise and realistic about your limitations, but don't let them stop you. As the old axiom goes, "Don't throw the baby out with the bath water." Learn to let God take you beyond your limitations by yielding to His Lordship and seeking to obey His will. Don't fret over your limitations, because it will only trigger more suppression of your ingenuity and desire. Instead, focus on your potentialities. As you learn to offer up to God your whole life—your strengths as well as your weaknesses—you will discover that, in God, the sky is your limit. No matter who you are, where you've been, or what you've done, you have within you many gifts, skills, talents, and capabilities that have not even been tapped into yet. Regardless of the size or number of your limitations, and sometimes the prevailing winds of adversity and suffering, they are all dwarfed by the magnitude of untapped potential God has placed in you. Don't get too big in a hurry. Trust Him, follow Him, and He will surely bring it to pass.

"Weeping may endure for the night (a season), but joy is sure to come in the morning!"

11

IT'S ALL ABOUT CHOICES

"You may believe you are doing right, but the Lord will judge your reasons. Depend on the Lord in whatever you do, and your plans will succeed."

— Proverbs 16:2–3 (NCV)

"Life is full of choices. God is not forcing us to do His will, He hasn't made us robots. We have an individual right whether to choose or not to choose."

— Bishop James A. Johnson

Understanding the Power of Personal Choice

CHOICES CARRY CONSEQUENCES. BAD CHOICES CAN BE VERY costly—sometimes even deadly. On June 25, 1876, Lieut. Col. George Armstrong Custer made a fateful and fatal decision that is still remembered today as one of the worst military and management decisions in American history. Custer was in southeastern Montana, near the Little Big Horn River, when he rashly chose to take the 210 men of the 7th U.S. Cavalry under his command into battle against a vastly superior force of over 2,000 Lakota Sioux, Cheyenne, and Arapaho warriors. Not surprisingly, he lost. In an engagement lasting less than an hour, Custer and all of his men were killed. This disaster was one of the consequences of the U. S. government's heavy-handed programs of oppression of Native American tribes; it was a conscientious effort backed by white European settlers who had an axe to grind, with the U. S. military as a co-conspirator for illegally invading and confiscating their reservation lands by marginalizing boundaries and property lines.

It need not have happened. Although there were many factors in play that led up to that fateful day, had Custer not made several incredibly poor decisions, he and his command might have survived. First, believing his judgment was superior to others, he refused to listen to them, even to the point of disobeying and ignoring orders from his senior commander. Brig. Gen. Alfred Terry had ordered Custer not to attack until he (Terry) arrived with reinforcements. Custer attacked anyway and died along with his men. Terry and his reinforcements arrived the next day. Second, Custer's arrogance caused him to vastly overestimate his own abilities and resources; he vastly underestimated the enemy, including their superior weapons, which were repeating rifles as opposed to the single shot rifles that Custer's men were equipped with. He was also unfamiliar with the rugged terrain his army had to pass through before they could engage the Native American warriors. Third, Custer was not focused on defeating the enemy, but was simply focused on trying to fortuitously prevent their escape. In this, he failed to recognize that his opponents were tenaciously spoiling for a fight, and had lured him into an ambush. Because he misread the situation and the enemy's intention, Custer split his command into three units, and attacked with only one of them. Fourth, Custer was out-managed. Very simply, he was done in by the superior military strategy of Sitting Bull, the leader of the Native American warriors, and Crazy Horse, Sitting Bull's highly capable field commander, both of whom lured Custer into battle on their timetable and in a place of their choosing

Because of these compounded errors of judgment, overestimating their strength of military might, and poor decisions, Custer took 210 underrequipped soldiers against one of the largest forces of Native American warriors (over 11,000 footmen) ever assembled in North America. Custer's defeat is still studied today as a model of how *not* to conduct a battle, especially when superior options are available, such as waiting for reinforcements. The consequences of his poor choices impacted his family and the families of the men who died with him for decades. This incident and many others like it exemplify how poor choices frequently lead to unnecessary suffering, pain, tragedy, and misfortune. Wrong life choices are a major part of the **root causes** of suffering, and often precipitate heavy repercussions with sometimes catastrophic or irreversible consequences.

The Effects of Decisions and Life Choices

Life is choices, not chances! Your life is the sum total of all your decision making and choices. Every one of your choices leads somewhere, either good or bad; they affect every area of your life. Undoubtedly, there will be times when some things from the outside may impact your life that you do not have direct control over. Some of the things that will happen to us in life are unpredictable and unexpected. However, we have all made uninformed decisions using creative rationale but inadequate information, resulting in incredulous, undesirable or even unimaginable outcomes. Wrong choices occur most often when you override your conscience and ignore the red warning flags that are clearly visible. Nevertheless, there will always be many choices that are within your sphere of control, and for which you must take personal responsibility. You must decide how you are going to live out your life. Are you here on the planet just to let the good times roll? Or have you decided to produce a quality life with lasting, spiritual fruit?

As I mentioned before, tragedies and human sufferings are a part of this fallen world. What choices will you embrace based upon the knowledge that suffering, pain, misfortune, injustices and, sometimes, rejection, are an unavoidable part of this earthly life? Trouble will seldom bypass you just because you hope and pray that it will. Trouble is everywhere! It's extremely hard to hide from it. Sometimes you can make the right decision, and things can still go terribly wrong; unexplainable, unpredictable events and circumstances can still show up. Oftentimes, these circumstances are just in the interim, and will change in the final analysis. If you have made the right decision, though you may suffer for a while, it will eventually turn out for your good and for God's glory, producing good final results. Be patient, not anxious; allow God to walk you through it. Pressure can often push you to the brink of hysteria. You need to understand that suffering and pain not only show your character, but more importantly, if you are wise, it will also develop your integrity. Trials and troubles show you who you are and what you are made of from the inside out.

On the flipside, you should never try to compound matters by creating your own crises through foolish and unwise decision making. We have all experienced some kind of misfortune or injustice in this life, but those of us who create extraneous troubles through unwise decisions cause unnecessary suffering and drama. There are few things more irresponsible than irrational and disingenuous decision making; living your life as a guessing-game. Far too often, wrong choices and poor judgment cause collateral damage to loved ones and others who had no part in those decisions, but who now are adversely affected or immobilized by them. We humans are created in the image of God, which means that we have moral freedom: the intrinsic free will to choose between good and evil, right and wrong, and blessing and cursing. God has made this explicitly clear in Deuteronomy 30:19:

> Today I have given you the choice between life and death, between blessings and curses. Now I call on heaven and earth to witness the choice you make. Oh, that you would choose life, so that you and your descendants might live! (NLT)

Doesn't it seem ironic to you that God foretells the outcomes of your choices and then informs you of what choice to make? Basically, there are only two different paths an individual can choose. On the one hand, there is life, good, and blessing; on the other hand, there is death, cursing, and perpetual suffering. Both options are potentialities in the hands of every individual. God makes it clear that His ability to choose for the individual does not figure into the equation; the choice of life or death is solely the responsibility of every individual.

God very plainly drives home the point that, in contrast to the permanent Word of God and eternity, everything in this natural human life, including our human existence, is transitory. The more proactive you become about limiting disruptive crises in your life, the more prepared you will be to implement wise strategies to your present way of living to help minimize avoidable crises in your future. The more you reverence the sanctity of life and execute purposeful actions in your *right now*, the more you will release yourself from obligations to things that will only serve as liabilities, depriving you of your future. Because nothing happens by chance, you make a conscious decision to refuse to be one of the **root causes** of bad things that happen to you. That decision will manifest itself in the way you choose for your future—next week, next month, and next year. It will manifest itself in a purposeful way in harmonizing with others. But it also will shine a glaring spotlight on deficiencies in your decisions, behaviors, and attitude; the challenge is for you to address them! As a believer, you must make sure that God's Word is the first and final authority in your life, and at the center of all your conscious decisions.

Conscientious decision-making is life-changing and future-shaping. There are the conscious decisions that make up a person's character. These are the waters we're swimming in. This is the good stuff, right here! These types of decisions are influenced by what you believe: your core beliefs, which reveal every facet of your character. By seeking proper wisdom in your decisions, you can proceed with courage and maintain a good attitude even when things don't go right, or as planned. These things are often revealed by your actions rather than by your words.

Many Christians with good intentions have adopted the same type of destructive mentality that the world's secular system lives by, and they act as though this earthy life is the immortal part of life. It certainly is not! In order to affect positive change in your life, you first must examine your thinking and upgrade your decision making and lifestyle choices. Your core beliefs are not measured in an assessment test or in who your closest friends are, but in the degree to which God's Word is the final authority in your life. Having God as your head means having His Word at the center of your consciousness, in where you spend your time, in what comes forth from your heart, in where you spend your money, in how you plan out your life, and the propensity in how you react to suffering, pain, misfortune, and hardship. Engaging in mischievous and foolish decision making will only heap a waiting harvest of destruction upon you and your family. Life comes complete with enough challenges and sufferings without creating more through mismanagement, flawed logic, faulty human reasoning, or blind ignorance. Don't get stuck on the suffering and pain of the past. Begin making better choices and rock-solid decisions today for your future. No! You will never arrest or block every bad thing that comes knocking at your door; however, knowing how to make solid decisions will have a tremendous positive and lasting impact on your life and greatly reduce future problems, sufferings, and hardships. You will not end up being totally dominated by the life circumstances of this world. Everybody gets only one-shot at living life.

10 Building Blocks for Making Solid Decisions and Life Choices

I have devoted most of the remainder of this chapter to the logistics involved with making solid and sound decisions. As you read through these profound, universal, building-block principles and life skills, consider seriously applying due diligence to implementing each principle into your everyday decisions and lifestyle choices. You will always be able to measure your quality of life by assessing what you need to do, observing the results of the steps taken, and reflecting thoughtfully on the outcome of your good and bad choices. Let's dive into a close-up examination of some of the most important, timeless, building-block principles for making quality, rock-solid decisions:

1. Let Your Inner Spiritual Compass Guide You.

The magnetic compass has been an invaluable navigational aid to humankind for centuries. Today it is an indispensable component for boats, ships, and aircraft; it is now even ubiquitous in automobiles, on smart phones, and other mobile devices. A compass, of course, consists of a free-swinging, magnetized needle in the center of a calibrated dial showing degrees of direction. The needle aligns itself with the Earth's magnetic field and always points to *true magnetic north.* However, *true magnetic north* is different from *true geographic north* (the North Pole). This difference poses little problem for those traveling hundreds and thousands of miles away. The closer one gets to these two poles, however, the more the difference between the two matters, until careful mathematical calculations must be made to adjust the compass to compensate, so that the ship or the plane can stay on course.

Just as magnetic compasses must be adjusted to compensate for the difference between *geographic north and true magnetic north* (which never changes), especially as one travels farther north, we must also adjust our lives to our *spiritual compasses,* our *"spiritual true north,"* the Word of God (which also

246

never changes). The Word of God and the gift of the indwelling Holy Spirit are the best things we Christians have going for us in life. Together they comprise our spiritual compass—the unshakeable foundation for making solid decisions and life choices. We must continually measure the *course* of our lives by the steady *compass* of God's unchanging, uncompromising, and unadulterated Word, or else we will inevitably stray off course and eventually end up somewhere we never intended to go. Tragically, many Christians have done this very thing and run aground on the *"junk-heap"* of erroneous beliefs and poor decisions, thereby wreaking havoc and residual destruction in their spiritual lives as well as in their natural lives. Being guided by our spiritual compass is not an automatic discipline; it is a matter of choice.

As Christians, we all have to make frequent *"course corrections"* in our lives, some big and some small, and we need the *spiritual compass* of God's Word to show us the way. More specifically, if you want to be able to make good and wise choices in your life consistently, then you must immerse yourself into spiritual things. Your intellect and reason alone will lead you astray; you must ask and trust the Lord to give you understanding through His Spirit. Read God's Word regularly—don't just read it—study it, and meditate on it; ask the Holy Spirit to reveal its meaning to you. Don't be afraid to avail yourself of written study aids prepared by others who have walked through life with the Bible as their *spiritual compass*. Couple your focus to immerse yourself in the Word with an equal focus on being led by the Spirit, and prayer. These are the *"needles"* of the *spiritual compass* in your life, by which the Spirit of God will show you the way to walk, and keep you on the correct path. For the believer in Christ, this is the path to take to ensure sound judgment, solid decisions, wise lifestyle choices, and a successful life journey. The psalmist said of God: "Your words are a flashlight to light the path ahead of me and keep me from stumbling" (Ps. 119:105 TLB).

2. Establish Strong Character.

It is said that Napoleon Bonaparte, the great French emperor and military leader, had a soldier in his army who was also named Napoleon. This lowly foot soldier, however, was very different from the general. He was cowardly; out of fear, he balked at doing almost anything he was told to do. In the face of intense battle and potential death, he would run away and hide at times. When brought before Bonaparte after one such disgraceful act, the general looked at him with disdain and said, "Either change your character or change your name."

Character always matters. It lies at the very core of who you are, and determines how you will respond to various scenarios and circumstances in life. Character is the moral code, the strengths or weaknesses, the inner qualities, and the traits that define a person—whether good or bad. Good character should be highly valued and sought after. Character is what you are made of, from the inside out. Character is who you are when no one else is observing you. Your reputation is what other people think about you, based only on what you allow them to see and know about you. Many people have established wonderful reputations and elicited the praise of others, but they exemplify poor character behind closed doors. Your character should match your reputation and outward image. You always have a choice in the type of character you choose to have. Abraham Lincoln said, "Character is like a tree and reputation like a shadow. The shadow is what we think of it; the tree is the real thing," and, "You may fool some of the people some of the time; you can even fool some of the people all the time; but you can't fool all of the people all the time." Yes, sir, and Amen!

The soldier named Napoleon lacked strong character, which was reflected in his cowardly behavior, phony disguise, frivolous rationalizing, and general untrustworthiness. Character can be faked, but not for long. It is easy to hide for a time our true self from others, while portraying an outward appearance of strong qualities. Sometimes we can even fool ourselves—until a crisis hits. Crisis reveals character—it never produces character. Difficulties and hardships bring out who we really are. People may say certain things with their mouths, but their hearts and actions eventually reveal the real story. The writer of Proverbs concludes the same, "People's words may be kind, but don't believe them, because their minds are full of evil thoughts" (Proverbs 26:25 NCV). In the face of ridicule, threat, imminent danger, or when everything you have—even your life itself—is at risk, suave façades fall; hypocritical posturing vacates, sophisticated masks melt, and all pretensions are stripped away so that the veracity of the inner self (good or bad) is on public display.

Shakespeare said of character, "This above all: to thine own self be true, and it must follow, as the night the day, thou canst not then be false to any man."

Crisis does not build character; it only reveals what is already there. When you're pushed to the brink and your back is up against the wall, your real character will automatically ooze out. For this reason, the time to deepen and develop your character is before crisis arrives. If you want to display strong character and integrity during tough times, then start cultivating them now. As in everything else, the Word of God will be immensely helpful in this area. The Word of God has a lot to say about character, including the blessings that come with good character and the consequences that result from poor judgment. Good character will help you show restraint under high-stress or pressure, rather than give way and allow your emotions, words, or your inflexible behavior to run rampant and lead you to an undesired consequence. The psalmist said: "Let integrity and uprightness preserve me, for I wait for You" (Ps. 25:21 NASB). A person's word is always the measure of their character.

All of the **character**-istics of solid character have their origin in Christ and are available to you through the Holy Spirit. You must pray to Him, and trust Him to build these qualities into your life. At the same time, you must be ready to work for the change you want to see in your own life. Decide now to do the personal and spiritual *"sweat equity"* needed to build and instill strong, solid character in your heart and mind, so you will be ready when the test comes. As you build and maintain your character, you must always be cognizant of the individuals you align yourself with. First Corinthians 15: 33 states very specifically, "Do not be fooled, 'bad companions ruin good character'" (TEV). Character is destiny!

3. Accept Responsibility for Your Actions.

Solid decision making begins and ends with accepting responsibility for all of your choices and actions—even the tough ones. One component of strong character is the willingness to own up to your mistakes and to accept full responsibility for yourself and your actions. Taking personal responsibility means doing what you know you should do because it is ethically, morally, or legally right, as well as making yourself accountable for your actions. People who are responsible seldom take on a victimization mentality or blame others for their mishaps; it's just the opposite. President Harry Truman famously had a sign on his desk in the Oval Office that said, "The buck stops here." He understood that great personal responsibility accompanied the Office of President, and that sign on his desk showed that he was willing to accept that responsibility. Blaming others or passing the buck for your own failures is not only dishonest, but it is also a sign of weakness and immaturity; immature people can't be trusted to make wise decisions or choices. That is why we don't let our young children make many of their own decisions, but instead decide for them, gradually allowing them to choose for themselves as they are able, growing into adulthood.

If you are experiencing ongoing difficulty and a barrage of trouble in your life because of poor decisions you have made and/or foolish actions you have taken, then understand that your conditions will never improve if you blame others for your mistakes. Refusing to acknowledge your own responsibility for your decisions is consequential. Blame-shifting has become the monolithic norm in our modernized culture. If life doesn't go the way you plan for it to go, or if you are unhappy, depressed, peeved, or angry, the *"blame-shifter's"* answer is to blame others for their own incredibly foolish and unwise decisions—always assuming it must be some else's fault. Accepting responsibility means you stop looking for an escape route for your poor habitual choices and stop demanding that someone owes you something in life. Defuse this kind of pretentious, arrogant, and bizarre thinking. If you regularly practice being lackadaisical and irresponsible, especially when the stakes are high, then it becomes much easier to seek to shift the blame. Your success, mental stability, and happiness are very seldom contingent upon the precipitous actions and behavior of others.

The first step in any recovery is recognizing that you have a problem, and that the person most responsible for the problem is you. Don't blame others. The blame game takes an exorbitant amount of focus and energy that otherwise could be harnessed for producing successful and positive results. Don't pass the buck. Don't change the touchy subject. Don't talk about someone else's *"problem"* in order to divert attention from your own. Man up! (or Woman up!) You control the power button every time you make a decision. You cannot grow beyond bad decisions for better ones and at the same time blame others for your mistakes and failures. This type of obnoxious behavior will only predispose you to residual injury and hardship. No one can change you except you, and you'll need God's assistance to do it. But the place you have to start is by standing up and saying, "*I'm responsible. It's no one's fault but my own.*" Once you can say that with all honesty and sincerity, you will have taken your first giant step toward recovery and promotion.

4. Seek Wisdom in Every Major Decision.

Many people value self-reliance as a cardinal virtue. Traditionally, the "*self-made person*" has been someone to be respected and admired. And, indeed, self-reliance is a good quality and an important asset to possess, but it only goes so far. Life is not and was never meant to be a go-at-it-alone proposition. Unbridled self-reliance easily breeds pride, which, unchecked, often leads to disaster. Pig-headed pride is incompatible with wisdom. Humility is wisdom's fertile soil. English poet William Cowper said, "Knowledge is proud that he has learned much; Wisdom is humble that he knows no more." None of us knows everything we need to know, and none of us can do everything we need or would like to do. To meet our goals and achieve our objectives, we need the support and help of other people. This includes our decision making and lifestyle choices. As the old axiom says: "No man is an island unto himself."

Most mundane, daily decisions we can make on our own, as well as some larger and more critical decisions, when we have the proper information and guidance. But we all need the benefit of godly wisdom and the collaborative effort of others in helping us make some of the major, potentially critical, or even life-altering decisions, especially in areas where we lack sufficient experience, knowledge, or expertise. Victory is often won in life where there is a multitude of advisors (see Prov. 11:14). If you suffer from health problems, you seek the wisdom of a qualified physician or healthcare professional to assist you in making the right decisions that will aid you in getting well. If your house needs major repairs, but you don't know which side of the hammer to hold, you would consult a competent carpenter or an expert in renovation, and restoration to help you decide what needs to be done and the best way to do it. Again, wisdom is the route you take when you don't know what to do or when you are unsure. God's Word is the first place to start and is always a safe guide to follow.

Proverbs 4:7 encourages us, "Getting wisdom is the wisest thing you can do! And whatever else you do, develop good judgment" (NLT). In other words, the perspective of wisdom is the starting point from which all wise decisions and choices are made first. This is so we don't have to keep repeating cycles of failures and mistakes, mismanagement of people and things, and/or starting all over from scratch after failing in repeated attempts to get something right. Wisdom is the principal element in making right choices and avoiding blind spots. You need not wait for an opportunity for wisdom to come to you. Seize the initiative. Seek wisdom first. It is readily available to those who proactively pursue it. Additionally, wisdom is the supreme crown jewel in any decision or undertaking. Every expenditure of one's time, energy, investment, and resources is worth the price when wisdom is the prize.

In contrast, the opposite of genuine wisdom is foolishness. Don't be a fool when it comes to life and the options you face. Benjamin Disraeli, nineteenth century English statesman and novelist, said, "The fool wonders, the wise man asks." Don't be afraid to ask for assistance. Don't depend impetuously on yourself alone when facing big decisions. Don't rely only on your own wisdom, knowledge, or understanding. Avail yourself of the wisdom and counsel readily available to you from different sources. Begin with prayer. You can't be a chit-chat-chatter-box, know-it-all, or thick-skulled kind of person and be filled with wisdom at the same time. Consult the Word of God, and ask Him to give you the wisdom to know what to do. He has promised to give supernatural wisdom "to all with simplicity and without reserve," to all who ask in faith (Jas. 1: 5–6 Wuest). Also seek the counsel of people whose track records and good judgment you trust and respect. And, where appropriate, seek the advice, prudent counsel, and assistance of godly and spiritual people, as well as trained, qualified, and experienced professionals. Yes, and Amen!

5. Live a Disciplined Life.

Pablo Casals, world-renowned Spanish cellist, was asked at the age of 81 why he continued to practice four to five hours a day. The great master replied, "Because I think I am making progress." He, like so many other musicians, artists, writers, athletes, and entrepreneurs, or anyone else who wants to be the best at what they do, recognized the indispensable role of discipline in the quest for success and achievement. Excellence in any endeavor requires discipline, but especially excellence and success in life. For solid decision making and sound choices to be effective, they need to always be accompanied by a disciplined life. Success will not come by accident; excellence cannot be obtained by osmosis. They are only acquired through consistent commitment and hard work.

One of the reasons so many people wrestle to instill discipline in their lives, and in the lives of their children, is the very fact that discipline is not easy. It never has been and never will be. Adding to the problem is the fact that ours is a society today where more and more people are developing an entitlement mentality; a mindset where they believe they should be given things that previous generations had to work to acquire.

It is human nature for us to appreciate and value most what we have worked hard for and achieved by fruit of our determination, the work of our hands, and the exercising of our minds, gifts, and abilities. At the same time, as fallen creatures corrupted by sin, we can easily succumb to the temptation to live off the labor and largess of others without bothering to try to pull our own weight or fulfill our personal responsibility, thereby depriving ourselves of the satisfaction and fruit of a disciplined life.

A mature Christian life is a disciplined life, and the disciplines involved relate to both the spiritual and natural realms. Spiritual disciplines, as well as natural disciplines are a part of a successful Christian journey. Discipline in the natural realm includes developing healthy and productive practices in every facet of life. This will take time and hard work, but the benefits of a disciplined life will be worth all the effort expended to achieve it. You can have the greatest intentions to make the right decisions in life, but that is not enough. You need to have more than just good ideas and good intentions in your heart and mind to do what's right. To make a quality decision, you have to be disciplined enough to get down to the nitty-gritty, set into motion your decisions, and act on them. Take stock of where you are now, and commit yourself to strengthen areas of discipline where you are weak. Once you start, don't give up, because the key is persistence. Persistence is the glue that makes discipline work.

Calvin Coolidge said, "Nothing succeeds like persistence." Persistence is at the heart of discipline. To be disciplined means doing what you need to do even when you don't want to, or don't feel like it; it means pressing ahead anyway even when you'd rather be doing anything else in the world than what you're currently doing. Establishing the habit of discipline builds into your life the powerful character quality of persistence, and persistence will lead you to success. Quality life decisions and choices can't stand the test of time without discipline.

Ironically, Mr. Murphy, a 69-year-old mid-town parking lot attendant, exemplifies the benefits of a disciplined life. Although he never made more than $14.00 an hour, by the end of his working career he had amassed a nest egg of more than $780,000. Mr. Murphy began working at the early age of 14. A short time later, he began educating himself on investing in the stock market, saving money from various odd jobs, and investing whenever he got the opportunity. A slow but steady, disciplined investor for over 50 years, Mr. Murphy made gigantic strides. He paid off his house, put five of his children through private universities and colleges, and traveled extensively around the world. Amazingly, Mr. Murphy didn't earn his high school diploma until his late 30s, having quit school around the sixth grade in order to assist his mother with family expenses. His dedication to a disciplined life of hard work, a willingness to learn new things, and a solid habit of saving and investing over the long haul brought him incredible success in his life endeavors. A disciplined life will do the same for you too. Successful people are self-disciplined people. The more you manage your life, the more you are able to accomplish in life. The discipline of hard work and perseverance always pays off in the end. Your quality of life and future depends on it!

6. Shaped by a Strong Value System.

Discipline, commitment, and persistence matter little in the long run if you are committed to the wrong things. Passionately wrong is still wrong. Persistence in error is still error. Right or wrong, your life and behavior are defined by the things you value. Everyone consciously or unconsciously lives by a value system. The values you live by will largely determine the choices you make, and the way you respond to the events and happenings in your life in any given circumstance. This will always be reflected in where you spend your time, gifts, and resources. Your quality of life will be decided by the value system you set in motion. If you want to consistently make good choices (spiritual as well as natural) and experience growth and success in your life, then you must make sure that you have embraced and are living sensibly by a system of values that are long-term, strong enough, and solid enough to take you where you want to go, and not just an outer-veneer and external trappings of having strong values and virtues.

So what values should you live by? Although there are many ways to answer that question, let me try to simplify it by breaking it down into three general categories: Faith, Family, and Fidelity. More specifically:

Faith. This means faith in God and in Christ as Savior and Lord. Faith is the starting point for any solid, strong system of values. It includes trust in the Bible as God's infallible Word, which is a completely reliable guide to life in all its aspects. Faith means having the Word of God resident inside your spirit, believing it, and then acting on it. Christianity is more than symbolism; it is a living faith in what God has spoken to be absolute truth. Audacious faith is at the core of the Christian life, and holds together our relationship with Christ, our church, our family, our communities, and what we believe. The virtue and value of faith play a vital role in all of your decision making and life choices. Faith is the bedrock virtue of the Christian witness. Faith is tantamount to the very thread that makes up the fabric of the Christian experience. Faith is the key that unlocks the door to overcome all of life's challenges and hardships. Solid decision making is impossible without active faith.

Family. A strong, faith-based value system encourages the development of healthy family relationships. The family unit is the most basic institution of society, that helps create and build strong communities. The nuclear family is the point of origin, where every individual's character, attitudes, behavior patterns, morals, ethics, beliefs, human relational standards, and norms are developed and shaped. The uncompromising Word of God is the foundational textbook for teaching a strong system of virtues and values. These virtues and values don't fluctuate, evolve, or eventually go out of style, nor become obsolete or outdated. Our methods for embracing them may change, but the virtues and values themselves are never volatile or visceral. If Judeo/Christian values and virtues are not rooted in the Word of God, then they are not Christian virtues or values at all.

Second only to your relationship with Christ, family should be your highest priority. Without a strong value system, relationships will often deteriorate and ultimately fail. The traditional nuclear family and traditional family values are under attack in America (and other parts of the world) as never before. Today, Christians are living under a constant barrage of secular values, and are far too often bombarded and challenged by images and messages of a radically opposing value system. Because of societal drift from biblical values, the abandonment of traditional marriage, rebellious children, teenage drugs, pregnancies, and suicides are on the rise. These pressing problems have been precipitated largely due to the absence and decay of strong family values and virtues. All of us who are followers of Christ need to be adamant, aggressive, and steadfast in standing for and modeling biblical family values and practices in everything we do. More expansively, family as a priority also includes our spiritual family, our fellow believers, and Christ-followers who we fellowship with in our churches on a regular basis. Even more broadly, we can also include our neighbors, who Jesus defined as anyone in need, and who we are in a position to help—people who are outside of our families (Luke 10:25–37).

Fidelity. In addition to a strong family, a strong value system facilitates the development of the essential character trait of fidelity. Fidelity means faithfulness—trustworthiness in word, deed, and life. Where faith is *what* you believe, fidelity is being *true* (faithful) to what you believe. Fidelity is being true to the Lord, living for Him, and serving Him alone. Fidelity is being true to your family—your spouse and your children. Fidelity is being true to your friends, your neighbors, your employers, and your fellow workers. Just as importantly, fidelity is being true to yourself by being brutally honest with yourself, as well as allowing God to shape you into the person He wants you to be. Fidelity is an ongoing virtue that is an unbreakable devotion of steadiness and commitment, placing other's self-interests and desires above your own. Fidelity promotes peace, healthy growth, and sanity in life.

Unfortunately, fidelity is fading fast in the minds of many today as a positive and essential value of life, and it is a test that, all too often, many simply don't pass. Today's postmodern social consciousness has been shaped by humanistic, psychological values and principles that encourage self-seeking, immoral, unethical, and even illegal behavior that disregards biblical virtues of any kind. This is not surprising, since postmodern thinking rejects the idea that morality, ethics, and personal behavior can be defined in any universal or absolute terms. Whatever is permitted by the culture is now regarded as morally acceptable. These immoral expressions in postmodern times are the primary systemic source of many social ills, such as suffering, pain, tragedy, and misfortune, which are intrinsically connected to an unhealthy and dysfunctional society.

All of these areas—faith, family, and fidelity—are characterized by the traits of honor, mercy, honesty, humility, integrity, purity, holiness, trustworthiness, fairness, tolerance, etc. These values are exemplified in what Jesus defined as the two greatest commandments, "Love God with your whole being, and love your neighbor as yourself" (Matt. 22:34–40). Paul was even more succinct in declaring, "The entire law is summed up in a single command: 'Love your neighbor as yourself'" (Gal. 5:14 NIV).

7. Allow Courage and Faith to Propel You Forward.

It takes courage to commit yourself to move forward from where you are—even if you don't like where you are—because moving forward means moving into unknown and uncertain territory, and that can be scary. It takes courage to make solid decisions and to stand your ground, to change course from a bad decision to a better one that will reshape your future. Courage is an inner braveness to stand against great opposition, suffering, danger, or hardship. It is to possess the strength, firmness, and unwavering determination of spirit to succeed or overcome in the face of extreme adversity with strong fortitude and resilience when pushed to the brink. Courage is not showing poor judgment or making rash decisions—abruptly jumping off a cliff hoping that things will turn out for the best. Anyone who possesses authentic courage is self-controlled, and is able to keep their spirit intact whenever they have been ostracized or threatened by opposing forces. Adverse situations always tempt us to quit or take the easy way out. Keep in mind, however, that what is unknown and uncertain to you (your future status and circumstances in life) is completely unveiled and perfectly clear to God, and He has your very best interests at heart. Confidence in this knowledge can give you the courage to move ahead even when you can't see the way yourself. Maya Angelou said, "One isn't necessarily born with courage, but one is born with potential. Without courage, we cannot practice any other virtue with consistency. We can't be kind, true, merciful, generous, or honest."

Courage is never the absence of fear. Courage is acknowledging your fears and going ahead anyway. Rick Stengel, who worked for two years with Nelson Mandela on his autobiography *Long Walk to Freedom*, shared this memory of the great man:

> In 1994, during the presidential-election campaign, Mandela got on a tiny propeller plane to fly down to the killing fields of Natal and give a speech to his Zulu supporters. I agreed to meet him at the airport, where we would continue our work after his speech. When the plane was 20 minutes from landing, one of its engines failed. Some on the plane began to panic. The only thing that calmed them was looking at Mandela, who quietly read his newspaper as if he were a commuter on his morning train to the office. The airport prepared for an emergency landing, and the pilot managed to land the plane safely. When Mandela and I got in the backseat of his bulletproof BMW that would take us to the rally, he turned to me and said, "Man, I was terrified up there!"

Mandela's courage in that scary situation was not in that he was unafraid —by his own admission, he was terrified—but in that he recognized that giving vent to his own fear would only make things worse for the other passengers, immensely feeding the growing panic. So, he tamped down his own fear, and his calm demeanor calmed and encouraged the others on the plane.

Strikingly, fear and courage are similar in the sense that they both involve energy. The difference comes in the result each produces. Fear will suck away your energy to act, and stifle you into paralysis. Courage, on the other hand, will channel that same energy into faith, and positive, productive action. Courage will propel you forward to do what you know you need to do even when your first impulse is to flee in fear. First John 2:28 points out, "And now, dear children, remain in fellowship with Christ so that when he returns, you will be full of courage and not shrink back from him in shame" (NLT).

Steadfast faith in God and immersing yourself in His Word and His love as a habitual practice will instill courage in you and drive out all fear. A little further in the same letter, John writes, "God is love, and all who live in love live in God, and God lives in them. And as we live in God, our love grows more perfect . . . Such love has no fear, because perfect love expels all fear" (1 Jn. 4:16–18 NLT). In making lasting decisions, courage is the ability to take brave steps forward by refusing to let fear and discouragement conquer your spirit. If you will have courage to stand by God's Word in making the right decisions in life, then God will stand by you—sailing you to victory.

8. Develop a Growth Mindset.

One of the basic realities of life is that, if you are not growing, then you are dying, or at the very least, you are stagnating. Although you reach the limit of your basic, physical growth once you reach adulthood, growth in every other area of your being—spiritual, emotional, intellectual, and psychological—should continue throughout your life. Learning to make quality decisions requires embracing a growth mindset, which involves the willingness to arbitrarily take on challenges, the flexibility to adapt to change, the strength to persevere through bitter waters and setbacks, the courage to shift one's paradigm when necessary, and a quickness to learn from past failures and mistakes. In fact, the ability to learn from our own failures and mistakes as well as others' is one of the most beneficial qualities of a growth mindset. A growth mindset carefully analyzes a situation, identifies the challenges, develops a plan for conquering those challenges, and then executes the plan. Afterwards, it evaluates the results to see what worked and what didn't, and make appropriate adjustments for the future. This is the way to build consistent success in effective problem-solving skills, visualizing every obstacle as an opportunity.

A fixed mindset, in contrast, rejects any efforts that foster growth. It is unwilling to adapt, resists change with rigidity, and supinely accepts the status-quo. The problem is that we live in a culture that is negatively focused in many ways, and that negativity has a way of draining hope and positive expectations right out of us, if we are not careful. Unfortunately, most people are not growing in their lives in any significant way, and their stagnated mindset can be contagious. More often than not, growth and development are not only byproducts of changes that take place within us, but they also come as the result of our taking advantage of potential opportunities on the outside that also foster our growth. It's not enough simply to recognize the potential of something to create positive change; we must draw up an action plan and then *act* on it.

Consequently, if you want to move forward in your ability to make wise choices and to deal with the challenges, struggles, and opportunities of life in a healthy and productive manner, then you must be determined to buck the norm, to rise above the mediocre, to pull yourself out of the clinging, suffocating clay of the rigid mindset around you, and position yourself on higher ground, and into a posture of growth. You need to decide early on to become a life-long learner, knowing that you seldom have all the answers up front. There is always room for adopting new strategies, embracing habits of assessing and reflecting, and facilitating continuous improvement. Be alert to the negative, stagnation-inducing stimuli around you in what you read, watch, or listen to on social media, and make some changes to expose yourself to things that promote your growth and development.

A growth mindset is much more than having bold, bombastic, flexible, and innovative ideas. Many people can be bold and flex in certain directions, only to flex back to their original state, eventually, and to their own detriment. A growth mindset has much more to do with changing and adapting to new paradigms, and being an open-minded learner, than it does with renovating older ones. It may seem very simple, but in reality, it's not. There has to be concentrated effort in fastidiously reinventing, rethinking, reworking, and replacing the old ways of thinking, and doing so in favor of new ideas and approaches that are more effective in meeting challenges and solving endemic problems. A lifelong learner is one who is able to learn new things, unlearn what's no longer relevant or beneficial, and relearn new concepts.

A top *Fortune 500* business executive reveals how a growth mindset has impacted his company and personal life. He says that without failure and the motivation to achieve, he would have never experienced dynamic growth opportunities in his professional and personal life. His business venture failures, a willingness to grow from them, and fine-tuning his unique capabilities made him a stronger executive, a stronger Christian, and an overall better father and husband. He lists five growth areas he learned from his failures and genuine ability to change:

1. *Failure automatically eliminates what will not work for you.*

2. *Failure often gives a needed boost to supply you with the energy, stamina and resilience to move forward.*

3. *Failure exposes others' challenges and hardships in similar areas that you didn't see before.*

4. *Failure gives credence to a heightened perspective on the authenticity of a quality life.*

5. *Failure helps orchestrate your future direction in areas of success and advancement.*

His failure became his instructor and motivator at the same time as he moved toward his goal. Failure was not the fixating obstacle hindering his success, but it was the very pathway to his success.

Paul the apostle affirmed the value of a positive growth mindset when he wrote, "I have not achieved it, but I focus on this one thing: Forgetting the past and looking forward to what lies ahead" (Phil. 3:13 NLT). Paul did not count himself to have grasped or achieved the pinnacle of life. But he carefully weighed the options that were under his consideration. A growth mindset and a clear focus in one's thinking and the follow through of one's actions are necessary to avoid the paralysis of a fixed mindset. Paul's past mistakes and failures were hindrances that threatened his efforts to move toward a better future. Paul's words illustrate clearly the success-oriented mindset required by athletes, inventors, students, businesspeople, Christian believers, or anyone else who has a goal that they passionately desire to reach.

9. Reaffirm the Right Direction.

As you move along life's journey, you must continually affirm and reaffirm that you have made the right decisions, and are headed in the right direction. All the zeal, effusive enthusiasm, and good intentions in the world won't mean anything if you are headed in the wrong direction. Affirmation is a declaration of agreeing with or consenting to a direction of assertion on a decision. When something is of good and sound judgment, it should be reinforced and affirmed. This is how you make a solid decision stick, forgoing whatever is pernicious, backwards, detrimental, or faulty. Every good choice and right decision may be challenged—as with any other choice. Just because a decision is challenged doesn't mean it is wrong. No matter what happens in life, if you continue to do the right thing, then it will pay off in the long run. You can't turn bad decisions into good ones unless you change course. It is impossible to choose a different outcome once the decision has been made. However, you can always analyze your bad decisions from the past to help you make better ones going forward. Your free will and occasions for decision making are with you every day, so you can always practice making good choices.

During the 1929 Rose Bowl football game between the University of California, Berkeley Golden Bears and the Georgia Tech Yellow Jackets, Roy Riegels, star center for the Golden Bears, recovered a fumble 30 yards from the goal line and began to run. While trying to evade a tackler, he got turned around, lost his bearings, and ran 69 yards in the wrong direction, finally being brought down at the 1-yard line of his own team's goal. The Golden Bears attempted to punt the ball away from their goal line, but the punt was blocked, thereby giving Georgia Tech a safety and a 2–0 lead. Georgia Tech went on to win the game 8–7. Riegel's error has been called the worst blunder in the history of college football, and earned him the nickname "Wrong Way" Riegels. Ironically, Riegels was an excellent athlete and ballplayer; he was even team captain. In fact, in the second half of that same Rose Bowl game, Riegels put in a stellar performance, even at one point blocking a Georgia Tech punt. The following year, he helped lead the Golden Bears to a 7–1–1 record.

There are a few *takeaways* we can learn from Roy Riegel's story. First, anybody can get turned around, get off track, and head in the wrong direction. It is foolish to think that just because you have made great decisions in the past, you are not susceptible to occasional slip-ups and wrong choices. Good judgment is when, having recognized that you have charted a wrong course, you correct it and change course. Second, no matter how far you go in the wrong direction, you can often turn around and recover from it, as long as you don't allow your mistake to define and paralyze you. Riegel's teammates didn't affirm his wrong direction; they disavowed it and tried immediately to help him turn it around, even though the team eventually lost the game. Third, every choice leads somewhere; nothing just happens. All choices have consequences. Even when we think we've made the right choices, we may find out down the road that they were the wrong choices.

So, what do you do if you are headed in the wrong direction in your spiritual life or in any other area of life? The first thing to do, once you become aware that you are off track, is to admit you're moving in the wrong direction. It's okay to acknowledge something was a mistake or a failure. This is the first step toward changing bad decisions into better ones. The second thing to do is to stop, turn around, and start moving in the right direction. Begin making solid decisions, and exercise good judgment.

But how do you know the right direction? As always, base your decisions on God's Word, and ask Him to affirm your choices when they are right. Proverbs 2:11 clearly teaches us, "Wise choices will watch over you. Understanding will keep you safe" (NLT). Being affirmed in your wise choices will help you immensely in withstanding the challenges and the wild curves of life, as well as help guard you against the potentiality of going in the wrong direction. God's protection becomes effective through consistent application of His Word. When you wonder which way to go, take your questions to the Word for the right answers. Trust in God's wisdom rather than your own, and He will show you which way to go. You can bank on it!

Even when you're headed in the right direction with the Lord, it is a healthy practice to periodically reaffirm your direction, to check your bearings, and to check your spiritual GPS to make sure you haven't gone off course. Because none of us are perfect, we all have to make occasional course corrections in our lives. This is a daily discipline in your lifestyle that is too important to ignore. "My son, listen, be wise, and keep your mind going in the right direction" (Prov. 23:19 GWT).

10. Maintain a Positive Attitude.

Your attitude is always a matter of your personal choice. Circumstances, people, or events in life do not choose your attitude. You do! A bona-fide, positive, and optimistic attitude is contagious; it will often breed enthusiasm and cause other positive things to attract themselves to you. Constantly thinking and speaking positive, faith-filled words with expectancy will help you build and maintain a positive outlook on life, no matter what's going on in your life. Faith is a positive force, but fear and its attendant, pessimistic spirit is a negative force. Whether you are a victim or a victor depends largely on your attitude. If you have a victim mentality, then your anemic thoughts, actions, and choices will reflect those of a victim. Most people who see themselves as victims have a vitriolic attitude with a chip on their shoulder; they pull all sorts of antics, huffing and puffing about how unfair life is, while many of them are actually victims of their own mistakes and failures. Many of these so-called victims become rhapsodically addicted to slipping and sliding into various forms of toxic negativity and paranoia; it's often like a repetitive ocean wave dashing against the beach's seashore. When you see yourself as a victim, you will allow others to victimize you and take advantage of you because, after all, you are a victim, and that is your lot in life. A victim mentality keeps you from success-oriented thinking because, as a victim, you believe that life and the world are against you. People with a victim mentality inexorably always expect things to go wrong, never achieving anything worthwhile or overcoming their handicaps and hardships. Life's trajectory always begins with attitude.

A victor mentality, on the other hand, sees handicaps and hardships as opportunities for growth, development and achievement. Victory-focused thinking goes hand-in-hand with a positive attitude toward life. Victory-minded thinkers dismiss all habitual, cynical, negative, and self-defeating thoughts from their minds. The caveat of possessing a positive attitude is that, when you think like a victor and not a victim, you will gregariously embrace the virtues of perseverance, hard work, determination, honesty, integrity, and excellence with enthusiasm. You will settle for nothing less than to exemplify these qualities in your life in ever-growing measure. Your winning attitude is what brings you triumph over hardships, with favorable end results. The apostle Paul described a positive attitude this way, "I can do all things through Christ who strengthens me" (Phil. 4:13 NKJV). Brian Tracy also said it best, "You can't always control what happens to you, but you can control your attitude toward what happens to you, and in that, you will be mastering change rather than allowing it to master you."

As you can see, each of these 10 *building blocks* for making solid decisions and life choices are distinct. Nevertheless, they are interrelated in many ways. There is an obvious connection between discipline, courage, a growth mindset, and a positive attitude; the fundamental grounding for these is found in your character, responsibilities, and the spiritual compass which is God's guidance through life. Learn to embrace each of these, and make them a part of your life. Depend on the Spirit of God to help you. The tedious growth process will be neither easy nor quick, but then nothing worthwhile in life ever is. Hang in there, keep going no matter what, and you will make it. As long as you don't quit, you will eventually succeed in making solid decisions and lifestyle choices.

Reflections on Making Rock-Solid Decisions and Lifestyle Choices

Whenever you don't follow through with good judgment and solid decision making, you rob yourself of your greatest potential, every worthy opportunity, the fullest blessings and benefits of God, and, eventually, your future. In the long run, your unresolved negative proclivities will only cause you further distress and anxiety without ever leading you to your desired results. In the end, all you will succeed in doing is damaging your most important relationships at the expense of unworthy and lesser things. Having to learn life's lessons the hard way means repeating monotonous, nostalgic cycles and patterns of failures despite the enormous amount of time, energy, and money wasted. Below I have selected five proven, healthy habits to help safeguard you against presumptuous actions and detrimental thinking patterns, and help you take the necessary steps for effective decision making.

1. **Learn to do the right thing from the start:** There is never a better time than now to start doing the right thing, no matter how long you have been doing the wrong thing. As long as you still draw breath, you still have time to change for the better. Mother Teresa said, "Yesterday is gone. Tomorrow has not yet come. We have only today. Let us begin." Your thoughts and actions today affect how your life will proceed tomorrow. Your life will always follow the dominant trajectory of your thinking and actions. As

Mahatma Gandhi observed, "The future depends on what you do today." So, don't delay. Start *today* to do the right thing.

God wants you to walk in the right way, and for you to succeed even more than you want to succeed. He will help you if you let Him. Start by taking inventory of your habitual thought patterns, actions, and responses to the different circumstances of your life. Don't expect God's grace to make up the difference; it certainly will not. God's grace is giving you the difference; take advantage of it! With a prayerful spirit, and with the Word of God as your guide, identify those habitual self-defeating thoughts, actions, and responses that are hurtful, harmful, and destructive. Then, consider how to substitute different thoughts, actions, and responses that will strengthen you and build you up in Christ, and greatly help you grow in Him and in your life in more positive ways. Consider this: Once you begin practicing this principle on a regular basis, it will lead you out of defeat and into new levels of victory. Don't allow the tendency of past failures to bind you to an apathetic and passive spirit—always resistant to change and insistent upon learning things the hard way. Don't waste time contemplating using the same old irrational and worn out excuses; start doing the right thing—right now, from where you are—it's never too late!

2. **Learn to say "NO":** Part of executing good judgment is adjusting your mindset to avoid bad choices by simply learning to say *NO*. It's a simple word, yes, but it's not always simple or easy to do, especially on a consistent basis, and especially when you are filled with trepidation for various reasons. You cannot exercise sound judgment and make solid decisions by glibly agreeing to every personal request or expressed desire of others.

Many people don't say no because they crave the praises, approval, and influences of other people. They end up sacrificing more important things (including relationships), to their own detriment. Their hunger for affirmation is so great that they will even knowingly make wrong decisions or engage in wrong behavior in order to get it. In so doing, they become masters of self-deception, inventing all sorts of creative justifications for their actions. Craving human approval and affirmation is always the wrong reason to say yes to something you know you shouldn't do. And, if you shouldn't do it, there *is* no good reason to say yes. Doing something bad in hopes of getting something good is the height of folly and self-deception, and it results in toxic messes, wasted lives, and unhealthy relationships, all chipping away at one's future potential, and often bringing financial ruin; this kind of thinking only leads to a cosmic amount of pain, disappointment, and disillusionment in the end.

As the saying goes, you will never be able to please all the people all the time. It's simply impossible. Learning to say *NO* goes back to the building blocks of discipline, courage, and a growth mindset that we discussed earlier. If you are caught up in an insidious vortex of bad habits that are dragging you down, holding you back, and stealing your future, then you need to build the discipline of saying *NO* to those things, and yes to better alternatives. A disciplined life will build enormous stamina and courage in you as you move forward to take the right steps. A growth mindset will develop healthy habits in you so you can avoid repeating destructive cycles that eventually lead to a complete fiasco. It is always easier to stay where you are than it is to change, even if staying where you are is uncomfortable. You probably are already keenly aware of your bad habits and other negatives in your life that you need to change. Think about those things, and then identify positive things you can replace them with. This is vitally important, because when you start saying *NO* to dubious options, critical attitudes, self-defeating thoughts, and neurotic behavior, you will be more successful if you can substitute them with positive thoughts of victory, and then take appropriate actions. Many don't link the consequences of their actions to their decision making and choices, but I can guarantee you, that bridge is there. Don't just say *NO* and let it rest with that; you're only asking for trouble. Make the necessary corrections and adjustments. Don't deny yourself something, even if it's bad, without something better to fill the gap. God has a victorious life planned for you!

3. **Guard your heart:** Proverbs 4:23 instructs, "Guard your heart, for it is the wellspring of life" (NIV). The natural heart is indispensable to life because it pumps and circulates the life-sustaining blood. If your heart is sick, your body will be sick; if your heart fails, your life will end. But in the Bible, the word *heart* also often refers to the inner core of your being, the

center of your thoughts and emotions, and who you are inside—in short, *your spirit*. So, this verse could just as correctly be stated as "Guard your spirit, for it is the wellspring of life."

Don't underestimate the insidious nature of negative and ungodly words or ideas, nor their propensity to corrupt you from the inside out. In Matthew 15:10–20, Jesus taught that it is not what comes from outside a person (food, drink, etc.) that corrupts, but it's what comes from inside (evil thoughts, murder, immorality, theft, lying, etc.). At the same time, you must guard your heart more closely against notorious negative and ungodly voices, ideas, bitter waters, and anything else that can stir up corrupting elements within you. Sin is a cancer that is always ready to metastasize with lightning speed at the slightest stimulation. The best way to guard your heart is to starve inappropriate thoughts and behaviors of those things that will prompt them to grow. You will become what you put into your spirit and mind. So be careful what you read, watch, or listen to, as well as of the people you hang around with. Fill your ears, eyes, and mind with good things, wholesome things, and godly things. Don't be anxious about anything, but pray about everything. "And the peace of God, which transcends all understanding, will guard your [heart] and your [mind] in Christ Jesus" (Phil. 4:7 NIV).

4. **Live with realistic expectations:** Too many people today live in a fantasy world—a *"pie-in-the-sky"* delusion by unrealistic expectations: winning the lottery, waiting for their grandiose ship to come in, achieving success without working for it and/or absent of infrastructure to hold it, and expecting their lives to change for the better while they continue in the same self-destructive patterns and self-defeating impulses that put them where they are in the first place. In the meantime, real life—and a potential life of great joy and satisfaction—passes them by without them ever knowing it. Benjamin Franklin said of expectations, "Our limited perspective, our hopes and fears become our measure of life, and when circumstances don't fit our ideas, they become our difficulties." Life swiftly moves on even when things don't always go according to our perfect plans. Real fulfillment and joy are not always wrapped in an extravagant

lifestyle, parading the outward signs of achievement, power, prestige, success, or having the "*big-bucks.*"

Many people desperately pursue an affluent life of luxury that is far above their means; all too often, burying themselves under a mountain of debt, exposing themselves to great suffering and hardship, and sentencing themselves to the bondage of spending the remainder of their lives doing damage control and trying to play catch-up. That's no way to live!

More than any other faith system in the world, Christianity is based solidly on a living faith and a living reality. It is based on a real God working with and relating to real people through real human history in a real world. As believers, your faith and hope are real. All of God's promises are Yes, and in Him, Amen (2 Cor. 1:20). But that does not mean that every promise or blessing from God will come to you without effort on your part. The promises of God don't fall on you like ripe cherries fall off a tree. I wish they did, but they do not. By all means, believing the promises of God means living in the faithful expectation that God will work His will and His plan in your life, because He will. But be prepared to practice the Word of God, follow the leading of His Spirit, and exercise faith and patience. Allow your faith to grow, and be built up over a period of time, because no one becomes a champion overnight. Growth is a dynamic process that involves being uncomfortable as well as experiencing pleasure, success as well as failure, and disappointment as well as satisfaction. Confidence in your glorious future should give you courage in your current struggles or circumstances as you work and wait with specific, realistic and pragmatic expectations—not wishful thinking, as God grows His purpose in and through you. Expect a bright future, stay focused on God's promises, and things will change in your favor.

5. **Manage your time and resources:** Time is one of the most precious commodities in life, yet one of the most flagrantly wasted. One of Satan's biggest deceptions is to convince us that we have all the time in the world, or at least more time than we really do. We don't. Our time and our resources both are limited. Once these commodities have been expended, it's impossible to get them back. Your physical life is on a timeclock. None

of us are promised tomorrow on this earth; all we have is today. That is why it is so important to learn to manage your time and resources well. Everyone on earth has the same amount of time each day—24 hours—but some people are more effective in life and achieve more than others because they have learned how to make the most of their time. And those who know how to manage their time usually know how to manage their lives and resources as well, because the general approach is similar for both: setting priorities and following through with a plan. God's design is that you excel, thrive, and not just survive.

Establishing sensible and realistic priorities with your time and your resources—and living by them—will allow you to concentrate on the most important things of life without getting out of balance and immobilized by overemphasizing secondary things. Don't get stuck in the same old rut repeating cycles of failures. *Buckle-down,* and align the various elements of your life according to purposeful priorities; avoid time-consuming, peevish distractions. A good way to begin is to use the three general categories of values we discussed earlier: faith, family, and fidelity. Some things in life are simply more important than others; nonessential things are not worthy of your valued time, resources, or attention. Stress the bigger ones, but lighten up on the rest.

12
MOVING FORWARD

"But here is the one thing I do. I forget what is behind me. I push hard toward what is ahead of me. I [move on] toward the goal to win the prize. God has appointed me to win it."

— Philippians 3:13–14 (NIRV)

"The future belongs to those who see possibilities before they become obvious."

— John Sculley

Moving Forward When Faced with Great Difficulties

ENTERTAINMENT ICON WALT DISNEY HAS HAD AN ENORMOUS impact on American culture and the world for more than three generations, but it might never have happened had he not persevered through multiple setbacks, that otherwise would have brought permanent failure. He began his career in humble means as a young animation artist, creating cartoon characters, designing special technical clips, and advertising business for magazines, newspapers, and movie theaters, for the modest salary of only $50 a month. One of his most popular and successful creations was Oswald, the Lucky Rabbit.

When Disney ventured out on his own and started his corporation in the 1920s, he lost the rights to a few of his most popular animated characters, including Oswald. As a result, he lost substantial revenue. Around that same time, the Great Depression hit the United States, and by the early 1930s, The Walt Disney Company was barely staying afloat and was constantly in danger of bankruptcy. The unrelenting hardships and monumental challenges he faced every day sorely tempted him to give up on his dreams, dissolve his struggling company, and go into another line of work. But he refused to quit. Fueled by a grand vision, and determined not to abandon his dreams, he made a firm decision to persevere no matter what.

In order to fund his ambitious project of the feature-length animated film *Snow White and the Seven Dwarfs,* Disney mortgaged his house and committed his modest earnings from earlier animated shorts, including Mickey Mouse. Little did he know at the time that the future of the Disney Corporation was wrapped up in these animated features and characters. The resounding success of *Snow White* began to turn Disney's financial fortunes around, but he still had a long way to go. By 1940, after the release of *Pinocchio*, Disney was over $4 million in debt.

He decided to diversify his production efforts, and this decision finally brought his company into solid profitability. He created films for international markets, wartime films for the government, television specials, and even sheet music through a subsidiary, The Walt Disney Music Company. Then, of course, there was Disneyland and, later, Walt Disney World. In the early days of diversification, however, Disney still found the need to cut expenses further, which he accomplished through the painful process of laying off more than 40 percent of his staff in 1946.

Because of his dogged determination and a firm belief in his vision, Walt Disney weathered relentless storms of adversity across many decades. Persevering against sometimes overwhelming odds and daunting setbacks, he eventually prevailed magnificently. At his death in 1966, his personal net worth was $5 billion. The company he founded has continued to grow and prosper in the years since his death, taking in $49 billion in revenue in 2014 alone. The company's net worth and assets could be estimated at well over half a trillion dollars—all from the vision of one man's dream. Many times during those early days he could have given up, but he didn't. Walt Disney was a man whose bold vision and confidence in what he had to offer compelled him to move forward against all challenges, disappointments, and obstacles.

How to Move Forward after Life's Setbacks and Hardships

Everything on earth and in the physical universe operates on a forward-moving time clock, and so should your life. No matter what setbacks you have suffered, what hardships you have borne, or what pain you have endured, you must decide whether or not to move forward. That is a decision only you can make. It is a personal choice. Moving forward in life after massive failure or debilitating misfortune is not always the easiest thing to do, but it is not optional if you desire to see an end to your present troubles. As I've said before, to stay where you are is easy. The first part of Isaac Newton's first law of motion, or the law of inertia, says that an object at rest will remain at rest unless acted on by an unbalanced force. In other words, all objects have the natural tendency to continue doing what they are doing; they resist changes in their state of motion. You will stay where you are unless some unbalanced force, external or internal, propels you to move. If you propel yourself to move rather than waiting for something or someone outside yourself to do it, you will have much more control over which direction you take and, therefore, where you end up. So, the choice is yours.

The way you respond to the challenges, disappointments, and the bitter taste that life can sometimes bring will determine whether you move ahead successfully to the next stages of life or stagnate where you are at present. Anything that stagnates degrades over time; it eventually dries up and dies. If you stop making progress in your spiritual and natural development after suffering bitter hardships or distressing reversals in life, you will not simply stop where you are and remain in a static state, but you will begin to degrade, to move backward, and to lose ground. Eventually, you will arrive at the end of the road of life, full of regret because you simply didn't embrace the mindset to move forward.

So, what can you do to prevent this? Following is a list of pertinent steps to take, and areas in your life that you must address in the face of challenges and setbacks before you can move forward successfully.

Moving Forward Means Pursuing Wholeness and Healing the Wounds, Pains, and Brokenness of the Past

Victor Alfsen said, "God can do wonders with a broken heart if you give him all the pieces." No one can mend a broken item better than the manufacturer. After all, who has more knowledge and understanding of how it is put together and how it operates than the one who designed and built it in the first place? No one is better than God in mending the human heart, because He **created** it. One of the reasons why God allows grievous suffering and hardship into our lives is because these things often realign our priorities. Because of our stubborn heart and lack of spiritual aptitude, we must be broken before He can do anything for us, in us, or through us. We must be forced to the end of our own resources, forced to recognize that we really don't have it *all together*, and forced to acknowledge that we need help from beyond ourselves. Yes, God can do wonders with your broken heart—or your broken life—but *you* must give him *all* the pieces. You have to pick up the debris of your life, hand it over to God, and say, "*I can't do anything with this. Please help me.*" And to do that takes courage, honesty, and humility. It also takes someone who knows where they are, someone who has been there and understands what it is like, and someone who can help us when we cannot help ourselves.

Fortunately for us, there is someone who can do this. His name is Jesus:

> So then, since we have a great High Priest who has entered heaven, Jesus the Son of God, let us hold firmly to what we believe. This High Priest of ours understands our weaknesses, for he faced all of the same testings we do, yet he did not sin. So let us come boldly to the throne of our gracious God. There we will receive his mercy, and we will find grace to help us when we need it most. (Heb. 4:14–16 NLT)

Jesus has been where you are, so He knows where you are. He knows what you are going through, and He cares. He strongly invites you to come boldly to Him, even in your brokenness—especially in your brokenness and He will heal you and restore you with His mercy and grace. And there is no limit to how often you can come to Him. Come whenever and as often as you need. Don't be afraid to come because you are broken; God specializes in broken people. In fact, He has never used any other kind. Our brokenness is essential to our usefulness to God.

Vance Havner said, "God uses broken things. It takes broken soil to produce a crop, broken clouds to give rain, broken grain to give bread, broken bread to give strength. It is the broken alabaster box that gives forth perfume. It is Peter, weeping bitterly, who returns to greater power than ever." It is a well-known fact that a broken bone, once healed, is strongest at the broken place. God does the same thing with broken lives. When you come to Him, bringing Him your brokenness for healing and restoration, He will make you stronger than you were before. He won't necessarily hide your scars or conceal your broken places, but He will make you more beautiful because of them.

Kintsugi, or *"golden joinery*," is "a Japanese art dating from the fifteenth century of repairing cracked or broken ceramics with pure gold which makes the broken pieces stronger and more beautiful than the original once they are repaired." Rather than trying to hide the cracks or broken places cosmetically, kintsugi deliberately highlights the damage by sealing the breaks and cracks with shining gold. Rather than flaws to be hidden away from view, the broken places become the aesthetic focal point. Most people would throw away a broken piece of ceramic as worthless. But the art of kintsugi salvages brokenness, and the golden-laced pieces, perfect in their imperfection, are more valuable than they were in their original, unbroken state. God is the Master kintsugi artist. Don't be afraid to give Him your brokenness. He will lace you with the precious gold of His grace, mercy, and presence to make you stronger, more beautiful, more valuable, and more useful than you have ever imagined.

Moving Forward Means Ending All Your Anger, Resentment, and Rage against God and Others

When it comes to living life in the face of suffering, pain, and misfortune, or any other life circumstance for that matter, you really only have two choices: to stay where you are and remain mean-spirted about life, bad breaks, and raw deals, or to grow and move forward. Another word for *staying where you are* is *paralysis*. You can stubbornly get so caught up in your pain, problems, sorrows, and other woes that you stop going anywhere at all in life. You find it extremely difficult to move forward, which puts you at risk of losing your faith and hope in God. You become paralyzed in mind and spirit, which means you stop growing. And when you stop growing, you start dying. *Stagnation* is another way to put it. As long as a stream is without external pollutants, the constant free-flowing movement of the current helps keep the water clean and pure. Any water that gets trapped in an eddy by the edge of the stream and stops flowing—when it gets out of the current and stops moving forward—stagnates very quickly, becoming stinking and discolored from impurities, and is awfully distasteful—even dangerous—to drink. The Dead Sea, near Jerusalem, receives a constant inflow of fresh water from the Jordan River, but since it has no outflow, only evaporation, the water in the Dead Sea is so alkaline, with salt and other minerals, that nothing can live in it. In the same way, if you allow your trials and sufferings to paralyze you, you too will stagnate like the Dead Sea. Moving forward is the only viable option.

Concretely, one advantage of moving forward is that the more you progress beyond your trials, hardships, and suffering, the more you will begin to see God working out in your life the purposes, pursuits, and blessings He had in store all along, but which could come your way only through the strengthening and maturing process of suffering. The measure of your character is always revealed, for good or bad, by the adversities in your life more than by the good times, when things have gone well. Your life is like a great canvas, with God as the Master Artist. The farther along you go, the more you will see His masterpiece plan in your life taking shape. No matter what you have been through, no matter what mistakes you have made, no matter how badly you may have messed up, and no matter how much pain external sources not of your making and beyond your control may have inflicted on you, God is committed to restoring you to your full beauty and glory. Like the experts who spent 20 years restoring Leonardo's *The Last Supper* to its original splendor, God is fully able to clean up all the dirt, grunge, pollution, and bad patch jobs that have made your life so vividly painful. And He is committed to do just that. Once you begin to see more of what He has in store for you—the wonders and greatness that He is preparing you for—all your anger, resentment, and rage will fade away, until they are only distant memories that no longer have any power over you.

But you still have to keep moving forward. Standing still because of your pain, anger, resentment, irrational hatred, or vindictive rage only allows these things to fester and become brackish and putrid, like water stuck in an eddy by the riverbank. Ecclesiastes 7:9 says, "Do not be eager in your heart to be angry, for anger resides in the bosom of fools" (NASB). You may have a legitimate reason to be intensely angry or even bitterly resentful because of suffering or disappointments in your life, but harboring a deep-seated, fretful, and irrational disposition is dangerous, and mainly characteristic of fools who know nothing but to continue repeating self-defeating behavior that only exacerbates suffering and tragedy. Fools always learn things the hard way. Don't let the small and insignificant things of life become the humongous uncontrollable stuff. It's perfectly okay to let some things go for your own sanity and mental health. Allowing anger, resentment, depression or rage to exasperate you will force you to spend the best years of your life agitated, frustrated, nervous, stressed, annoyed, and fatigued about things you are unable to change. The way to restoration and growth is always forward. Let the past be the past. Step forward in eager anticipation of the great destiny that awaits you; it is the destiny God planned for you long before you were born. No doubt about it!

Moving Forward Means Accepting, Knowing, and Resting in God's Eternal Love

Author Tim Hansel, in his book *You Gotta Keep Dancin,* tells of the day he and his son Zackery were exploring in the countryside, climbing and hiking some high peak bluffs and range cliffs. Suddenly, Tim heard his son yell from above, "Hey Dad! Catch me!" As Tim looked upward, he was surprised to see his son Zac already in mid-air, having just jumped joyfully off a rock cliff. Instantaneously, Tim imitated the most agile of acrobatic performers and managed to catch Zac. The force of Zac's falling weight hitting his father caused both of them to slam to the ground. Stunned by his son's circus stunt and their sudden impact with the ground, it took Tim several seconds to catch his breath.

"Zac!" he gasped in exasperation when he was finally able to speak, "Can you give me one good reason why you did that?"

Zac responded with remarkable certainty and calmness. "Sure! Because you're my Dad."

Zac's whole rationale for suddenly jumping off that cliff was his confident, trusting certainty in his father's love, and his unquestioned confidence that his father would catch him. Zac was fearless in life because he rested in the secure knowledge that he could trust his father. In a similar way, moving forward in life means you have accepted God's love in greater dimension, and that you trust Him implicitly and completely to "*catch*" you no matter what.

One of the greatest indicators that we have moved forward from our hardships and sufferings is that we are resting in God's eternal love. Whenever you are experiencing hardship or are afflicted with suffering, it is easy to conclude that you are alone in your pain. God seems far away. He may even appear deaf to your prayers and cries for help and, in the depths of your sorrow and despair, you may begin to doubt that He loves you. After all, if God really loves you, why doesn't He answer? Why doesn't He come to your relief? Why doesn't He rescue you?

These are perfectly natural questions when you are in pain, and life seems to make no sense. It is in times like these, most of all, that you need to remember one rock-solid, unchangeable truth: *God loves you!* You are infinitely precious to Him, and nothing will ever change that. Whenever you begin to doubt God's love for you, just look at the cross, where Jesus died for you in the ultimate expression of self-giving love. God proved His love for you once and for all at Calvary. His redemptive, restorative love for you should be a settled matter in your heart. God is eternal, and so is His love, because God *is* love (1 Jn. 4:8). God is unchanging, and so is His love, because God *is* love. In simple terms, God loves you *forever!* Nothing you have done in the past and nothing you may do in the future will ever change that fact. God will never love you any more than He loves you right now, because He already loves you perfectly, fully, and infinitely.

God's eternal love is the anchor that holds our lives, our relationships, and our whole being together. Without knowledge or confidence in God's love, life quickly falls apart at the seams. Whenever the tough places in life hit (and they certainly will), the anchor of God's love secures everything in one place so nothing drifts away. Before Hurricane Sandy in 2012 cut a swath of death, destruction, and severe flooding from Jamaica to Cuba to the Bahamas, and up the entire Eastern Seaboard of the United States, everyone in its rugged path had plenty of advance warning to prepare for it. Meteorologists identified the storm quickly, and accurately predicted its path days in advance. And although it was the deadliest and most destructive hurricane of that season, advance warning and preparation helped prevent its consequences from being even worse.

Oftentimes we can foresee the storms of life on the horizon. God never told us to run, hide, and hope for the best. No, He has told us to trust Him, believe His Word, and rest in His love. Many of the residents on the Eastern Seaboard anchored down or otherwise secured their property and possessions in the face of the approaching storm. Otherwise, their property would have drifted away with the sand, and possibly become hazardous debris propelled by the violent vortex of wind. When the storm hit, anything that was not anchored down was blown away. Likewise, when the storms of life hit, we, as children of God, must anchor our faith on the firm foundation of the Word and the love of God, who is our strength, hope, and peace. Resting in God's love is healthy medicine for our wellbeing. Those who have personally experienced and accepted the love of God grow steadfast in their faith (1 Jn. 4:16).

If you're still having trouble believing that God loves you unconditionally and completely, perhaps the apostle Paul's inspired words will convince you. For the child of God who chooses to walk and remain in His love— there never has to be any separation. From God's standpoint, He's already set you up to win in spite of whatever happens. In very succinct terms, he makes it clear that God's love for us is completely unconditional:

> *The one who loves us gives us an overwhelming victory in all these dif-*
> *ficulties. I am convinced that nothing can ever separate us from God's*
> *love which Christ Jesus our Lord shows us. We can't be separated by*
> *death or life, by angels or rulers, by anything in the present or anything*
> *in the future, by forces or powers in the world above or in the world*
> *below, or by anything else in creation. (Rom. 8:37–39 GWT)*

Did you catch that? Don't miss it! God loves you so much that He has already given you overwhelming victory! You have to first become convinced, as Paul was, and then decide to trust Him and remain in His love. God will never walk away, even if you decide too. You choose! It's up to you to rest in His eternal love. Know it. Embrace it. Rest in it. Yes, sir!

Moving Forward Means Changing Course from
Wrong Decisions and Bad Choices to Better Ones

Changing course from bad life decisions to good ones is not always simple, because it is very easy to fall into a pattern of bad habits that is hard to break out of. Sometimes, nothing short of a major life crisis is needed to immediately wake us up and propel us into changing our ways for the better. There's nothing quite like a life or death emergency to give us crystal clarity about what is truly important and what is not when life hangs in the balance. When the captain of a ship in arctic waters spots an iceberg dead ahead, he does not ignore it and continue on his current course—that would be disastrous! Instead, he changes course to avoid the iceberg, thus he ensuring the safety of his ship and everyone on board.

How would your life change if you received a terminal medical diagnosis? What if a doctor gave you only six months to live? What effect would that reality have on your priorities? On your behavior? On your plans and dreams for the future? On your relationships with family and friends? What would you give your attention to during those six months, and what would you ignore? Every decision we make every day, good or bad, affects our future to some degree, either short-term or long-term. How would your life change if you suddenly received a reprieve from death? What if your terminal diagnosis was wrong, or you were healed as a result of your trust in God's promises? Would you return to life as it was before, or would you maintain the life changes you had made because you knew they had made your life better? It is never too late to change the course of your life and do the right thing. While you may suffer unpleasant, temporal consequences for your bad judgment and poor decisions, even as a Christian, God always rewards obedience in one way or another. So, regardless of your problematic circumstances or mind-boggling issues, regardless of how far away from God you have turned, or how long you have been gone, your future is not already etched in stone. You can still change your ways or direction and begin to live according to God's will, principles, and commands.

In ancient times, King Hezekiah was one of the best and godliest kings of Judah (the Southern Kingdom of the Israelites). Scripture describes Hezekiah as one with wholehearted devotion who "did *what was* right in the sight of the

LORD, according to all that his father David had done" (2 Ki. 18:3 NKJV), so that none who came before him or after him were like him. He faithfully followed the Lord and obeyed His commandments. Yet even this godly man and king faced two major crises, and his response to them had a significant impact on his life and the lives of the Israelites.

The first crisis occurred when Hezekiah's kingdom was invaded by the cruel, arrogant, and aggressive kingdom of Assyria to the north, who regarded the Israelites as inferior. Faced with the ominous threat of conquest by a kingdom that was stronger militarily than his own, Hezekiah prayed to God, and God gave them a miraculous deliverance, killing 185,000 soldiers in the Assyrian camp during the night. This disaster forced the proud king of Assyria to return home in disgrace, where he was later assassinated by two of his own sons. You can read this amazing story in 2 Kings 18–19 (with a parallel account found in Isa. 36–37).

Hezekiah's second crisis was more personal. Sometime after Judah's deliverance from Assyria, Hezekiah fell deathly ill; he was so ill, in fact, that God sent the prophet Isaiah to the king to tell him that he was going to die, and to set his affairs in order (2 Ki. 20:1). Once again, Hezekiah responded with prayer, "Remember, O LORD, how I have always been faithful to you and have served you single-mindedly, always doing what pleases you'" (2 Ki. 20:3 NLT). Despite his faith, Hezekiah broke down in bitter weeping over his plight. Perhaps, underneath the words of his prayer, was the unspoken complaint: Is this what I get for years of faithful obedience—death by sickness? Even faithful and godly people are still human and sometimes prone to weak or unworthy thoughts or words, especially during a crisis. Nevertheless, God responded favorably to Hezekiah's faith and faithfulness, despite his human weakness. He sent Isaiah, the prophet, back to the king with these words: "I have heard your prayer and seen your tears. I will heal you. . . . I will add [15] years to your life, and I will rescue you and this city from the king of Assyria." (2 Ki. 20:5–6 NLT) His request was promptly granted. When Hezekiah humanly asked for a sign of assurance of his healing and extended lifespan, God caused the shadow on the sundial to move backwards 10 degrees (2 Ki. 20:8–11).

During much of his reign, Hezekiah had faced danger and ominous threats from implacable enemies, the Assyrians in particular. After his close call with death, his healing, and throughout his extended lifespan of 15 additional years, however, Hezekiah's reign was peaceful and victorious. There were no more threats to his kingdom that he had to deal with. Through Isaiah, God revealed to Hezekiah that, after his death, the kingdom of Judah would be defeated and carried into exile by the Babylonians. But Hezekiah had peace and rest during the remainder of his life.

Ironically, it was Hezekiah's son, Manasseh, who succeeded him on the throne and who clinched the disaster that was going to befall Judah. Manasseh was 12 years old when he took the throne, which means he was born during the additional 15 years of life that God gave to Hezekiah. Scripture reveals that Manasseh changed course for the worse, not the better, and ended up as the most evil and godless of all Israel's kings, in the northern and southern kingdoms—even worse than Ahab. Although God eventually judged the people of Judah for their repeated idolatry, wickedness, and faithlessness, it was the singularly evil and idolatrous reign of Manasseh that locked in God's judgment on the nation as inevitable. Not even the godly and reforming reign of Manasseh's son and successor, Josiah, could forestall it. The Bible even says that, late in his reign, Manasseh himself repented to God of all his evil, and God forgave him—but Judah's judgment remained certain. It's never too late to turn from bad choices to better ones.

God has both the power and the will to turn any circumstance, no matter how bad or negative, for His purpose, and bring good out of even the most devastating or catastrophic situations. So be encouraged! There is nothing bad or foolish that you have done that God cannot turn around and bring a blessing out of it, if you will simply humble yourself, change the course of your life from frantic, insecure thinking and poor decisions, and start moving forward in a positive direction; ask and allow God to lead you in establishing healthy habits and a lifestyle that honors Him. Life is usually not unalterable if we will change direction from wrong to right. Proverbs 4:26–27 says, "Take heed to the path of your feet, then all your ways will be sure. Do not swerve to the right or to the left; turn your foot away from evil" (RSV). Changing your mind and your choices in this way will have a powerful and positive impact on your life for growth and restoration that will also bless the lives of those around you and set you up for a future of great benefit, fruitfulness, and purpose in God's grand design.

Moving Forward Means Embracing an Optimistic Attitude and a Positive Perspective about Life and the Future

Les Brown is widely regarded as one of the world's leading motivational speakers. An acknowledged authority on achievement, success, and leadership, he has spoken worldwide before audiences as large as 80,000. Considering his long and storied career as one of the world's foremost experts on achievement, Brown's humble beginnings make his success story even more remarkable. Born in an abandoned building in Liberty City, FL in 1945, at six weeks of age, he was adopted by an unmarried cafeteria cook. He began his life in abject poverty, received a poor education, and witnessed constant depression and hopelessness everywhere he turned. Life wasn't easy for Les in any sense. But from an early age, he adopted a contagious, positive, and optimistic spirit that nurtured a mindset of possibility thinking, which convinced him that his future could be much better than his past and present. As an elementary school student, he was mistakenly labeled as "educable mentally retarded." Throughout his early adulthood and into his formative careers, Brown continued to believe in himself and do his very best. Through determination, persistence, and a firm belief that he could achieve more, Brown evolved into a one-of-a-kind personality who has impacted the world through his multi-million dollar company, which he built on positive leadership concepts for promoting and developing optimism in business.

A positive, confident, and optimistic attitude begins first with generating enthusiasm within yourself to move your sense of eagerness and interest in the right direction. How do you see the glass of life—half empty or half full? Robert Schuller said, "Most of us think that enthusiasm is the result of circumstances around us. But enthusiasm is that which you consciously choose to generate from within yourself regardless of circumstances." Proverbs 23:7 says, "For as he thinks in his heart, so is he" (NKJV). In other words, your heart condition determines your mental position, growth, and posture for restoration. You are (or become) what you think. Attitude is everything. In fact, someone has said that *"your attitude determines your altitude."* You can only fly as high in life as you believe you can. Suffering and hardship can keep you grounded for life if you allow a *"stinkin'-thinkin'"* attitude to become embedded in your mind. You can soar to the heights, however, if you keep your trials and troubles in perspective and learn to use them as stepping-stones to help you grow and courageously move forward instead of building a monument to your failure. Some people get so beaten down by the adversities of life that they quit trying. They simply give up. They cease any further attempts to move forward or to improve their circumstances, because they have convinced themselves that it is useless —because they fear more pain, or even worse, failure. The old axiom is true that says, "Nothing ventured, nothing gained." Those who never dare to try—and possibly fail—never accomplish anything. In fact, the only true failures in this world are those who never try or who give up trying. Even failure can be an advancement or progress toward victory and discovery. Remember Thomas Edison, who said that his failures taught him thousands of ways how *not* to make a lightbulb. He kept trying and eventually succeeded.

Bethany grew up in a family that loved the water. She and her brothers took up surfing at a young age, and by the time Bethany was in her teens, she was already winning awards for surfing, and was regarded as an up-and-coming champion of the sport. Then the day came when a shark attacked her while she was surfing, and bit off her left arm just below the shoulder—terribly disfiguring her body. Weeks of therapy and physical recovery followed. But there were psychological and emotional traumas as well. She struggled with depression, anxiety, suicidal thoughts and many unanswered questions of why this unimageable bad thing had happened to her. She could have given up and concluded that life was no longer worth living and that her surfing pursuits were over, along with her bright dreams for the future. Her strong, audacious faith and the support of her family members sustained her, however. With the Holy Spirit's help, Bethany determined to make the best of her situation and be optimistic about the future, and to look on the positive side of life after her accident. Having the support of her family and friends, she returned to surfing and excelled once more, proving that her disability was no hindrance to success. In addition, thousands of people have been encouraged and strengthened in their own struggles and problems by the story of her life.

Ultimately, there is nothing that you, as a child of God, cannot do in the will of God if you rely on His power through the Holy Spirit. No matter where you are in life, and no matter what has happened to you along the way, if you are a child of God, there is no reason—and no excuse—for you to slip into and wallow in negativity and pessimism. God has destined you for success, and even your trials and sufferings serve to prepare you and bring you into that destiny. Don't blow things out of proportion, but keep all things in proper perspective. With the work of Holy Spirit in your life, you have everything going for you, because God is going to complete what he began in your life—if you allow Him to do it. As Andrena Sawyer encourages us, "God restores. Completely! That's our Blessed assurance."

Philippians 4:13 says, "I can do all things through Christ who strengthens me" (NKJV). In context, Paul is talking about having learned to be content in whatever circumstances he finds himself. What this verse means is that, no matter what the circumstances, whether good or bad, that God allows into your life, He can and will empower you to prosper and overcome in the midst of and even in spite of them. In commenting on this verse, Israelmore Ayivor said, "I can do ALL THINGS through Christ who empowers, enriches, equips, enlightens, energizes, recreates, revives, promotes, strengthens, purifies, sponsors, and prepares me! Yes, I can . . . ALL THINGS, I can!" Anything that God wills for you to do—ANYTHING—you can do because He will enable you. Nothing will stop Him from working good in your life so that you can fulfill the purpose, plan, and destiny He has for you. Again, Ayivor said, "God is willing! God will save! God will rescue! God will restore! God will revive! God will empower! God is willing and He will do it!" He's waiting on you to believe His Word.

Reflections on How to Move Forward in Life after Extreme Challenges

Moving forward in life is about making a quality decision to step-up to the plate, and place yourself in a posture to bat again in life, regardless of your past hardships and adversities. Cutting right to the chase, if you put into practice this five-step process, then it can assist in helping you to move forward from life's challenges and setbacks.

1. **Commit yourself to the challenge of becoming a lifelong learner.** Truth be told, times change, seasons change, people change, and so do circumstances; you have to be ready to change with them if you don't want to

get left behind. Don't be afraid to learn new things; increase your ability to learn and relearn. Nurture your creativity to learn new and innovative things. Moving forward means giving methodical thought to your past heartbreak experiences, taking the knowledge of the past to relearn and recalibrate from the negative aspects of life in order to develop a new direction, and concentrating and focusing on shaping the future for achieving your goals. Your past failures don't have to equal your future. Exercise your mind by reading on new subjects and rejuvenating your thinking with new information. Take advantage of training and other educational opportunities that come your way. Learn to think of yourself as an astute, perpetual student, always searching, always curious, and always eager to learn something new. At the same time, be practical in your approach to new things, build your spiritual life, and develop other things that will help you become more successful in your life, family, career, and other areas of interest. Most importantly, put God's Word first in your life. One thing is for certain: The more you forge ahead to learn and know about conquering life's adversities and monopolizing on life's realities, the better equipped you will be at making wise decisions in every facet of life. Resilience and strength are the keys to bravely learning and moving forward from life's daunting challenges and inescapable disappointments. Decide immediately to become, and a lifelong learner, a better listener, no matter what you encounter along life's journey. Never stop learning!

2. **Seize the opportunity as part of your Christian walk to learn and know God's Word so you can better hear His voice.** The only way to get to know a person is to spend time with that person. It is the same way with God. You can't expect to hear God's voice or know Him in close fellowship unless you spend time talking to Him and listening to Him. The best way to condition yourself to hear God's voice is to commit yourself to learning God's Word by spending time every day reading the Bible, listening to your pastor, meditating on its meaning, and praying for the Spirit's enlightenment. God's Word is the place where you learn to build your spirit to know the voice of God. The more you take in God's Word by making it relevant, the more you will begin to think like God, and see life and the world from His perspective. There is a satisfying life of fulfillment after failure and misfortune. As your heart beats more in rhythm with

His, and the more your mind aligns with His, the more you will hear His voice and the more you will recognize Him speaking in ways you never saw before. God's way is the best kind of thinking and learning you can develop. It will take a lifetime to know God's ways, but it is never too late to start. So, start now.

3. **Identify your past failures and mistakes and learn from them.** If you simply try to forget or ignore your past failures rather than learning from them, then you will likely end up repeating them to your own detriment and demise. Failure can be a great teacher if you have a teachable spirit, are willing to accept instruction, and a willingness to grow and develop. Don't allow pride or shame over your past to prevent you from examining your mistakes and failures in order to learn why they happened. Identify the lessons in your past mistakes, and learn from them. Uproot the negative seeds of the past, and stop trying to please everyone all the time—it's just impossible. A critical juncture in moving forward is understanding why you failed, and then applying that knowledge. This will be of immeasurable benefit in helping you avoid the same failure in the future. God's grace is always available to give you the strength and the help you need to avoid the sticky spots of repeated failures, mistakes, and unhealthy cycles, as well as to establish a sense of well-being in you. However, it will never excuse any unscrupulous behavior, poor decisions, or refusal to make corrections. Once you learn those lessons you need to learn, then you will be able to move on to better and bigger things in life.

Many people are looking for the get-rich-quick or happy-go-lucky life without any discipline, discretion, restraints, or responsibilities; however, it doesn't exist; it's an illusion. The first step toward change is to acknowledge the problem, with a sincere desire for change and growth. Begin living your life in a way that reflects God's wisdom, grace, and empowerment for change. Make declarations that you have the supernatural strength and wisdom of God to succeed in life. Expect things in life to change for the better. God's hand of blessing is ready to move on your predicament, if you can stay in a mindset of faith and expectancy. Do you want things in life to change for the better? As the old axiom goes, "If you want something you've never had, then you've got to do something you've never done before." You'll be amazed at the new doors of opportunity that will come open for you. It's all up to you!

4. **Develop a strategy for the vision of life that you would like to see materialize for your future.** When you are in the midst of suffering or hardship, it is difficult to think about anything else. The inescapable reality of your pain and inward misery banishes all other considerations. But, as painful as your adversities may be, they are only temporary and eventually will pass. Then what? Unless you know where you want to go in life, and have a plan for getting there, you will remain stuck where you are, like a sitting duck that's waiting for more trouble. You can't reach your destination in life if you don't know where you're going, and you can't know where you're going without a vision. I'm not talking about a mystical trance, but a personal dream or vision for the future. What do you want to do with your life? Where do you want to go personally, educationally, professionally, and spiritually? What dream has God etched in your heart? What possibilities for your life has He enabled you to see? For every exit in life opens new doors into fresh opportunities. A dream gives hope to aspirations, hope gives strength to endure and to vanquish all obstacles, and a vision gives momentum to make gigantic strides in pursuit of your dreams. Don't ever give up hope, and never quit trying to make your dreams become reality.

Ask Yourself: Where do I want to be in 1 year? 2 years? 5? 10? Or even 20? If your dream has become dulled by the difficulties or perplexities of life, ask God to revive it, rekindle it, and infuse your heart and mind with new energy and enthusiasm for pursuing it. If you don't have a dream, ask God to give you one. Ask Him to show you where He wants you to go, and how He wants you to get there. He may not give you all the intricate details upfront, but He will give you enough to get you going and following Him by faith. Many people attempt to begin a new direction, but fail due to a lack of follow-through. Always remember that life is fragile and not always fair, but it can also be purposeful and meaningful. Life isn't a 100-yard sprint, but it is a marathon. Things will not always work out exactly as planned in your mind, but they will work; so, expect them to work in your favor. Never give attention to the provocations of naysayers and haters;

it's a waste of your energy and time. Take their misguided criticism and cynicism with a grain of salt, and keep moving ahead. Certain aspects of your plan will probably change along the way, which is perfectly normal, but having a plan, acting on it, and making necessary adjustments along the way means that you are moving forward rather than standing still, and that's where you want to be—enjoying life to its fullest at every season.

5. **Use positive affirmations to initiate your path forward and lay a foundation for your future growth and success.** Don't be fooled; the devil plays dirty. He's a trickster. He'll knock you down and kick you while you're down. He'll gnaw, scratch, and curse you from every angle to steal your joy, pulverize your peace, shatter your confidence, and smother you in guilt and shame like a burial shroud. Unless you know how to counter his onslaught, and know your rights in Christ, he can stop you in your tracks before you've taken a single step to move forward, and then keep you there.

If you want to overcome Satan's vicious attacks and insinuations, you must learn not to be timid, and proactively counterattack. Don't budge or give the devil any ground in your life. Not one bit! Whenever he slams you with inferiority, feelings of inadequacy or condemnatory thoughts, and tries to make you become disenchanted and disillusioned, use your faith to pounce on that rascal! Don't allow him to snatch your zest and zeal for life by getting you upset and bent out of shape over the little bitty stuff in life. Let me assure you up front: Positive thinking and affirmations are not magic; they're not new age philosophies or feel-good remedies, but are part of having a positive attitude for maintaining an optimistic spirit. Courageously fight back by speaking and filling your mind and heart with positive affirmations from God's Word about yourself and the love God has toward you because of His great grace. Begin to visualize and make positive affirmations daily: *"Today is going to be a great day." "I will successfully handle whatever comes my way—with God's help." "It's a good thing to be alive and well." "No weapon that is formed against me will prosper." "God is on my side and He is helping me working out the difficulties of life." "I expect good things to happen to me." "My life will not fall apart, and things are getting better."* Life is worth living. Believe you are the blessed of God, and speak what God says is yours, and who you are in Christ. Before you ever achieve anything worthwhile in life, you must first begin seeing yourself as successful. Keep your vision fixed and set on the promises of God. Life may be unfair, but God will always have the last say-so in your situation. Remember that God has a victorious and a unique plan for your life, no matter what you have gone through. Positive thoughts and spoken faith-filled words will always lead you out of defeat and into victory.

As the anonymous axiom says, "The things that you have cried about yesterday and today, you will laugh and rejoice about tomorrow." Yes, sir, and Amen!

Summary

WHENEVER CRISES OF VARIOUS KINDS—SUFFERING, PAIN, tragedy, misfortune, or death, whether it is sudden, unexplainable, or even premature—strike innocent and righteous people, it challenges our faith in God—that He is a **Good God**, that He really cares, and that He is an all-wise, all-powerful being who is concerned about the affairs of humanity. How could a perfectly good, loving, intelligent, omnipotent, and omniscient being allow such egregious evil, suffering, and human misery to touch His creation, especially those He lovingly created in His own image? This is the age-old conundrum of understanding why evil exists.

Sometimes, particularly horrific instances of evil or misfortune have caused even some devout Christians to turn their hearts from God in befuddlement, bitterness, and disillusionment, wrestling with and ultimately blaming Him for inflicting such *unfair* and *vindictive* pain and suffering upon them or upon the ones they love. Many nonbelievers today, if they think of God at all, view Him as the *"big-bad monster,"* and the control freak who uses humans as pawns for His every capricious whim. The problem with this argument is that we, as finite humans, have limited information and, worse, refuse to acknowledge that we are part of the pressing problem of evil itself. No! Life is not always fair, but God is and will always remain eternally good.

God's providential intent is that His children have the best that this life can offer in this fallen, broken, stained, and cursed earthly realm. Even so, God doesn't always stop every bad thing from happening to us, but trusts that we will keep faith in Him and His Word to eventually bring salvation, restoration, and healing, no matter how extreme the adversity or prolonged the suffering may be. For us, it is not a matter of if, but when things will go wrong. No matter how much we try to avoid it, sooner or later we all run into some level of misfortune, pain, or suffering in this life.

Satan works extremely hard to destroy the faith of the children of light in their heavenly Father, but his power is limited as far as what he can and cannot do. Yes, the devil comes to steal, kill, and destroy our quality of life and existence as believers while here on earth, but Christ came to give abundant life, to counteract humanity's sin, and to restrain the devil's free will and destroy his evil works. God is both just and righteous; He is the perfect Judge of right and wrong. He is a holy, sovereign God who is concerned with the smallest details of our lives. Trusting God under the pressure of adversity and suffering is much harder than when things are going well. True faith—persevering, overcoming faith—is more than just words we speak. It is more than simply declaring, "*In God we trust.*"

Invariably, we must remember that God is more powerful than Satan and all the other evil forces present in our world. For reasons we cannot fathom (but should trust His wisdom and righteous character), God allows the devil, demons, and evil a limited amount of space, time, and freedom to act in our world, but it's only for a season. God has not yet revealed the role that the continuing presence of evil and suffering in our world plays in His overall redemptive plan for humanity and all of creation, and whenever He does so, that's His prerogative alone. In the meantime, our part, especially as believers, is to do the best we can in an evil, fallen world to consistently make good, moral decisions, work to minimize evil and Satan's influence, strive to remain sensitive to the presence of God around us, and give priority to living righteous and godly lives here on this planet.

Unequivocally, God's decreed-will is that we live in this world and fulfill our purpose without the world's godless influence and decay destroying us prematurely, but that's up to us. Hardships, trials, adverse sufferings, and temptations are an inescapable reality, but they also play a part in our spiritual development as well. It is true that in this world we often suffer for our own mistakes and failures; we reap the consequences of our poor decisions and foolish actions. Yet even our very worst behavior cannot overpower God's mercy, love, and grace when He intervenes. All of us know of some people who got what they rightfully deserved, and others who did not, at least in this life. God is gracious and merciful, but He is also just, and justice will ultimately prevail and be served on everyone who has ever walked this planet when He ushers in the final judgment of all things.

Because God is a righteous Judge, He will someday render a complete, final, and eternal judgment on all who practice evil. This will mean the complete demise of Satan and his demonic kingdom, along with all humans who have served his cause, whether knowingly or unknowingly, and have rejected God's grace and the Lordship of Jesus Christ for their eternal salvation (Eccl. 12:14; Rev. 20:11–15). God doesn't always judge or fix everything at every interval in the span of time. He has left the resolution of some things for the future judgment and age of His eternal reign. Just because justice hasn't been served on all evil and sin yet, and they haven't been totally eradicated, does not mean that they won't be in the future. One day soon, God will usher in His complete and thorough remedy, fashioned in eternal ages past to be revealed at His chosen moment. Pay day is on its way!

Speculatively, atheists, agnostics, and other skeptics alike are often *haters of God*, disingenuous, deceiving themselves with blinders, always following intoxicating human logic, and oscillating between not believing anything at all to demanding that God show all of His cards up front, and repeatedly challenging His justice and fairness. God doesn't work that way. God is God—He's calling the shots! He doesn't cater to people's demands, fascinations, and whims. It is important to remember that the grace and love of God has appeared to all humanity, and He has brought salvation and redemption to all who will receive it. He brings His grace to everyone, although no one deserves it and no one can ever merit it. And that means all of us, without exception. But His grace ultimately abounds only to those who will freely respond and receive it, and for those who remain in Him. Make no mistake: Grace will never cover those who deny, walk away from, and reject God's redemption plan and salvation.

Our faith in God holds us until the day we come face to face with Him and receive full, concrete disclosures of what the sufferings in this world really meant (Rom. 8:18–19). The devil and the kingdom of darkness are certainly partly responsible for the suffering, evil, pain, and misfortune in this world. And some of the responsibility is ours as well. Remember, God gave us free will, and allows us to exercise it, even though some of our choices are not in our own best interests or the best interests of others. We, not God, are responsible for every choice we make. We can't expect God to always rewrite our past to rectify every experience that was unfair to us. When He does, it is because He chooses to do so. We must ask God to help us accept those things that can't be changed and embrace change for the things that we can change. He is an expert at working out painful and difficult things for our good and our future.

Finally, we may never in this life have all the answers to our questions about why good people suffer bad things—especially righteous believers. But we can shut the door, diminish the devil's effects, and deny him many opportunities to take advantage of us in our lives simply by living under God's divine, limited umbrella of protection through the new covenant that He has provided, by doing the right thing, and by choosing to make good and wise decisions. Taking our God-given responsibility and allowing the power of God to be manifested in us, through us, and for us is the beginning of God dismantling the works of evil, and limiting as much as possible evil and suffering for us while we live in this broken world.

Why do good people suffer bad things? Here are 10 illuminating, solid principles for life on earth that I would like you to take away from what you have read in this book:

1. **God's goodness and grace will prevail.** The nature of God is goodness. God is light, and there is no darkness or evil in Him at all (1 Jn. 1:5). He is the author of life, not death, evil, or destruction. Everything that emanates from Him is good. God is the eternal source of all goodness, mercy, compassion, redemption, grace, and perfection. God's saving grace, found only in Christ Jesus, is an extension of His goodness that is available to the whole world. However, the salvation of Jesus Christ is conditional, and human free-will plays a vital part in its acceptance or rejection without any external or internal control. God's grace is His remedy, and eternal solution for saving us from our sins; it eventually brings us into His everlasting kingdom, preserves us from the present evil that is in the world, as well as safeguards us from the wrath that is yet to come.

2. **Evil in the earth is real and powerful.** Not everything that happens in this hostile world is an endorsement or expression of God's will. The earth has been infected by the curse resulting from the fall of humanity, which also gives

Satan ample opportunities to inject even more sin, evil, destruction, pain, and suffering into the world. We humans are quick to express our moral outrage and utter astonishment at the lawlessness, evil, and suffering in the earth while at the same time we are obstinately resistant to recognizing our own personal sins, rebellion, disobedience, and misbehavior or the sins of others that contribute to them. There is no such thing as random fate. Everything that exists is the cumulative result of cause and effect to some degree and at some level. The devil, sin, suffering, and evil are no illusions, but are stark and sobering realities.

3. Faith and trust in God is the key to victory and fulfillment in life, both now and forever. Trusting God in every facet of life should be at the core of every Christian's belief system. Trusting God means that you will not always have all the answers up front, and maybe not even at all in this earthly life. Christians are to hold on to their faith, and trust God and His Word. But at the end of the day, you trust that God knows what He is doing and that it is in your best interest to trust Him, whether or not you understand it right now. Apart from faith and trust in God, there really are no ultimate or conclusive answers to all the questions regarding evil, suffering, and the meaning of life, only continual pondering and systematizing. Indeed, outside of Jesus Christ, there is no hope of salvation and eternal life in the presence of God beyond the grave; there is only the prospect of eternal and infinite separation from His presence, accompanied by unending torment and suffering on a celestial scale. If we believe that there is a God and an eternal everlasting kingdom, then salvation in Jesus Christ and peace with God is certainly the most important truth to know and experience in this mortal life.

4. The ultimate judgment of the devil, evil, and all ungodliness is certain to happen eventually. There is a final judgment and restoration of all things that is still to come. There are many things that we cannot see or know now that one day will be revealed as to *"why."* Questions of the ages will finally be answered. All things that are hidden will eventually come to light in the future, on a day that God has reserved to Himself alone. Despite all the unspeakable evil and wickedness that pervades the earth today, God is yet sovereign, and firmly in control over all human life, the course of history, and the universe.

The day is coming when God will bring into judgment the deeds of the righteous and faithful, then give their due rewards, as well as judge the deeds of the evil and wicked, then pass their eternal sentencing and punishment (Rom. 2:5–11). God will one day in the future make things right for all the evil, suffering, pain, misfortune, and tragedy that happens in the earth. The certain future judgment of the wicked should give us all the more reason to follow God's commands today. All of the secret acts, hidden things, and unanswered questions, whether good or bad, will be revealed in the course of time, and we shall all see it together. The final judgment is when God will make all things right and known through His Son, Jesus Christ.

5. **God has placed limits on the proliferation of evil in the earth.** While the curse is enforced in the earth, God has ordained times, seasons, boundaries, and limits to evil, destruction, suffering, pain, and misfortune, including restrictions on Satan's power and influence. Like humans, Satan has limitations. God, on the other hand, has no limitations; He is infinite and uncontained in every characteristic. God never evolves or changes; He just *is*. That is very difficult for the finite mind to conceive. It should also be understood that not all pain and suffering are beneficial to the human experience. God's sovereignty limits evil and Satan from achieving the total destruction of the earth and the annihilation of all life, especially human life.

God is neither limited nor diminished because of His choices. Some people observe God's apparent lack of response to the world's troubles and conclude that He is limited in power. This viewpoint ignores human responsibility. God has never withdrawn humanity's role of intervention, choices, and stewardship (responsibility) in the earth. With his limited freedom, Satan dazzlingly arrogates the hearts and minds of sinful people to aid him in his arduous quest to commit as much damage as he can to God's creation. While God has given limited information about the purpose of evil and suffering in the earth with regard to His ultimate plan, He has given us so much more on how to limit its influence in our lives.

6. **There are "unknowns" or secrets of time, that God has withheld from this world and will reveal them only in eternity.** Humanity has received many *"knowns"* as gifts from God. When it comes to many of our questions,

particularly the *"why"* questions—the deepest, puzzling perplexities of life—God sometimes reveals the full answer, a partial answer, or no answer at all. Who can fully know and understand what God is doing in the world? God mostly has remained silent on the origin and the workings of evil. It is obvious that humanity does not possess all knowledge. If we did, we would have no unanswered questions. God possesses unlimited wisdom and knowledge that abounds within Himself. Why God chooses to reveal some things and conceal others is hidden within His sovereign will. We humans must be content to let God be God and reveal or conceal as He chooses (Deut. 29:29; Job 21:22; Rom. 11:33–35).

7. **Purposeful Christianity actively dismantles and fights against the kingdom of darkness and evil in this present world.** As Christians, we have a moral duty and responsibility to help limit the liability of evil, suffering, pain, and misfortune in our personal lives and the lives of others through the knowledge of Jesus Christ and the Word of God by, yielding to the law of love and by exercising obedience and self-restraint, all through the work and power of the Holy Spirit. Christian responsibility goes a long way in minimizing bad things. God stands willing and ready to help us in our fight of faith and survival in suffering. In modern times, society has moved away from personal responsibility. Christian responsibilities in taking precautions and God's Word guarantee some level of shield and protection against the evil forces that permeate the earth realm with the sole purpose of wreaking havoc and destroying humanity.

8. **Human freedom necessitates the existence of choices.** The freedom of choice (decision-making-power) can't exist without both good and evil coexisting. You cannot have the freedom of choice without having the option to choose evil or good. We humans are made in the image and likeness of God in that we possess both a will to choose and an eternal spirit. All humans possess the capacity and ability to freely reject righteousness (good) and accept evil, or to spurn evil and embrace righteousness. Every act of evil, suffering, pain, misfortune, and tragedy can be traced back to some human decision influenced by Satan. God does not stop humans from choosing, but He allows them to learn from their mistakes and failures, thus reorienting their priorities. Bad choices can often be great lessons. The existence of evil on earth is

inextricably tied to the decision of the original man, Adam, whose sin opened the floodgates to perpetual suffering and evil in the earth.

9. Nature is under a curse because of the fall of humanity. When Adam sinned, a curse fell upon the ground and, to a greater extent, the earth itself. Not only is the ground cursed, but the apostle Paul calls Satan the *"Prince of the Power of the Air"*; air is the atmosphere. Satan's influence is apparent in chaotic, natural disasters such as tornados, earthquakes, hurricanes, tsunamis, floods, droughts, severe heat or cold, and other violent aberrations of nature that are not in and of themselves morally evil. We often call these weather or climate events *"acts of God"* which is factually inaccurate. In the original state, everything that God created was good and in proper order; the atmosphere acted as a covering and protection against the elements. Adam's rebellion produced adverse consequences (Gen. 3:17). This is never an act of God. It is the curse that is in the earth that lies behind much of the destruction that emanates from natural disasters. Although God's breathtaking beauty, character, creativity, and awesomeness can be seen in nature, the curse nevertheless runs rampant throughout the whole earth because of humankind's wretched sin and Satan's influence. Humans today are still contributing to the curse in the earth to an even greater degree by poisoning and abusing the environment. All creation lives in a state of frustration, and groans for the day of deliverance from its bondage (Rom. 8:20–22).

10. Identifying the *Root Causes* of suffering and evil in the world is important in learning how to mitigate its influences and minimize its effects in one's personal life and the lives of others, as much as possible. Everyone suffers at some point in life; however, because each of us is different, our environment, backgrounds, and opportunities may set us apart. The conclusion to our particular suffering may often very, even if external circumstances appear similar, our outcomes may be totally different. While it would be impossible to name all the various specific types, reasons, and degrees of suffering that people consciously experience we can nevertheless, categorize all suffering into one or more of three fundamental *root causes:*

A. **The sin of Adam and Eve in the Garden of Eden resulted in the fall of humanity**. Their single act of disobedience to God started a cascade effect of disaster that has echoed and amplified throughout human history. It corrupted their bodies, minds, and character; it brought down the curse that God permitted to come upon the land. The physical earth, nature in all its forms, is still reeling from the effect. Adam's sin also opened the door of opportunity for Satan to flood the world with his evil, wickedness, catastrophic disasters of every kind, and seductive influence, which leads to the further corruption of humanity—a direct result of Satan's onslaught. In short, the disobedience of Adam and Eve became the primary *root cause* of all the enormity of human suffering in the world—past, present, and future.

B. **The demonic free will and influence of Satan throughout this fallen world is currently under his sway, power, and dominion.** This is the secondary *root cause* and origin of why so much evil and suffering pervade our world. Satan is aggressively proactive in capitalizing on our fallen human nature, and on a natural world that is severely out of order to further his dastardly designs to destroy as much of God's creation as possible, especially the humans that are recreated in His image. Satan hates God with every fiber of his being, and therefore hates with equal passion all those who bear His image and His name. He passes up no opportunity within his powerful, though limited, authority to inflict as much evil and to perpetrate as many circumstances, intensifying sorrow, pain, suffering, tragedy and misfortune upon as many people as he possibly can.

C. **Humanity's free will, in its fallen state, continually leads to poor decisions, and engagement in wrongful behavior.** In other words, humanity's wrong choices are the tertiary fundamental *root cause* of human suffering and pain in this world. Our universal, God-given human capacity of free will to make conscious, deliberate choices is directly connected to the origin and *root causes* of all human suffering and evil. Some of our troubles and suffering are directly related to our actions, while other circumstances are indirectly related, but all are a part of the *root causes* of our suffering. Scripture bears this out. Human history and the Bible provide many clear and precise examples of the cause and effect of actions and responsibility, along with the dangerous consequences of irresponsibility. Wrong choices often precipitate heavy repercussions that are sometimes reversible and repairable, but they also sometimes carry paralyzing or disabling, and final or fatal consequences.

These are the three fundamental reasons *why good people suffer bad things.*

Notes

Introduction:

"Challenger Explosion," History.com, http://www.history.com/topics / challenger-disaster (accessed April 12, 2014).

"Biography: Christa McAuliffe," Biography.com, https://www.biography.com /people/christa-mcauliffe-9390406 (accessed April 12, 2014).

Chapter 1: Life is Fragile

Aaron Peckham, *Urban Dictionary* (Kansas City, MO: Andrews McMeel Publishing, LLC, 2012).

Neil Gaiman, *The Graveyard Book* (New York: HarperCollins Publishers, 2008).

"A Duke University Study: Peace of Mind," http://www. Bible.org/illustration /duke-university-study/ (accessed May 2, 2015).

Lavaille Lavette, 86,400: *Manage Your Purpose to Make Every Second of Each Day Count* (Nashville: Faith Words, 2011).

Chapter 2: The Fall of Humanity

David Breese, *Living for Eternity: Eight Imperatives from Second Peter* (Chicago: Moody Press, 1988), 99.

The Boy Who Lost His Boat (Wheaton, IL: Good News Publishers, 2002).

Matt Carter and Halim Suh, *Creation Unraveled: The Gospel According to Genesis* (Austin: The Austin Stone Community Church, 2011; published by Lifeway Press, Nashville, TN), 10.

C. S. Lewis, *Miracles* (San Francisco: Harper, a division of Harper Collins Publishers, Inc., Harper Collins edition 21001; Copyright 1947, C. S. Lewis Pte. Ltd. Copyright renewed 1974), 198.

Mark Water, *The Bible and Science Made Easy* (Peabody, MA: Hendrickson, 2000).

Ibid.

Warren Wiersbe, *The Strategy of Satan* (Carol Stream, IL: Tyndale House Publishers, 1979).

Chapter 3: God's Goodness

C. S. Lewis, *Christian Reflections* (Grand Rapids, MI: Wm. B. Eerdmans Publishing Company, © THE EXECUTORS OF THE ESTATE OF C. S. LEWIS, 1967. Renewed 1995 by C. S. Lewis Pte Ltd.), 80.

Lee Strobel, "*Why Does God Allow Tragedy and Suffering?*" www.biblegateway.com/blog/2012/07/why-does-god-allow-tragedy-and-suffering (accessed February 16, 2015).

Maya Angelou, *Letter to My Daughter* (New York: Random House, 2008), xii.

George Washington Carver, "*How to Search for Truth,*" a letter to Hubert W. Pelt, February 20, 1930.

John W. Wenham, *The Enigma of Evil: Can We Believe in the Goodness of God?* (Grand Rapids, MI: Zondervan, 1985).

Ibid.

Norman Geisler, *God, Evil, and Dispensations* (Chicago, IL: Moody Press, 1982).

Martin H. Manser, *Dictionary of Bible Themes* (London: Martin Manser, 2009).

Matthew G. Easton, *Easton's Bible Dictionary* (New York: Harper & Brothers, 1893).

Spiros Zodhiates, *The Complete Word Study New Testament* (Chattanooga: AMG Publishers, 2000).

Chapter 4: God's Sovereignty vs. Human Choice

William Peterson, *How to Be a Saint While Lying Flat on Your Back* (Grand Rapids, MI: Zondervan, 1974).

Witherington daughter dies story: http://www.christianitytoday.com/ct /2012 /april/when-a-daughter-dies.html?start=1/ (accessed June 5, 2017).

Alan Cairns, *Dictionary of Theological Terms*, (Greenville, SC: Ambassador Emerald International, 2002), 314.

Millard J. Erickson, *The Concise Dictionary of Christian Theology* (Wheaton, IL: Crossway Books, 2001), 80.

A. W. Tozer, *The Knowledge of the Holy* (San Francisco, CA: Harper Collins, 1961).

Martin Luther, *The Bondage of the Will.*

Philip Yancy, *The Question That Never Goes Away* (Grand Rapids, MI: Zondervan, 2013).

C. S. Lewis, *The Case for Christianity* (New York: Touchstone, 1996), 42.

Thomas H. Huxley, from an address on university education, Baltimore, MD, September 12, 1876.

Chapter 5: The Life and Times of Job

Nyomi Graef, "Inspirational People Who Triumphed Over Tough Times: Matt Golinski Looks to the Future after Immense Loss," Extrahappiness.

com April 28, 2013 http://extrahappiness.com/happiness/?p=6006. (accessed August 27, 2015).

Helen Keller, "Hellen Keller Quotes," BrainyQuote.com, Xplore Inc, 2017, https://www.brainyquote.com/quotes/quotes/h/helenkelle109208.html/ (accessed August 27, 2015).

J. E. Smith, *The Wisdom Literature and Psalms*, (Joplin, MO: College Press Publishing Company, 1996).

Ibid.

Chapter 6: Life Lessons from The Book of Job

Nelson Mandela, "Biography of Nelson Mandela," Nelsonmandela.org, https://www.nelsonmandela.org/content/page/biography. (accessed August 29, 2016).

Nelson Mandela, *Long Walk To Freedom: The Autobiography Of Nelson Mandela* (Boston, New York, London: Little, Brown and Company, 1994).

Spiros Zodhiates, *The Complete Word Study Old Testament,* (Chattanooga: AMG Publishers, 2000).

Paul W. Powell, *When the Hurt Won't Go Away* (Wheaton, IL: Victor Books, 1986).

Ibid.

William D. Mounce, *Mounce's Complete Expository Dictionary of Old and New Testaments Words*, (Grand Rapids: Zondervan, 2006), 566.

Nosson Scherman, *Tanach* (Brooklyn, New York: Mesorah Publications, LTD, 2012).

Chapter 7: Restoration

"Early Restoration of Leonardo's Last Supper," Bibliotecapleyades.net, https://www.bibliotecapleyades.net /davi/project/restoration.htm (accessed October 13, 2015).

Scot McKnight, *A Community Called Atonement* (Nashville: Abingdon Press, 2007).

Candy Arrington, *"Pruning with Purpose,"* © 2014. www1.cbn.com/devotions/ pruning-purpose. (accessed November 13, 2015).

Ibid.

C. S. Lewis, *The Problem of Pain* (New York: Harper One, an imprint of Harper Collins Publishers, ©1940, restored 1996, C. S. Lewis Pte. Ltd.), 91.

Chapter 8: The Impact of Open Doors

Timothy Keller, *Walking with God through Pain and Suffering* (New York: Dutton, 2013), 47.

Thomas Newberry, *Interlinear Literal Translation of the Greek New Testament* (Bellingham, WA: Heaven Word Inc. 2004).

Kenneth S. Wuest, *Wuest's Word Studies from the Greek New Testament: For English Reader* (Grand Rapids, MI: Eerdmans, 1997).

Chapter 9: Responsibilities of the Christian Life

Al & Laura Ries, *The 22 Immutable Laws of Branding* (New York: HarperCollins, 2002).

John Henry Thayer, *Thayer's Greek Lexicon* (Transliterated Greek), (New York: Harper & Brothers, 1889).

Ibid.

Chapter 10: Overcoming Life's Challenges

Elizabeth Street, "Overcoming Obstacles: How Louis Zamperini Remained 'Unbroken,'" Learningliftoff.com, January, 9, 2015, http://www.learningliftoff .com/overcoming-obstacles-how-louis-zamperini-overcame-his-biggest-challenge-after-the-war/#.WP-2mNIrKM8 (accessed August 12, 2016).

"12 Famous People Who Failed Before Succeeding: Sir James Dyson," Wander lustworker.com, https://www.wanderlustworker.com/12-famous people-who-failed-before-succeeding (accessed August 29, 2016).

"Forbes Profile: James Dyson," Forbes.com, accessed August 29, 2016, http: // www.forbes.com/profile/james-dyson (accessed August 29, 2016).

American Psychological Association. www.apa.org/research/action /lemon. aspx. (accessed July 16, 2016).

Adam Wenger, "If Happy People Live Longer Lives, This is Why," Healthline .com, February 25, 2015, www.healthline.com/health/happy-healthy-living#2 (accessed July 12, 2016).

Lissa Rankin, "Scientific Proof That Being Thankful Improves Your Health," Mindbodygreen.com, November 27, 2013,www.mindbodygreen.com/0-11819/scientific-proof-that-being-thankful-improves-your-health.html (accessed July 20, 2016).

William F. Arndt, *Greek English Lexicon of the New Testament and Other Early Christian Literature* (Chicago: University of Chicago Press, 1979).

A. T. Robertson, *Word Pictures in the New Testament* (Grand Rapids MI: Baker Books, 1960).

Chapter 11: It's All About Choices

John Hollon, "The Lessons Of Custer: 5 Things to Consider On 'Bad Management Day,'" TLNT.com, June 25, 2012, http://www.eremedia.com/tlnt /the-lessons-of-custer-5-things-to-think-about-on-bad-management-day/ (accessed April 22, 2016).

Kharunya Paramaguru, "5 Great Stories About Nelson Mandela's Humility, Kindness and Courage," Time.com, December 6, 2013, http://world.time.com /2013/12/06/5-great-stories-about-nelson-mandelas-humility-kindness-and-courage/ (accessed April 19, 2016).

Chapter 12: Moving Forward

Mary McCoy, "6 Celebrities Who Recovered From Financial Failure Before They Became Famous: Walt Disney," Moneycrashers.com, story: http://www.moneycrashers.com/celebrities-recovered-financial-failure-before-famous/ (accessed August 9, 2016).

Kathryn Slattery, "The Beauty in Our Brokenness," Guideposts, https://www.guideposts.org/better-living/life-advice/managing-life-changes/the-beauty-in-our-brokenness/ (accessed March 19, 2016).

Tim Hansel, *You Gotta Keep Dancin* (Colorado Springs: Cook Communications Ministries, 1985).

"Biography: Les Brown Facts," Yourdictionary.com, accessed August 27, 2016, http://biography.yourdictionary.com/les-brown/http://www.Lesbrown .com/ (accessed August 27, 2016).

Robert H. Schuller, *Move ahead with Possibility Thinking* (New York: Doubleday and Company, 1967).

Roy Lessin, *Today is Your Best Day: Discovering God's Best for You* (Green Forest, AR: New Leaf Press, a division of New Leaf Publishing Group, Inc., 2012).

About the Author

TR Williams is a gifted lecturer, author, communicator, family counselor, and spiritual-life coach. He is the founder and president of Empower Life Inc.: a nonprofit whose aim and mission delivers a message of hope, empowerment, encouragement, and leadership to individuals who seek success and advancement in life. TR Williams holds a Bachelor of Arts Degree in Communications from North Central University in Minneapolis, Minnesota; a Master of Arts Degree in Organizational Leadership from Bethel University in St. Paul, Minnesota; and an Honorary Doctorate Degree in Humanities from St. Thomas College in Jacksonville, Florida. He has received numerous accolades and awards for his contributions on leadership development. TR Williams and his wife are the proud parents of three children.

Coming Soon

TRUSTING GOD

WHEN BAD THINGS HAPPEN

Effectively Navigating Through and Overcoming Life's Most Severe Challenges, Disappointments and Disruptions.

TR Williams

CPSIA information can be obtained
at www.ICGtesting.com
Printed in the USA
JSHW040849150322
23638JS00001B/1